P9-CFV-115

THE WHIGS IN OPPOSITION
1815–1830

THE WHIGS IN OPPOSITION

1815–1830

BY

AUSTIN MITCHELL

OXFORD

AT THE CLARENDON PRESS

1967

Oxford University Press, Ely House, London W. 1

GLASGOW NEW YORK TORONTO MELBOURNE WELLINGTON
CAPE TOWN SALISBURY IBADAN NAIROBI LUSAKA ADDIS ABABA
BOMBAY CALCUTTA MADRAS KARACHI LAHORE DACCA
KUALA LUMPUR HONG KONG TOKYO

© *Oxford University Press 1967*

PRINTED IN GREAT BRITAIN

PREFACE

NUMEROUS debts of gratitude have inevitably been incurred in the writing of the present study. Mr. Michael Brock of Corpus Christi College, Oxford, was a continuous source of stimulating ideas and very kindly made available his transcripts of some manuscript collections which I was unable to inspect personally. The owners and the librarians responsible for the various manuscript collections mentioned in the bibliography all provided friendly and generous help. The D.Phil. thesis on which the book is based was supervised by Professor A. Aspinall. Mr. Philip Williams and Dr. A. F. Madden of Nuffield College, Oxford, both devoted considerable time and effort to reading through and advising on the early drafts of the manuscript and their advice has been invaluable. Miss Penny Dawson, the secretary of the Department of Political Science, University of Canterbury, typed out the final drafts of the book. To all of them, and to the friends and fellow students who read through the different drafts, my gratitude.

AUSTIN MITCHELL

Department of Political Science
University of Canterbury
Christchurch, New Zealand

CONTENTS

INTRODUCTION

THE study of early-nineteenth-century English politics has tended to suffer from the wealth of documentation available. An age when contact was curtailed through distances and the shortness of the parliamentary session has yielded a massive ransom to the historian, in correspondence, journals, and diaries. Much of this has been published in the heavy volumes which Victorian publishers thought appropriate. Professor Aspinall has published large sections with minimal commentary, and much remains, unpublished but newly available, in family archives all over the country. Collection and publication have their obvious importance, but concentration on these tasks has combined with the inevitable difficulty of digestion, to produce a comparative failure of analysis.

Contemporaries were willing to use terminology such as 'whig party', 'tory party', 'country gentlemen', 'independent', 'neutral squad', and similar terms, but rarely bothered to explain them. Enthusiasm for describing at length the immediate and the obvious is a more modern phenomenon. Unfortunately, repetition of the contemporary stock phrases without further amplification has been the resort of most historians. Some evade the issue by making little or no attempt to describe the party system; Keith Feiling managed to write a history of the second tory party without effectively defining it; Michael Roberts devoted just over three pages to describing the party political framework within which his whig party operated. Others have confined their description of parties to the names and opinions of a few leading figures or a vague background to a biographical study.

The present study is an attempt to go behind the stereotypes and examine the working of the political system from the point of view of one party, the whig opposition. The new availability of several whig manuscript collections such as the Brougham, Fitzwilliam, Grey, Holland, and Lansdowne papers now makes it possible, not only to describe in detail the attitudes and internal workings of the opposition party, but also to analyse the politics of the period and the nature of the political system, so far as they affected and were affected by that party.

The study falls into two sections. The first three chapters are concerned with the principles and organization of the whig party, and the reasons why it remained in opposition and never achieved power until the end of the period. The remaining chapters describe the party in action from 1815 to 1830, a year in which it drew together again, and the problems which had prevented it from coming into office were one by one solved or removed. Thus, as well as being the conclusion to one long and difficult section of the history of the whig party, the penultimate chapter provides the starting point for the next phase of whig history, the long period of power.

ABBREVIATIONS IN FOOTNOTES

Althorp — Papers of the second and third Earls Spencer, Althorp, Northamptonshire.

Brougham — Papers of the first Baron Brougham and Vaux, University College, London.

Broughton — *Recollections of a Long Life* by Lord Broughton, edited by Lady Dorchester, London, 1910.

Camden — A. Aspinall, *The Formation of Canning's Ministry*, Camden Society, third series, vol. lix, London, 1937.

Carlisle — Papers of the fifth and sixth Earls of Carlisle, Castle Howard, Yorkshire.

Devonshire — Papers of the sixth Duke of Devonshire, Chatsworth, Derbyshire.

E.H.R. — *English Historical Review*.

Fitzwilliam — Papers of the fourth and fifth Earls Fitzwilliam, formerly preserved at Wentworth Woodhouse, Yorkshire, Sheffield Public Library.

George IV — A. Aspinall, *The Letters of George IV, 1812–30*, Cambridge, 1938.

Graham — Papers of Sir James Graham, Netherby, Cumberland.

Grey — Papers of the second and third Earls Grey, Prior's Kitchen, Durham.

Heron — Sir R. Heron, *Notes: Printed but not Published*, Grantham, 1850.

Holland — Papers of the third Baron Holland, British Museum.

Lambton — Papers of the first Earl of Durham, Lambton Castle, Durham.

Lansdowne — Papers of the third Marquess of Lansdowne, Bowood, Wiltshire.

Maxwell — H. Maxwell, *The Creevey Papers*, London, 1905.

Milton — Papers of the fourth and fifth Earls Fitzwilliam, formerly preserved at Milton, Northamptonshire, Northamptonshire Record Office.

Monteagle — Papers of the first Baron Monteagle, National Library of Ireland.

P.D. — *Parliamentary Debates.* (N.S., New Series.)

Wynn — Papers of Charles Williams-Wynn, National Library of Wales.

I

PARTY AND PRINCIPLES

THE new insight conveyed by Sir Lewis Namier's pioneering study of the 1760's has, in the years since 1929, hardened into a new orthodoxy with claims to a dominion far wider than the narrow area of history originally covered. The Namier method, essentially the application of the techniques of sociology and research in depth to historical studies, has enormous and obvious importance to all those periods of history which can provide grist to the mill. Whatever the virtues of its finished product, the mill also turns out less desirable by-products. Analysis in statistical terms has a built-in bias against the politics of principle; ideas do not lend themselves to tabulation, and dissection in depth draws attention away from differences of viewpoint to concentrate it on the similarity of mechanical factors. Less inevitable is the over-enthusiastic attempt to export Namier's conclusions to areas of history where the same foundations of basic research have not been provided and where the climate is less favourable.

The early nineteenth century has been an obvious export market for deep-frozen Namier concepts. Emphasis on factions in the 1760's has drawn attention to those existing in the period of George IV: the Canningites have been much studied and Donald Read has claimed that 'the whig party in 1819 was not so much one coherent organised body as a collection of loosely connected groups'.[1] The demonstration that political parties did not exist in the earlier period has been reflected in a tendency to minimize the importance of early-nineteenth-century parties: Professor Gash has criticized the late A. S. Turberville's book on the house of lords because 'whigs and tories are accepted as the natural dichotomy of late eighteenth and early nineteenth century politics as though Sir Lewis Namier had never existed'.[2] Inevitably too, much play has been made on a comparison with

[1] D. Read, *Peterloo: The Massacre and its Background*, Manchester, 1958, p. 198.
[2] *E.H.R.*, 1959, p. 304

the 'modern' party system. Professor Gash contrasts this with party in Peel's period, and Robert McKenzie has stated that 'at the end of the third decade of the nineteenth century it was still almost impossible to identify within parliament or outside it anything that resembles the modern party system'.[1] Namier has attached the seal of his own authority to this development by arguing that in 1809 it is still possible to discern

> the basic structure of eighteenth-century parliamentary politics, with increased regard for the country gentlemen but no trace of a two party system, or at all of party in the modern sense. . . . Nineteenth-century parliamentary historians now seem agreed in deferring the full emergence of the modern party till after the second reform bill: what preceded it were intermediary forms which should not be treated anachronistically in terms of a later age.[2]

Study of the early nineteenth century provides undoubted warrant for all such attempts to emphasize 'non-party' elements and create a 'soft' concept of party. As in the 1760's, it is possible to discern factions, tiny groups of M.P.s and peers plying for hire on the most favourable terms. The Grenville group, the Canning group, and the tiny and idiosyncratic Wellesley group are the examples inevitably produced, and the party splits of 1827 to 1829 created splinter groups which could be described in the same terms. Again, large numbers of M.P.s laid claim to the virtues of independence and smaller numbers would stress their impartiality, and haphazard voting, unrestrained by party ties, was a characteristic of at least a section of M.P.s and peers. Where contemporaries discerned a party clash it was not one between two sharply opposed bodies but rather a divergence, on the pattern of modern differences between Republican and Democrat, between two centres of gravity with some degree of overlap between them. Parliament contained a spectrum of opinion which party cut with sometimes artificial boundaries. The range from ultra tory, through liberal tory, to neutral, and then reaching out through the opposition side of the house, was a gradual one.

As a final item in the indictment it is clear that on many questions party did not function. Tithes, poor-law reform, game

[1] R. T. McKenzie, *British Political Parties*, London, 1963, p. 1.
[2] L. B. Namier, *Crossroads of Power*, London, 1962, p. 231.

laws, and humanitarian reforms including legislation on chimney sweeps and corporal punishment in the army, were the preserve of minorities of enthusiasts. The question of the currency can be placed in the same category after the agreed measure of 1819 had removed the demand for the resumption of cash payments, once a useful stick with which to beat the government.[1] Major questions such as the corn laws, protection of industry, help for agriculture, trading monopolies, the navigation laws, combination laws, and factory legislation, were areas of disagreement between interests, but hardly between parties; ministerial and opposition sides of the house were not united internally on them. Finally, questions of slavery and the slave trade were mostly broader than the dimensions of party. Taken with minor legislation, local bills, and such procedural and privilege questions as were not drawn into party warfare, these matters inevitably occupied a substantial proportion of parliament's time. Indeed by the 1820's such non-party questions occasioned nearly as many, and sometimes more, divisions than the party political conflict.[2]

[1] C. C. Western, who was both whig and inflationist, admitted, 'I am a party man; that is to say, I acknowledge the necessity of acting generally, though by no means invariably, in a party with those who concur in opinion upon great fundamental principles; but on this question, no such feelings can exist.' *P.D.*, N.S. ix. 834.

[2] In sample sessions the number of divisions on which the voting figures are recorded shows the following patterns:

	1816	1818	1819 (I)	1819 (II)	1822	1825	1826
Foreign policy	5	2	3		2		
Repression (incl. aliens)	12	18		17	18	6	
Parl. reform and electoral		4	2		1		2
Scotland		1	3		5		1
Law reform			3		2	1	1
Catholic Q.	1		1		2	6	
Economy and finance	35	11	22		48	16	10
Bank questions	7	5	2				
Miscellaneous issues	4	6	5		8		5
General questions	2		1	3	2		1
Total 'party' divisions	66	47	42	20	88	29	20
'Non-party' questions	15	15	18	2	25	26	29
Local and particular questions	15	7	21		12	26	4
Total 'non-party' divisions	30	22	39	2	37	52	33

Factions and neutral groups, ranges of opinion within the house, and non-party issues, all help to explain any tendency to discount the importance of a two-party system. Yet to treat these as the dominant features of the political scene is to distort. There remained but three factions, and the open opportunism and place-hunting of one, the Grenvilles, was subject to widespread condemnation, while the breakdown of parties from 1827 to 1829 produced such a volume of comment as clearly indicated its exceptional nature. The independence claimed by so many amounted to real neutrality only in a few cases. For the most part the members in the central zone of the house were ultimately subject to the attracting or repelling power of one of the two political poles. The range of opinion always resolved itself in discussion, and divisions into two sides and the differences within parties were variations on the same theme, not disharmonies. The existence of non-party divisions does not eclipse the fact that political ones in which ministry and opposition, or sections of them, clashed were in a majority most of the time. They certainly received much the greater share of public and press attention.

Contemporary opinion regarded party as dominating the scene. Most observers acknowledged that there were, as Croker put it, 'two marked and distinct parties in the country, which might for brevity be fairly called whig and tory', and many, particularly those most committed to either the government or the opposition side of the house, saw important benefits accruing from the existence of party; Castlereagh argued that

> public business could not be better managed, or so well managed, if it were not for the system of parties; and on his conscience he believed that whatever of human happiness was to be found in this country in a greater degree than in the other countries of Europe was to be attributed to that conflict of parties, chastened by the principles of the constitution, and subdued by the spirit of decorum.[1]

Soon the period before the great reform bill came to be regarded in retrospect as the hey-day of a strong two-party system. Writing in 1833 J. A. Roebuck describes a scene of parliamentary chaos with members laughing, groaning, and braying, and one mem-

[1] L. J. Jennings, *The Correspondence and Diaries of J. W. Croker*, London, 1884, i. 401; *P.D.* xxxv. 270.

ber hooting like an owl 'to the great disturbance of the gravity of the assembly and evident annoyance of the speaker'. Such disorganization, Roebuck comments, had not occurred in the pre-reform house because

in former times there were two distinct and organised parties; these parties had well known leaders, upon whom devolved the business of advocating and opposing the measures before the house. Everybody knew this; and no one interfered with the part assigned to a given individual. The debate then went on quietly. . . . But now there is no organisation.[1]

Lord Brougham, a party man turned bitter critic, helped to further this trend by his own attacks on party, many of them illustrated by examples from the period before the reform bill.[2]

There were many groups critical of party but their criticisms were explicit recognition of its importance. Members with pretensions to independence were frequent complainers; Sir William Geary lamented in 1818 that 'in the late parliament all things were guided by party, by votes from party feeling alone: an independent man could not do the service he wished'.[3]

The radicals, though a newer phenomenon, were equally vociferous. J. C. Hobhouse complained that

it is a great mistake to suppose, that party co-operation renders necessary a sacrifice only of minute differences; it requires a sacrifice of vital principles. The leaders of such a co-operation will naturally keep back the agitation of such questions as are likely to show any difference of opinions in his battalion. . . . It will be the object of such a leader never to bring before the public any but vague questions to catch all latitudinarians.[4]

Finally, Greville, an outside observer, argued that

The spirit of party influences every man's opinions. It is not extraordinary that each individual of a party connected by general similarity of opinion should adhere to the great body, even in cases where he may not happen to agree with them . . . but it is very improbable that on a particular question, unconnected with any general system, where arguments are adduced from opposite sides, and submitted to

[1] R. E. Leader, *Life and Letters of J. A. Roebuck*, London, 1897, pp. 52–53.

[2] See his Introduction to the *Life, Letters and Speeches of Lord Plunket*, by D. Plunket, London, 1867, p. 20, and his own *Historical Sketches of Statesmen who Flourished in the Time of George III*, London, 1858, i. 373–80.

[3] *The Times*, 26 June 1818.

[4] *An Authentic Narrative of Events of the Westminster Election*, London, 1819, p. 61.

the enlightened judgement of an assembly, the same arguments which are looked upon as satisfactory and unanswerable by one set of men should be deemed without exception utterly fallacious by another.[1]

Sir Ivor Jennings's so-called 'sham fight' is no modern phenomenon.

These contemporary comments are a clear proof of the existence of parties. They were not, indeed, 'modern' parties, but to think in these terms is not an historian's job, nor is it useful to point out that the nineteenth century is not the twentieth. Since we have no useful measure of 'modernity', the historian should inquire whether contemporaries recognized a party system, and also if large numbers of M.P.s can be shown to be acting together for the furtherance of common aims and principles. He is concerned to describe the nature of the early-nineteenth-century party system rather than to define a degree of approximation to modern examples.

Contemporaries do, in fact, provide clear descriptions of the nature of party; it was something to 'keep men to a point' by enforcing common principles. Lord John Russell describes, in terms which ring truer of the nineteenth century, the evolution of a young politician in the reign of Queen Anne.

He adopts, if you please, the general opinions of the tories. He votes generally, but not always, with that party. He naturally becomes acquainted with some of them. He talks over the questions that are coming on for some time before. These conversations lead to a more intimate union: his opinions are listened to, and his doubts melt away in the course of amicable discussion. Sometimes, when the measure is one of party policy rather than of principle, he surrenders his own opinion to that of the statesmen most respected by the society of which he is a member. He thinks it more probable that several able, and a large body of patriotic men, *arguing from the same principles as himself*, should form a right decision, than he alone in the whole house of commons should, from given principles, have derived a true conclusion. He is, in short, a party man. Thus it is that without any violation of conscience party is formed.[2]

[1] L. Strachey and R. Fulford, *The Greville Memoirs, 1814–1860*, London, 1938, i. 76–77.

[2] Lord John Russell, *An Essay on the History of the English Government and Constitution*, London, 1821, pp. 133–4. See also *Edinburgh Review*, no. lix, 1818, pp. 183–6.

Lord Grey leaned more heavily on Burke, defining party as

the connection of honourable and independent men to support their common principles, which they can do more effectually by united than by divided efforts. This supposes a general agreement on great public questions, and occasional concessions on points of minor importance where such become necessary for the general advantage of co-operation; but none on leading and material principles; the moment there arises a disagreement on these the party is dissolved, on the same honourable ground on which it was first united. It was upon this principle, when very young that I originally connected myself with the whig party, and I was glad to have the advantage of being assisted and directed in my course, whilst I sacrificed nothing of my independence, by those for whose experience, integrity and talents I had the highest respect.[1]

Principle was supplemented by social and personal ties, and long association tended to develop loyalties of its own, so that those who changed their opinions could not drop away without being treated as traitors, as Sir John Leach, W. C. Plunket, William Lamb, and others found to their cost.[2] Yet such bonds were supplementary, not basic. Agreement on common principles was the essential tie, and if it were broken then union 'must cease, or at least be suspended', as the whig experience with the Stafford group and then the Grenvilles was to show.[3]

In an age when parties were hardly based on the diverging interests of social and economic groupings it was inevitable that party differentiation should rest on disagreements over principles, which in turn were the product of the past. The definition and discussion of these principles was more a whig pastime than a tory; the opposition needed to define its position and outline its alternative, while the government was more pragmatic. Nevertheless, both sides had their theorists and their propaganda, and both tended to interpret present issues and controversies in the light of a body of inherited principles, prejudices, and attitudes. The past exerted its influence in three main ways.

[1] Grey to S. Whitbread, n.d. [May 1820], copy (Grey). In this quotation, as in all others in the present study, abbreviations in the original are rendered in full in the text, and dates given are taken from the original or from endorsements on the letter.

[2] For example see D. Plunket, *Plunket*, pp. 17–19; *P.D.*, N.S. viii. 1030–1; *P.D.* N.S. ii. 269–70.

[3] Grey to Wilson, 29 July 1818 (Grey).

As with modern American parties, party mythology (the party's interpretation of its own history) helped sustain differences. Deep-seated attitudes, the frozen postures of the past, also made their effects felt. Most important of all were differences over issues which had arisen in the recent past, or were arising in the present; all of these fitted into place like the pieces in a jigsaw to produce a coherent body of attitudes.

Myth was the least important tributary, though it provided a continuous flow of psychological solace. Early-nineteenth-century whigs had a satisfying feeling of being part of a long historical continuity. Tracing the history of their party back to the seventeenth century, they regarded themselves as the 'descendants and representatives' of the revolutionaries of 1688, and their principles as 'strictly those of the revolution'.[1] In the view of nineteenth-century whigs the whig party had struggled with the tories under Anne, maintained the succession under George, and then held power, ruling through the house of commons, for a half-century of English greatness, until, on the accession of George III, they had been sacrificed because of their reluctance to become the subservient tools of prerogative.[2] As a governing group they had then been replaced by the tories, recalled from their rural fastness by George III's advisers, and joined by new apologists of royal power and by subservient ministers such as Grafton, North, and then, an apostate from whiggery, the younger Pitt.[3] Support was given to this interpretation by the presence in the nineteenth-century party of descendants of the great seventeenth-century opposition families, Russells, Cavendishes, and even a reputed descendant of Pym, as well as Bentincks and Keppels, the heirs of William III's favourites, Lord Holland, a Townsend, and a Walpole, the present representatives of the Venetian oligarchy.

While it was a comforting food for the speech course at party dinners, the whig interpretation of history became rather more dangerous when used to explain nineteenth-century differences. Some still talked in terms of passive obedience and the right of resistance, or of differing attitudes to the personal power of the

[1] Lord Erskine, *A Short Defence of the Whigs*, London, 1819, p. 4; Sir G. Byng in *The Times*, 20 June 1818.

[2] Lord John Russell, *An Essay*, p. 161, and Mackintosh in *P.D.* xli. 1484

[3] The fullest whig interpretation of party history is in G. W. Cooke, *The History of Party*, London, 1837 (3 vols.).

crown.[1] Others, slightly more up to date, looked for a contrast between the old Rockingham doctrine that ministers were a collective entity, responsible to parliament, and a tory acquiescence in the king's wishes.[2] All this was irrelevant. No whig would have thought of invoking the ultimate safeguard of the right of resistance, and resignations of tory ministers against the king's wishes in 1827, and the frequent refusals of Liverpool's cabinet to defer to the monarch, could hardly be explained in terms of traditional toryism. The most the whigs could assert was that the existing administration was prepared to give way to the king more than they would.[3] This could hardly be tested, although it may be that a tory administration, having few disagreements on principles with the king, would take fewer stands. Thus all that remained of the old doctrines was an enduring suspicion of the crown.

A feature of the traditional interpretation is its pride in the party's forebears in opposition, the Rockingham, the Portland, and then the Foxite whigs. Here was a clearer continuity, for Fitzwilliam was Rockingham's political heir; Lauderdale, T. W. Coke, and Sir William Lemon had opposed the American war; and many others, including Grey himself, had followed Fox's opposition to the French war.[4] This long conditioning in opposition had helped to produce quite distinct whig attitudes on public opinion and economy. An eighteenth-century opposition inevitably looked to public opinion for support against the government and attempted, whenever possible, to stir up popular agitation against ministers. This deference was facilitated by traditional whig emphasis on the people, as opposed to the crown; Coke defined his whig principles as meaning that 'the rights of the people had ever been more dear to him than the honour of the crown; for they taught him that the king was

[1] Lord John Russell, *An Essay*, pp. 131–2; *Edinburgh Review*, no. liii, 1816, pp. 249–50; *Manchester Guardian*, 13 October 1821.

[2] *Morning Chronicle*, 5 July 1819.

[3] Grenville regarded Liverpool as a minister pliable to the system of court government practised by George III and the regent. Grenville to Grey, 10 November 1812 (Grey).

[4] Of fifty-two voters and tellers who backed Fox's opposition to the address in the crucial month of December 1792, twenty-one were returned to the 1812 parliament and still in opposition. To go even further back, four of the 108 M.P.s who had opposed the address in October 1775 were still in both parliament and opposition.

made for the people, and not the people for the king'.[1] The increasing tendency to translate the word 'crown' by executive government facilitated this trend. Long habit, supplemented by principles, made deference to public opinion a conditioned whig reflex.

Yet the whigs were no democrats. The opinion they would defer to was not that of the masses but of 'the intelligent class of the English public, those who from property, and from education and from place in society, are entitled to sway the opinion of the legislature', and a more specific definition would probably have been the opinion of the 'middling classes', as expressed through the traditional channels of town and county meetings, with the participation of urban middle classes and county freeholders.[2] Even to this opinion their attitude was condescending, for the whig aristocracy regarded themselves as intermediaries between crown and people.

> The power of great families [argued the whig organ, the *Edinburgh Review*] is indeed a most necessary part of the array to which the people must look for their security against misgovernment. . . . They afford a counterpoise from their wealth, rank and station, to the resources of force and corruption at the crown's disposal: they are a rallying point to the scattered strength of the inferior partisans, and a more permanent mass in which the common principles may be embodied and preserved among the vicissitudes of fortune: . . . they are eminently useful in tempering the zeal, as well as in fixing the unsteadiness of popular opinion.[3]

The whig belief that theirs was the party of the aristocracy, of 'Earl Grey of spotless character, followed by the Russells and the Cavendishes, by all the ancient nobility, and all the great property of the realm', was a myth.[4] The opposition in the commons was no more aristocratic than the government members, although it was possible to argue that the whigs were the most aristocratic section of the opposition. The whigs peers may not even have constituted a majority of those members of the aristocracy whose titles were created before 1760, although

[1] *The Times*, 22 October 1812.

[2] Plunket in *P.D.* xxiv. 813; *Edinburgh Review*, no. lxi, 1818, pp. 191–2.

[3] *Edinburgh Review*, no. lix, 1818, p. 192. See also W. J. Denison in *The Times*, 24 June 1818.

[4] J. Gore, *Creevey's Life and Times*, London, 1934, p. 55.

they did form a higher proportion among this group than among later creations. Yet whigs had little time for dull statistics and, though a half truth, their belief in their own high ranking in property and status strongly influenced their attitudes. Seeing themselves as the aristocratic party and visualizing the role of the aristocracy as that of giving 'a tone' to public opinion, the whigs considered that their task was that of guiding opinion and making change safe. Lord John Russell pointed out that 'if great changes accomplished by the people are dangerous, although sometimes salutary, great changes accomplished by the aristocracy, at the desire of the people, are at once salutary and safe'.[1] In this way 1688 continued to provide an inspiration and an example. The attitude was, however, also one of enlightened self-interest, for whigs had grasped the danger of damming up discontent. As Grey pointed out in 1819, when urging his fellow peers to protect the people, 'their character as a party, their interests as individuals, deeply involved in the maintenance of the constitution as the only safeguard of their property and their rank, equally prescribe a firm and active discharge of their duty'.[2]

The party's history was also reflected in its attitude to finance. One means of winning public support was by tax reductions through economy in government, and this popular demand had been an inevitable programme for every eighteenth-century opposition. It was, too, one to which the whigs were deeply conditioned. Moreover, this was also a programme to which their other whig views predisposed the party, for economy and tax reductions were ways of reducing the power and influence of both the executive government and the crown. Whigs had long urged economical reform, the reduction of the numbers of unnecessary offices and sinecures, as a practical means of reducing that government influence in parliament which, as an opposition, they saw as the main obstacle they had to contend with. Now, however, this argument about the power of place in politics was being subordinated to more general arguments. The savings from economical reform had proved small and the reforms carried out up to 1815 had hardly changed the

[1] *The Substance of the Speeches of Lord John Russell on Moving Resolutions on Reform of Parliament*, London, 1822, p. 85.

[2] Grey to Devonshire, 23 September 1819 (Devonshire).

parliamentary situation at all drastically. Creevey therefore claimed that

it is the *indirect* influence of the crown in the house of commons, which now bears down everything before it. The unions with Scotland and Ireland have in themselves altered the very face and nature of the house of commons. Then the enormous debt which has been created within the last thirty years, with the endless patronage arising from the collection of the revenues to pay it; the vast and almost unbounded increase of our colonial possessions, during the same period, with all the establishments of every species belonging to them: —these are the united circumstances that have given the crown an *indirect* influence in the house of commons.[1]

Economical reform became one point of a three-pronged attack which also urged tax reductions and retrenchment in the costs of government. The traditional arguments assumed a new force after the Napoleonic wars, for the whigs, now, as in 1780, saw heavy taxation as the cause of existing distress, and economy as both the universal solution, and an essential means of conciliating opinion outside the house.[2] The three-pronged attack thus became a continuing preoccupation of the opposition. It was also the major single point at issue with the government.

Deep-seated attitudes on public opinion and retrenchment were supplemented by broad differences on a series of specific questions. In their interpretation of party history the whigs over-emphasized the element of continuity and underrated the importance of the new crop of issues planted and harvested in the reign of farmer George III. The extent of the power of the crown, the position of the ministers, the legitimacy of royal influence over parliament, the nature of popular control over the commons, the question of the American colonies and then the French Revolution, were issues which had divided the political world on questions of principle. These issues had been drawn into the existing conflict between ministry and opposition, so that both sides had tended to become committed to a point of view. It was this development, rather than any continuous two-party system dating from the reign of Anne, which created the

[1] *Remarks on the Last Session of Parliament by a Near Observer* (Creevey), London, 1822, p. 59. Others would have added the increase in the size of the army to Creevey's list. See Milton in *P.D.* xxxiv. 518.

[2] *Edinburgh Review*, no. li, 1816, p. 155.

basis of the division between whig and tory in the nineteenth century. New divisions had received old names. The Rockingham whigs usurped monopoly patents on the brand name 'whig', and gratuitously conferred the title 'tory' on their opponents, and 'toryism' on the collective principles and practices of the governments they opposed. Long reiteration brought the words back to the political vocabulary and the new allocations had been widely, though not universally, accepted by both sides by the end of the Napoleonic war as the titles Foxite and Pittite began to fade.[1] Faced with agitation and radicalism, the French Revolution, and then war, feeling the mantle of responsibility on its shoulders, and needing to take account of the inclinations of the king and of its own country backbenchers, the government had taken up broadly conservative stands. Their opponents had taken up contrasting and more liberal views, so that Grey could argue that 'the party principle which distinguishes us as whigs is a principle of moderation and liberality, both in religion and government'.[2] Thus the new differences between whig and tory, as distinct from the dead differences of the early eighteenth century, emerged as a broad differentiation between a liberal and a conservative attitude. Indeed, these two terms themselves began to enter into the political vocabulary in the years before 1830.[3]

This dichotomy can be discerned on a range of issues. One is catholic emancipation which, since Fox's day, had become a central doctrine of the whig party, so important that Tierney once described it as 'the only tie by which for some time past we have even appeared to be kept together'.[4] Where a substantial majority of tories opposed emancipation as a dangerous infringement on a protestant constitution, the whig replied,

[1] 'Tory' was tacitly accepted rather than generally used, and the Duke of Newcastle even told the king in 1827 that he preferred to be called a whig rather than a tory since in his view the real tories were jacobites. (Newcastle papers, Nottingham University, NeC. 5, 143. Quoted in G. I. T. Machin, 'Catholic Emancipation as an Issue in English Politics, 1820–1830', Oxford D.Phil. Thesis, 1961, p. 2.)

[2] Grey to Holland, 17 January 1817 (Grey).

[3] The terms were originally importations so that tories could occasionally be referred to as the *parti conservateur*, and the principles of the whigs as *liberaux*. See *George IV*, ii. 390. Campbell was referring to himself as a liberal in 1820; Mrs. Hardcastle, *Life of Lord Campbell*, London, 1881, i. 396. See also Broughton, iii. 30. On the other side Peel admitted, 'I may be a tory, I may be an illiberal'; N. Gash, *Mr. Secretary Peel*, London, 1961, p. 437.

[4] Tierney to Grey, 3 March 1814 (Grey).

on the theoretical plane, that rights should not be denied on religious grounds, and, on the practical level, that emancipation was essential if peace and order were to be restored to Ireland. A tiny number of whigs were against emancipation: Erskine is reported to have feigned sleep whenever the question was discussed in the 1806 cabinet, and opposition members for Bristol always opposed it, as did William Dickinson, the opposition member for Somerset, and Captain Webb, member for Gloucester and chairman of the local whig club. Rather more were lukewarm, wishing with Lord Mulgrave that the emancipation millstone were at the bottom of the sea, or anxious, like Sir Robert Wilson, to seize any opportunity to escape from an unpopular commitment.[1] On the other side a minority of tories supported emancipation and the whig leaders normally conferred closely with prominent government advocates such as Castlereagh or Canning to determine procedure on motions related to the question. Despite this competition the whigs still had the bulk of the market, while the majority of their opponents were against emancipation. The same was true of the other religious issue discussed in parliament, concessions to nonconformists by the repeal of the test and corporation acts.

Mass agitation and mass discontent, prominent features of the scene after the war, raised problems approached by tory and whig in different ways. More strongly influenced by fears of social revolution, the tory tended to see mass discontent as being deliberately fostered and exploited by 'Jacobins' for revolutionary ends.[2] His antidote was repression and coercion.[3] Though not without their own fears, whigs tended to argue that discontent had positive causes, exclusion of catholics from parliament in Ireland, distress and high taxation in England, and that repression would simply drive it underground to reappear in more dangerous forms. Their solution was concession and conciliation. Though the whigs always eschewed the radical doctrine of natural rights, they still believed in free speech, free press, freedom of meeting, which they saw as guarantees of

[1] *The Journal and Correspondence of William, Lord Auckland*, London, 1862, iv. 385–6; Wilson to Grey, 22 August 1821 (Wilson Papers, Add. MSS. 30123, f. 248).

[2] See, for example, Robinson in *P.D.* xli. 1051–2.

[3] See Burdett's description of a tory as 'a person of contracted, bigoted, and arbitrary disposition, who would . . . make fear his instrument instead of love' (*P.D.*, N.S. xxii. 1219).

liberty. The invasion of these rights they saw as a dangerous step towards slavery which would accustom the public mind to submission.[1] Their arguments never proved acceptable to parliament, for up to 1830 mass agitation always stampeded support to the government; the relationship was so close that some whigs argued that panic was being exploited as a deliberate tool of government.[2]

Attitudes to change show a further differentiation. George Wilbraham told the Cheshire whig club that

> the whig seeks to support the constitution of his ancestors by a frequent recurrence to its principles: that *he* wishes to amend what through time has become defective and to adopt it to the purposes, and the improved habits of the age. The tory, on the contrary, feels a sort of religious abhorrence to touch what he calls the sacred fabric, which he would rather see crumble to pieces under his feet than he would lend his assistance to render it immortal by reforming and amending it.[3]

This exaggeration was not too wide of the mark up to the 1820's, for whigs like Sir Samuel Romilly, Sir James Mackintosh, and Henry Brougham, were prominent advocates of reform, both of the law and of the court of chancery; Lord Archibald Hamilton, James Abercromby, and Thomas Kennedy, pressed for changes in the burgh system, the electoral framework, and the system of justice in Scotland. Irish whigs, including Spring Rice, drew attention to abuses in their country. Most saw abolition of sinecures and inefficient offices and reform of the civil list as ways of streamlining the constitution.

Parliamentary reform posed more problems. Whig opinions on renovation and responsible public opinion naturally predisposed a large section of the party to it. Materialistic calculations pressed in the same direction, for, once taken up by a body of responsible public opinion, reform would become a prerequisite for the consummation of whig courtship of that opinion and indispensable if any marriage was to bear fruit. Without it some saw little chance of turning the ministers out. Others thought that even if power could be attained it could not be retained, in the face of royal hostility, without reform. For these

[1] *Edinburgh Review*, no. liii, 1816, pp. 250–2.
[2] *Edinburgh Review*, no. lxv, 1820, pp. 195–6.
[3] *Manchester Guardian*, 18 October 1823.

reasons sections of the party had already advocated reform at times when there was any semblance of popular demand for it, and at the close of the war at least ninety sitting members had already voted for reform, while Bedford, Somerset, Albemarle, Norfolk, Tavistock, Brand, and others were enthusiastic advocates. Yet there was little agreement on what could safely be done. A few, including H. G. Bennet, were prepared to follow Sir Francis Burdett off the whig horizon. From 1818 J. G. Lambton was urging a plan for disfranchisement of rotten boroughs, equal constituencies, extended franchise, and triennial parliaments, and Romilly, Brand, and Perry had envisaged similar, though less far-reaching, plans.[1] Many were taken up with the theory of representation of interests, which had the attraction of ruling out a universal suffrage certain to swamp the house with one interest, that of the mob.[2] Most reformers, however, satisfied themselves with vague formulae of moderate reform, or still vaguer expressions of sympathy.

Rather more of the party's members were cool. For Grey, querulous doubting middle age had succeeded the glad confident morning of two decades before. Alienated by the extreme demands of the radicals he was no longer prepared to go as far as his reform plan of 1797. Much of the time he appeared to be a friend to a 'moderate and gradual reform' only because he was a greater friend to consistency. Even Althorp admitted that he himself could see little good that reform would do, and Holland liked it less the closer he looked at it.[3] Such attitudes created a basic division between those who wanted to put the whigs in the vanguard of the reform movement and those content with the guard's van.

Others declined to travel at all. The Grenville group were opposed to reform, and even Thomas and Lord Grenville, prepared to proffer a cold welcome in theory, always considered that practical circumstances were never opportune. The Fitzwilliams, the Earl, his son Lord Milton, and his member William Elliot, all shared Burke's phobia of reform and for Burke's reasons. Carlisle, Devonshire, Spencer, and their ilk were unsympathetic, Darlington and his sons were openly opposed, and

[1] Lambton to Wilson, 3 July 1818 (Wilson Papers, Add. MSS. 30108, ff. 405–6).

[2] *Edinburgh Review*, no. lxi, 1818, pp. 175–7.

[3] Althorp to Milton, 17 May 1818 (Milton).

several others shared Lansdowne's cautious reserve. This made it impossible for reform to be a party question at the end of the war. In Grey's words

> agreement upon that question is hopeless. It must be left, as it hitherto has been, for individuals to act upon according to their respective opinions. It may undoubtedly assume so much importance as to make this hereafter impossible; but for the present it must be set aside in any consideration of our party politics. To get any declaration in favour of it assented to by the party is obviously out of the question.[1]

This was to remain the position until growing pressure for reform among representatives of 'responsible' public opinion produced a new situation.

On all reform, parliamentary and otherwise, the whigs were walking a delicate tightrope. They were urging changes which the bulk of their tory opponents refused to accept. Even when tories in office began the work of reform, the whigs could still argue that they would enter the task more confidently and more effectively.[2] At the same time the whigs would proceed neither as far nor as fast as the radicals. Whig change was conservative, designed to bring institutions up to date, the better to preserve them. Its method was a 'moderate and cautious policy of gradual improvements founded in whig principles'.[3] The whigs saw the radicals as doctrinaires and themselves as practical men. They looked to the historical processes of change, decay, and renovation and eschewed schemes of reform based on abstract theories. It is no coincidence that there were few theoreticians like Ricardo in the ranks of the parliamentary opposition, but several historians, including Mackintosh, Lord John Russell, Henry Brougham, and Charles James Fox himself. Some whigs were inevitably influenced by reformers such as Jeremy Bentham, but when these influences were felt, as they were by Brougham, they were always diluted by whig attitudes.

In foreign policy, too, the whigs were the advocates of change. With Europe dominated by an oligarchy of conservative powers, the whigs, Palmerstonian before Palmerston, urged the twin

[1] Grey to Holland, 17 January 1817 (Grey).

[2] *The Times*, 17 April 1826.

[3] Grey to Wilson, 24 October 1819 (Wilson Papers, Add. MSS. 30109, f. 56). See also *Morning Chronicle*, 26 October 1813.

principles of national independence and national self-determination. These they hopefully saw as the basis for the encouragement of liberal governments and constitutions on the pattern of the British; in the words of the party paper: 'The Americans first, then the French, and now the Spaniards and Neapolitans have been our pupils. They have each caught a portion of that spirit which animated the founders of our liberties. The revolution of 1688 has served them as model.'[1]

All other whig principles were subordinate to this encouragement of liberal régimes. Non-intervention was never advanced in absolute terms, and could be promptly put aside in the case of the British intervention in 1826 to protect constitutional government in Portugal.[2] To the advocates of liberal constitutional régimes the holy allies, Austria, Russia, and Prussia, constituted a permanent *bête noire*, a threat to liberty on the Continent and even in England itself. Their treatment of small states at the Vienna congress and afterwards aroused whig horror. Ministers, by contrast, regarded themselves as practical men, unable to afford high-flown idealism and unwilling in any case to subscribe to it. They saw co-operation with the continental powers as the guarantee of peace. It was not until the 1820's that Castlereagh hesitantly and quietly, and Canning boldly, and with due deference to public relations, began the work of severance.

Whig and tory attitudes can be distinguished on questions entering into the liberal–conservative dimension and on issues relating to public opinion and economy. It was on these subjects, too, that government and opposition differed. With the normal tendency of the politically involved to exaggerate and over-dramatize, the *Edinburgh Review* argued that

the present ministry are in their hearts and in their whole conduct the enemies of every reform, and of none more than of retrenchment. They will yield nothing of the patronage of the crown; and, until forced, they will lessen none of the people's burdens. They are friendly to large military establishments; patrons of arbitrary power abroad.... At home, they undervalue the rights of the people, and carelessly treat the most sacred parts of the constitution.... In one

[1] *Morning Chronicle*, 23 August 1820.

[2] For early reservations about non-intervention see Grey to Holland, 17 January 1817 (Grey), and *Morning Chronicle*, 23 November 1813.

word, abuse of every description finds in them protection and palliation . . . they shrink back from amending any part of our jurisprudence. . . .[1]

Inevitably the whigs saw theirs as a sharp alternative. It was described by Grey. In a letter to Holland he says:

to the catholic question we are pledged. Equally so to a system of moderation and conciliation, in opposition to that of coercion and terror, in our domestic policy. Strict economy and retrenchment the circumstances of the country imperiously prescribe, and not less a system of non interference, where our honour and interests are not immediately in question, in our foreign policy.[2]

However embroidered, the fact that these differences were also differences of attitude between whig and tory means that in practice ministerialist and tory, opposition and whig, have to be regarded as synonymous. This is, in some respects, a distortion, because ministers who would have eschewed the label, or claimed only to be Pittites, backbench tories whose conservatism was dyed deeper than that of the government, and the cautious moderates of lighter hue, have all to be defined as tory and ministerialist. It is justifiable because all shared a distaste for the principles described by the opposition as whig. The whigs were the pace-setters of party because they agreed, broadly, on a set of principles; the government side was a *de facto* party, for though bonds were looser, principles more diffuse, in the last analysis its members wanted to keep the whigs out.

Within the opposition, too, there was a range of opinion. On the one extreme, approximating most nearly to government, stood the Grenville group: Lord Grenville, a handful of peers including Cawdor, Carysfort, Auckland, and Stafford, and about a dozen M.P.s, all held together by blood, background, and Buckingham's borough patronage. They had begun to co-operate with the whigs after the break-up of Pitt's long administration, and a loose association, agreed in 1804, had been cemented by common support of catholic emancipation, opposition to existing war policies, and office shared under the 'talents'. Subjects of difference remained and became more

[1] *Edinburgh Review*, no. lix, 1818, pp. 204–5. See also C. H. Hutchinson in *P.D.* xli. 1030–1.

[2] Grey to Holland, 12 April 1820 (Grey).

important with the end of the war, but even then a break was envisaged only reluctantly. Ties of friendship and respect had developed; the group, though small in numbers, consisted of 'men of great weight and character', and its members had views in common with others in the party, for alliance with the Grenvilles had been accompanied by reunion with Carlisle, Fitzwilliam, Devonshire, Spencer, and their associates, all groups which had broken away from Fox in 1792. Lord Carrington, a follower of Pitt until 1806, had also moved towards the whigs. All these sections shared the caution of the Grenvilles; though their personal friendships with the party were stronger, they probably attached more importance to the whig association, and some of their relatives and heirs, such as Lord Milton, Lord Althorp, and Lord George Cavendish, were more liberal in sentiment.

At the other extreme stood the radicals. Immediately after the war they were a tiny handful, Burdett, Cochrane, and few others; but later this Westminster rump was joined by men such as Alderman Wood, Colonel Davies, Joseph Hume, and T. W. Beaumont, all flaunting an aggressive independence. More important were the radical whigs, perhaps thirty strong, and including such impeccably aristocratic figures as Bedford and his sons, or Lord Ossulston, his brother H. G. Bennet, and Lord Folkestone, together with newer men like Peter Moore, Edward Ellice, Thomas Brand, and J. G. Lambton. In the last years of the war many of this group had tended to act independently with Samuel Whitbread, but after his suicide in 1815 they gradually returned to the fold, and by 1817 the former 'mountain' was no longer a force to be reckoned with. Divergence began again in the 1820's, when many of the radical whigs were prepared to follow the independent initiatives of Joseph Hume, but this never separated them from the main body of opposition in the way Whitbread's leadership had done. Whatever their position, their role was the same. Normally there was little love lost between whigs and extreme radicals outside parliament. Cobbett, Hunt, Cartwright, and even Burdett, until he became respectable in the 1820's, were regarded by whigs as spreading dangerous and impractical delusions. These radicals responded with the same bitter hatred for the cautious whigs that a communist might feel for a social democrat. The radical whigs, therefore, saw their role as that of bridging the gap between the party and 'responsible' radicals, and displacing the more violent radicals through progressive whig leadership of popular demands. They were a pressure group pulling the party to the left in the same way as the Grenvilles were mooring it to the right.

These pressures were exercised on a political centre consisting of those who had followed Fox up to his death and the later recruits of similarly moderate but liberal sentiments. It was from this zone that the leadership of the party was exercised: in it that the leading figures, Grey, George Tierney, Holland, Mackintosh, Lansdowne, and Sir James Macdonald, were found. Even here there were shades of difference, for Albemarle, Romilly, and Brougham, after his early Westminster flirtations, were more progressive and radical than cautious elements such as Carnarvon, Lord George Cavendish, and James Abercromby. Such differences were minor compared with the measure of agreement and the length of shared experience, but they did make the political centre a continuous spectrum between Grenvillite and radical, rather than a firm block.

All this made for a party unwieldy and difficult to handle, as well as one which required a continuous process of consultation and negotiation. Complaints were frequent, and there were even occasional suggestions that the party should be reduced in size and changed from a church into a sect which could be in full agreement. Nevertheless, it was a recognizable party. Even the extreme radicals and those opposition voters who eschewed party were, in practice, whigs. George Lamb warned his Westminster electors in 1820: 'If Mr. Hobhouse was returned, the moment he entered the house of commons, from that moment he must become a whig; for his services in parliament could only be rendered available by voting with the whig party in opposition to the measures of government. If he did not do that he could do nothing.'[1]

All opposition voters were part-time soldiers in an army generalled and largely manned by whigs. Differences of opinion among those who did actually regard themselves as whigs were also unimportant before the fact that they were 'a party banded together to obtain office upon certain principles'; and whatever their differences of emphasis among themselves, all could agree

[1] *Morning Chronicle*, 14 March 1820.

that their system was preferable to that of the men in power.[1] Such an objective in turn made it necessary that the opposition should act in united fashion and counter ministerial blandishments by an agreement to take office only as a body. This was the basis of party co-operation. When Wellesley was negotiating with the Whigs in 1812, Grey made it perfectly clear that the only acceptable arrangement was a union characterized by 'a full and unreserved communication of our respective views and opinions . . . and above all by the immediate and firm rejection of every invitation which may be held out by the court of separate favour, and the absolute renunciation of all separate pretensions on that account'.[2] This agreement extended to offices outside the political arena. Asked by Robert Adair about accepting a diplomatic post from the ministry, Grey advised against it:

looking at such a party as ours, as constituted on a public principle, and in itself forming a great public interest, it resolves itself into the weight of one public duty, balanced against another. Generally speaking therefore, the harm that is done to public character by such a connection with political opponents . . . and the example and encouragement it gives to others, without the same motives or the same justification, for a defection from the cause on which they are engaged, are evils which in my mind greatly over-balance the partial good.[3]

Similar advice was given to Sir John Leach in 1814, and when he accepted office two years later it was one personal to the regent and then only at the cost of breaking with his party and resigning his seat.[4]

A party dedicated to defeating and displacing ministers was committed to continuously fluctuating hope and doomed to intermittent despair. To those who felt that only hopes of power and prospects of office could hold a party together, these periods of despair seemed likely to dissolve the whole body.[5]

[1] Tierney in *P.D.* xl. 491. See also *Edinburgh Review*, no. lix, 1818, p. 186.

[2] Grey to R. Adair, 28 October 1812; copy in Grey papers and in *Historical Manuscripts Commission, Report on the Manuscripts of J. B. Fortescue Esq.*, preserved at Dropmore, London, 1927, x. 317.

[3] Grey to Adair, 1 January 1813 (Grey).

[4] Leach to Grey, 7 February 1816; Grey to Leach, 12 February 1816 (Grey).

[5] Brougham to Lambton, n.d. [1817] (Brougham). '*The hopes of place* are so slender that there is a disposition in all the shabby ones to leave us. Besides some

Their prophecies were never fulfilled. This was partly because of the ties of long association, but it was also because the whigs could, even when office seemed furthest away, still derive comfort from the fact that opposition had a recognized role in the state. Its usefulness in keeping constant scrutiny overministers, and even in standing ready as an alternative government, was generally acknowledged.[1] This encouragement was supplemented by hopes of being able to check some government measures. Finally, there was the prospect of putting the case against ministerial men and measures so that it should go on record and, amplified by press and *Hansard*, go out to the country and abroad to encourage the like-minded, and possibly to gain converts.[2]

W. H. Lyttelton once expressed the hope that the whig leader, Tierney, would not go into office, since this would make him less popular and limit his ability to do good.[3] For most whigs, however, opposition was a second best with several marked disadvantages. Resisting bad principles was less satisfactory than implementing good ones and ambition was always better gratified on ministerial benches. Only a few whigs had to suffer overt discrimination at the hands of government, but others thought that they did, and the whole party was inevitably condemned to suffer some deprivation. Those bonds of place and patronage which led Grey to argue that 'on the side of the government there will always be a regular, systematic, and well organised party' were lacking. Also, the opposition member lost the local patronage accorded to ministerialists, and ran against that declining influence which government could still bring to bear on elections.[4]

During the war and the immediate post-war period the whigs had to combat the prevailing hostility to the liberal principles they advocated and to protect groups who responded with scant gratitude. Grey wrote:

others less shabby are tired of opposition.' See also Samuel Romilly, *Memoirs of the Life of Sir Samuel Romilly*, London, 1840, iii. 318–19.

[1] See Castlereagh's description of opposition as 'those gentlemen opposite, who, he trusted, would fill official situations hereafter, if the confidence of the crown should be withdrawn from the present ministers' (*P.D.* xxxv. 271).

[2] See W. Roscoe to T. W. Coke, n.d. (Roscoe Papers, Picton Library, Liverpool), for a good expression of this view.

[3] *P.D.* xli. 614.

[4] Grey to Wilson, 20 July 1818 (Grey).

I have on every occasion which my parliamentary life has presented, defended popular rights when I thought them dangerously attacked, and resisted the extension of the power and undue influence of the crown. This system of conduct has during thirty four years . . . excluded me from office, but it has not protected me against the reproaches and distrust of the very people whom I have endeavoured to serve.[1]

Even when liberal sentiments began to gain ground in the changed political climate of the 1820's, bringing the whigs more nearly into accord with the prevailing mood of the political nation, they were still condemned to the somewhat impotent role of supporting measures which they felt could be more effectively and fully implemented by whig ministers.

Undoubtedly many whigs had a martyr complex which predisposed them to exaggerate the difficulties of their position. Yet such a complex was at least partially justified, for it was, as Sir James Mackintosh pointed out,

their lot to devote themselves to a life of toilsome, thankless, and often unpopular opposition, with no stronger allurement to ambition than a chance of a few months of office in half a century, and with no other inducement to virtue than the faint hope of limiting and mitigating evil; always certain that the merit would never be acknowledged, and generally obliged to seek for the best proof of their services in the scurrility with which they were reviled.[2]

The fact that the body of volunteers which constituted the whig core of the opposition continued to hold together and to function as a party in the face of these difficulties is the most effective testimony to the strength both of their principles and of the ties that bound them together. Perhaps it is a feature which makes them a new type of party on the political scene.

[1] Grey to Wilson, 19 November 1820 (Grey).
[2] *P.D.* xxx. 896.

II

PARTY AND ORGANIZATION

PARTY represented opinion, but to be effective it had to be organized opinion. The parliamentary struggle required leadership, consultation, and some form of secretariat. The strengthening of party ties necessitated a meeting place and social functions. Elections created a need to find seats for suitable men and men for likely seats. Responding to such needs in an environment of mass electorate and mass communications, late nineteenth- and twentieth-century parties naturally developed a mass membership and a rigid framework. In the early nineteenth century the response to the needs was similarly influenced by the prevailing social and political background. In a period when the total electorate numbered a few hundred thousand, when under a third of the constituencies were contested at general elections, and when national issues were usually less important than local, extra-parliamentary organization inevitably depended on personal initiatives, rather than elaborate machinery. At a time when the social world was small and intimate, personal connexions and social ties obviated the need for formal ties. All the functions necessary to a political party were performed. The methods by which this was done were those appropriate to the period.

The party leader, a key figure, was less important than his counterparts either before or since. Eighteenth-century factions had centred on one man, who was often the *raison d'être* of the group. Later leaders have held tight the reins of party discipline. The early nineteenth-century whig party was too large to allow its leader the easy superiority of the faction leader, or even for him to have the influence of a Fox, who had practically formed the party after his own image.[1] Instead he was the first among

[1] 'As to a leader who is more than the mere agent and instrument of the general opinion of his party, that is whose authority shall create for them the opinions they espouse, it is a phenomenon, which whether desirable or not will never occur again in our days and I believe is hardly adapted to the state of society in which we live' (Holland to T. Grenville, 24 July 1818; Grenville Papers, Add. MSS. 41858, f. 288).

equals, the head of a coalition of faction leaders. The party was also too loose to be controlled in modern fashion; a wide spectrum of opinion made the leader a conciliator rather than a driving force. His strengths as leader were largely personal, for a leader established his primacy through his abilities and his reputation as a statesman. He would take the major position accorded to his party in any ministry, and the experience of 1806, and later of 1830, indicated that if his party was dominant in the administration, he would become prime minister.

His standing in the political world thus became a major asset to the party, and hopes of place under him a bond of unity. Stature could be supplemented by the attractions of personality and principles. The charm of Charles James Fox so bound the whig party that Creevey could describe his political creed simply as 'devotion to Fox'; and both Fox's passionately vague and Grey's austerely high-principled liberalism attracted followers, even though, after the creative phase of the 1790's when Fox had largely dominated and shaped the party, the leader's position in respect of party doctrine was that of a presbyterian moderator rather than a pope. Essentially the leader's importance was negative rather than positive. He could check fissiparous tendencies, but not end them: he could make the party a more effective fighting force, but not give it power.

Even these negative functions were not effectively performed. The leader at the end of the war was Grenville, accepted by Fox when their two parties allied, and confirmed in office by the death of Fox and the experience of the 'talents'. Though Grey, as leader of the Foxite section, deferred automatically to Grenville, the more radical members of the party accepted him with bad grace, and his icy aloofness and diminishing activity maintained his own reputation as a statesman at the expense of the party's for vigour. Grenville had seen the need to end this situation as early as 1812, when, though only 54, he had felt years and lassitude growing on him and had written to Grey to request him to take over the leadership.[1] Grey responded by deprecating his own abilities and industry, and, less explicably, declaring his own intention of withdrawing from all formal position at the same time.[2] The matter was deferred for a

[1] Grenville to Grey, 10 November 1812 (Grey).

[2] *H.M.C. Dropmore*, x. 311–13.

personal explanation in the coming session, and apparently this changed nothing.[1] Thus an unsatisfactory situation was prolonged with both leaders curtailing the scope of their activity; Grenville announced his intention to attend as little as possible, Grey stayed at home in 1814 and 1816 and took soundings about withdrawal in the intermediate year.[2]

Even the rupture between the two sections of the party did not bring definition, for in June 1817 both Grenville and Grey rose in the lords to announce their intentions of withdrawing from active politics.[3] Grey described his own position slightly later:

the declaration I made last year was not a hasty or an unpremeditated opinion. It proceeded from a deliberate conviction of the impossibility, after the course that events took in the course of last session, of my being able to do any good, and of the necessity both on account of my health and the circumstances of my family, of my residing less in London, and withdrawing myself from any active lead in public affairs . . . though I by no means intend to abandon all concern whatever in politics or to preclude myself from taking such a part as I may hereafter may [*sic*] be able to take, if an opportunity should arise which might afford a hope of my being able to serve either my friends or the public.[4]

The effect of Grey's declaration was slight. There was a brief burst of speculation, Whishaw and Althorp conjecturing that Lansdowne would become leader, and Brougham suggesting the Duke of Bedford, 'if the Duchess will let him do the needful', but nothing came of this, and towards the middle of next year Brougham acknowledged that Grey's supremacy was beyond question.[5]

There could be no change. Grey perversely and paradoxically continued to regard himself as leader and continued to talk of retirement, writing in 1818: 'every succeeding year impresses me more strongly with the conviction that to lead, for which I

[1] Grenville to Grey, 28 November 1812 (Grey).

[2] Grenville to Holland, 14 January 1817, copy (Grey); *H.M.C. Dropmore*, x. 360–4, 397–8; Rosslyn to Grey, 25 December 1815 (Grey).

[3] *P.D.* xxxvi. 1005 and 1013.

[4] Grey to Fitzwilliam, 29 January 1818 (Milton).

[5] Brougham to Lambton, n.d. [1817] (Brougham); Lady Seymour, *The 'Pope' of Holland House*, London, 1906, p. 184; Brougham to Lambton 'Tuesday', n.d. [July 1818] (Brougham); Althorp to Milton, 21 March 1818 (Milton).

was never perhaps sufficiently qualified—I am now altogether unfit'.[1] Much as Grey might afford himself the exquisite pleasure of offering to resign, he was not prepared to make the act definite. This was brought out in 1818 by a short-lived attempt, inspired by George Tierney, to secure a definite understanding on the leadership. Tierney was apparently convinced of the need to install Lord Lansdowne as leader. He began to point this out to Holland and others: 'we can hope for no material accession to our present strength before it is distinctly felt under whom new recruits are to be controlled, and to whom for the maintenance of his principles or to the furtherance of his political views a man who joins the opposition is to look'.[2] Grey, informed of Tierney's desire for some decision on the leadership by Holland, by his own son-in-law J. G. Lambton, and, more tactfully, by Tierney himself, reacted strongly.[3] His reply to Tierney gave a clear indication that the point should not be pressed. Privately he commented to Holland:

I can see no possible advantage, and still less any necessity for urging such an arrangement as he appears to call for in the house of lords. I suppose he must mean the public declaration of some acknowledged head of the party there. As far as I am myself concerned, such an attempt can only have the effect of obliging me to withdraw myself, more decidedly than I have yet done, though what I have said two years ago I intended to have that effect, from all pretensions to that situation. In the opinion which you seem to entertain of the importance of my refusing it, and in all the feelings you express upon that subject, I can only see proofs, not of my fitness for it, but of your partiality and kindness. These undoubtedly I cannot transfer to any other person, nor could I ever for a moment dream that I had any right beyond my own abdication. Even this I should not have considered as a matter within my own choice or justifiable on any other ground than my consciousness of my inability to discharge the duties which I owe to my friends and to the public. In the appointment of another I could not under such circumstances consider myself as having even a voice. It must result from the opinion

[1] Grey to Lambton, 16 November 1818 (Lambton); Grey to Devonshire, 23 October 1819 (Devonshire).

[2] Tierney to Holland, 23 August 1818 (Holland); Fazakerly to Milton, 11 August 1818 (Milton).

[3] Holland to Grey, 6 November 1818 (Holland); Holland to Grey, 13 November 1818 (Holland); S. J. Reid, *Life and Letters of the First Earl of Durham*, London, 1906, i. 107.

and confidence of the party in the person, whoever he may be, on whom that opinion and confidence may devolve.[1]

This ambivalent position was a veto on any alternative leadership. As Ellenborough pointed out to Grey in 1822: 'I consider you as the real leader, because if you belong to a party you must be its leader.'[2]

Ties which were based on respect and affection could hardly be transferred at will, and important figures in the party were not prepared for any change. They were ready to accept Grey's inactivity in the hope that prospects of office would bring him once more into the field. Holland told him:

> If a season were to arrive in which a government could be formed with you at the head and your friends in the body of it—what a silly reason it would be to forgo such an advantage because some time before you had said you would not avail yourself of it—they at the time might think and probably would think it dishonourable and inexpedient to do anything but with you and under you.[3]

More important, there was no real alternative. Tierney pointed out to Grey: 'I can assume that you will say you have not the authority which you ought to possess, but it still is, however limited, the only authority we have.'[4] Lord Holland, whom Grey had unsuccessfully asked to take over the leadership in 1812, was disqualified by his diffidence, his gout, and his idiosyncratic views on foreign policy. The most he was prepared to do was to act as Grey's self-effacing *locum tenens* in the 1816 session.[5] Lansdowne was more respected by the moderate section of the party and was adept at conciliation, yet his character was colourless, his disposition retiring, his habits dilatory, and his integrity unalloyed with ambition, drive, or decisiveness. All the other leading magnates were ruled out even before consideration; Carlisle and Fitzwilliam as too old, Darlington as incapable, and Bedford and Devonshire as too little active in politics. All possible remedies were worse than the disease.

[1] Grey to Holland, 9 November 1818 (Holland).

[2] Ellenborough to Grey, 18 November 1822 (Grey).

[3] Holland to Grey, 13 November 1818 (Holland).

[4] Tierney to Grey, 10 January 1820 (Grey).

[5] Grey to Holland, 14 November 1812 (Grey); Holland to Grey, 17 November 1812 (Holland); Holland to Grey, 7 January 1813 (Holland); Holland to Grey, 8 December 1816 (Grey).

Grey stayed as leader, and the party remained saddled with a largely unsatisfactory figurehead. Perhaps Grey's most striking characteristic was a deep and abiding pessimism about the possibility of changing, or even influencing, the political scene. This attitude was behind both the frequent talk of retirement and withdrawal and the occasional public declarations of such an intention.[1] It was reinforced by laziness, ill health, and distance from London. Each session the pleading letters would flow north to Howick. In some sessions they were answered promptly, in others they received only the partial answer of a late arrival; in some they were ignored or countered by a series of excuses based on the futility of action, family convenience, personal illness, and the illnesses and pregnancies of Lady Grey (even though, as Lady Glenverbie pointed out, Grey was hardly a male midwife). Uncertainty as to Grey's movements made it difficult to plan the session's tactics in advance, and without positive decisions advance notification could not be issued to bring party supporters up to London. This hampered party activities, while Grey's aristocratic reserve, concealing as it did a brooding sensitivity, weakened personal ties. Indeed, perhaps the most surprising factor about the situation is that a leadership so debilitating for the party received hardly any criticism.

The problem solved itself with Grey's withdrawal from politics in the course of the 1820's, though even then he regarded his inactivity as a means of resigning without formal announcement. In 1823 he informed Holland that he would take no part in future political arrangements though throwing no obstacles in the way of others who might think it expedient to do so.[2] Two years later he wrote to his old friend:

> Our views as to office are, I believe, much the same: except that I may perhaps conceive myself more out of the question, in all cases, than you do: or ought to do. My conduct, for the last two years, must have made this sufficiently clear to all who take an interest in it: and I have no reason to believe that anybody, yourself and Tierney excepted, looks at all to my opinion as in any degree influencing their conduct.[3]

[1] See, for example, *P.D.* xli. 479 and 494.
[2] Grey to Holland, 23 February 1823 (Grey).
[3] Grey to Holland, 2 September 1825 (Holland).

Grey now regarded Lansdowne as the leader of the party, a conclusion to which the bulk of its members had probably been driven by Grey's absence and Lansdowne's presence in parliament. Yet Lansdowne was in a very difficult position until some formal understanding had been arrived at, Holland pointed out that Grey had a duty to keep Lansdowne informed and should make it quite clear whether he himself intended to be active or whether the party were to consider him as no longer a figure to be consulted.[1] This jolt was the only way to end Grey's drift, and it had the desired effect. Grey reported early next year:

remembering what you said in our correspondence of last year, I have told Lansdowne that I wish him decidedly to understand that I stand out of the way, and look to him as the person best qualified to undertake the chief direction of the party, if a party can now be said to exist, whether in or out of office. He received this kindly and with a sort of *nolo episcopari*, but I think I could perceive both at the time and since that he feels that this situation is more defined by it, and that he will act with greater confidence than he did before.[2]

It is completely characteristic that even now Grey should not have made any public announcement of his resignation. He communicated it only to Holland, Tierney, and Lambton. He also misunderstood Lansdowne's reaction, for the diffident peer was unwilling to become a party leader, feeling himself neither inclined nor able to fill the position adequately.[3] Lansdowne took neither a more active nor a more dominant role, and later pointed out to Holland: 'I have at no time considered myself, or ever allowed myself to be considered by others as a party leader.'[4] The final abdication had left an uncertain situation and a leaderless party.

The weakness of the over-all leadership situation was further amplified by the situation in the commons, where the decisive parliamentary combats were fought. With the main leader in the lords there was a need for an additional leader in the commons. He was inevitably something of a subordinate figure, a channel of consultation and communication rather than a focus of decision. Responsibility was heavy, power minimal. It was

[1] Holland to Grey, 2 September 1825 (Holland).
[2] Grey to Holland, 16 February 1826 (Grey).
[3] Lansdowne to Brougham, 4 January 1827 (Brougham).
[4] Lansdowne to Holland, 31 May 1827 (Holland).

a wearing process keeping the party in lords and commons in step without being able to decide the marching orders, just as it was difficult to unite the larger and more heterogeneous party in the commons behind a policy and a strategy which, in part at least, were decided elsewhere. Real as the difficulties were, they were too often turned into excuses for doing without a commons leader, a situation which weakened the party, for a recognized leader could guide and encourage its efforts, help to co-ordinate its strategy, and give it a greater degree of coherence.

The leader since 1807 had been George Ponsonby, a cautious and conciliatory figure, no great speaker, and the object of sarcastic hostility from the radical wing. Historians have tended to echo contemporary criticisms of Ponsonby, though these ignore his sensible clear-headed approach, and also his difficulties. In the last years of the war and the first years of peace no leader could resolve the disagreements or straddle the range of opinion within the party. Only Tierney was generous enough to admit that a leader's job was difficult 'because of all the confusions, cabals and divisions by which we are distracted. It is not in the power of any one man to compose them and produce order.'[1]

Ponsonby died in 1817, and the first reaction was a consensus against filling the vacancy in the leadership. Some thought with Abercromby: 'I see no man who is fit to be called by that title—at least there is no one who would accept it, that is fit.'[2] Others were oppressed with the difficulty of choice, and both groups took refuge in the idea of doing without a leader. Brougham reported to Lambton: 'Romilly and I have come to a very clear opinion in which Sefton and indeed every sound man among us concurs, that to talk of any leader in parliament at present is absurd, that we shall do far better and be a much more formidable party without one.'[3] Lambton and others accepted this situation, Althorp so heartily that he was shortly proposing that the party should be controlled by a committee of twenty selected by ballot, a system which would allow all sections to be represented and the new leader to emerge from the com-

[1] Tierney to Grey, 28 January 1813 (Grey).
[2] Abercromby to Devonshire, 8 July 1817 (Devonshire).
[3] Brougham to Lambton, n.d. [1817] (Brougham).

mittee.[1] Such republican enthusiasms dimmed only when lack of a leader produced difficulties. Althorp reported to Milton in 1818: 'The experienced people in the opposition say it is impossible for us to go on without an acknowledged leader. Duncannon says that without one we must certainly go entirely to pieces and that he has never had so much difficulty in getting an attendance as this session.'[2] Tierney too shared these trends of thought and emphasized the need for a leader if the party were to be mustered in full.[3]

From such sentiments there sprang a move to appoint a leader. This settled its choice on George Tierney, who, though less striking in personality than his two main rivals, Sir Samuel Romilly and Henry Brougham, did not arouse the same degree of antagonism in the more moderate sections of the party, and if less inspiring was considered more stable. As an able debater Tierney had been coming to the fore ever since the death of Ponsonby, and Wilberforce was referring to him as the leader of the opposition as early as March 1818.[4] At the same time Brougham, his main rival, lost ground heavily by ill-judged manœuvres in 1817, and in 1818 was purposely keeping in the background and deferring to Tierney.[5] The choice, originally difficult, became suddenly easy. It was made, not by Grey and the aristocratic members, who, after the experiment of appointing Ponsonby, appear to have stood clear, but by a spontaneous movement among the party in the commons. Sefton and Duncannon were the leading figures, though Grey was consulted in the early stages, being shown a letter, to be signed by M.P.s, which asked Tierney to take office as leader. Grey was neither helpful nor sanguine, though he half-heartedly agreed to the experiment, feeling that 'if a leader is to be appointed, this is the only choice that can be made at present'.[6] With this faint praise the preliminary discussions were followed, on 12 July 1818, by a meeting at Brooks's club of all M.P.s still in London. This gathering, nearly forty strong, included representatives of all sections of opinion, and in addition Sefton was able to produce a letter from Brougham, then campaigning in Westmorland,

[1] Althorp to Milton, 21 March 1818 (Milton). [2] Ibid.
[3] Tierney to Grey, 11 April 1818 (Grey). [4] *P.D.* xxxvii. 859.
[5] Brougham to Lambton, n.d. [1818] (Brougham).
[6] Grey to Wilson, 20 July 1818 (Grey).

expressing his cordial support. This wise precaution went far to guarantee success, for though he could not be leader himself, the lawyer could, had he been ill disposed, have made the life of any other impossible.[1] The meeting agreed unanimously both on the need for a leader and on the appointment of Tierney. The letter of invitation, which bound signatories together 'to strengthen and consolidate by every possible means, that union by which alone these principles which we think essential to the general welfare of the nation can be upheld and brought into action', was approved for circulation and submission to Tierney.[2] After a busy month of letter-writing and canvassing Duncannon secured the signatures of 113 M.P.s, and letters of support from ten others, while fourteen M.P.s, though well disposed, declined to sign for fear of alienating constituents by a close identification with party.

The hardest part of the whole operation proved to be that of persuading Tierney to take office, for his first reaction was to decline, largely because of his concern that some decision should be taken at the same time about the leadership in the lords.[3] Only in the face of reiterated persuasion from Duncannon and Holland did he at length give way. Nevertheless the first effects of the experiment were striking. Castlereagh admitted that

> a great improvement had certainly been effected by giving the command to the right honourable gentleman. Now all was order—everyone was in his place—all with 'eyes front' looked to the right honourable gentleman for instructions ready to obey the word of command. Bound to acknowledge the infallibility of their political pope, they took their places at five o'clock, and hardly left them to obtain natural refreshment.[4]

Even the militants praised the new leadership, Brougham commenting that 'nothing can do better than Tierney and our discipline is perfect', while Wilson added: 'Tierney has gained quite decisive over the new parliament. His triumph is decisive

[1] Duncannon to Grey, 13 July 1818 (Grey); Duncannon to Elliot, n.d. [13 July 1818] (Milton).

[2] Fitzwilliam to Grey, 18 July 1818 (Grey); Tierney to Grey, 21 August 1818 (Grey).

[3] H. K. Olphin, *George Tierney*, London, 1934, pp. 187–8; Tierney to Grey, 21 August 1818 (Grey); Tierney to Holland, 23 August 1818 (Holland).

[4] *P.D.* xl. 502.

and no effort on the part of the enemy has made any impression to his prejudice.'[1]

Momentum soon passed and Tierney's efforts to recover the situation were marred by the failure of his own health, always precarious and now quickly undermined by exertion and late sittings. In December 1819 he broke down in the house through complete exhaustion, and wrote to Grey:

I have been, and still am most anxious to do all I can for the common cause, and the more so as I am afraid my withdrawing myself would in the present state of things, produce the worst effect in our ranks, but I feel that it is impossible for me to continue my attendance in the house of commons as I have done. Whether the sort of functions I have to perform are capable of being discharged with any advantage unless executed to their full extent is very doubtful. Much will depend upon the temper and spirit of conciliation with which our friends conduct themselves towards one another. As far as depends upon me I can only say that I will make every exertion in my power to assist, but I am compelled to add, my exertions must now be upon a limited scale.[2]

To this end he warned Duncannon before Christmas that his health would not allow of anything like a full attendance.[3]

Early next year Tierney reiterated his desire to withdraw, and Lambton and Althorp consulted about the means to get Brougham quietly seated in Tierney's place, but Althorp was only too well aware of the strong objections felt by many to Brougham, and the scheme foundered.[4] Nothing was done until Tierney took the definite decision to withdraw from his official position, which he did early in 1821.[5] Though the experiment had failed it had neither done so through Tierney's fault nor demonstrated the advisability of doing without a leader. Tierney had had to face serious difficulties, not the least of them being lack of active support from Grey, which left him like 'a captain without an admiral' for much of the time.[6] He had suffered too

[1] Brougham to Grey, 6 February 1819 (Brougham); Wilson to Grey, 5 February 1819 (Wilson Papers, Add. MSS. 30123, ff. 33–34).

[2] Tierney to Grey, 31 December 1819 (Grey).

[3] Tierney to Grey, 5 April 1820 (Grey).

[4] Lambton to Grey, 13 May 1820 (Grey); Althorp to Spencer, 15 May 1820 (Althorp).

[5] *P.D.*, N.S. iv. 4812; C. W. Wynn to H. W. Wynn, 12 March 1821 (Wynn, 4816); *The Times*, 13 March 1821.

[6] Tierney to Grey, 19 January 1820, and 5 April 1820 (Grey).

from the opposition's inability to bring down the government, for the high hopes engendered by the occasional success threw into gloomy perspective the depth of disappointment and disillusion which automatically followed. Despite such difficulties Tierney had brought a new cohesion and force to the opposition, and led it through its most vigorous phase until his health could stand no more exertion.

The resignation left a real need for a leader, and Brougham standing head and shoulders above all possible claimants. Yet the hostility of a section of the party created the possibility of a split should he be appointed, while he himself was extremely reluctant to take the position, and deeply involved in his legal practice.[1] This created a very difficult position, for Brougham led in debates, made the major speeches, and played the leading role in consultations, establishing such a primacy as would prevent any alternative emerging. Yet he himself neither could nor would be installed. Holland summed up the position in a letter, written in 1828, but relevant to the earlier period.

> No party can be conducted with satisfaction to itself and with advantage to the country without a leader *of authority in the house of commons.* 2. Certain very rare qualifications are necessary to constitute such a leader. 3. Brougham who has some of these qualifications (but perhaps not all) in perfection, is a lawyer and neither can nor can be expected to take such an office. 4. There is no body else that has hitherto shown himself equal to it. The consequence is and necessarily will be till some such man arises, disunion, jealousy, inconstancy and what not.[2]

This was clearly shown by whig ruminations on the possibility of office in 1822. Grey and Holland were then both satisfied that the whigs might not be able to take office unless Brougham would lead in the commons, but despite strong persuasion he refused to consider the position. Similarly in 1823, when Duncannon proposed a scheme to strengthen party unity with regular opposition dinners[3] and a written bond, Lord John Russell urged that

[1] Grey to Holland, 16 February 1826 (Grey).

[2] Holland to E. D. Davenport, 20 October 1828 (Bromley–Davenport Papers, John Rylands Library, Manchester).

[3] Althorp to Brougham, 17 March 1823 (Althorp); Russell to Brougham, 23 March 1823 (Brougham); Abercromby to Brougham, 19 and 26 March 1823 (Brougham).

a committee should be appointed of from seven to ten members to put business into some form previously to general meetings. This will be a sort of cabinet which, in a party of 200 I think is necessary to bind different opinions together, or rather different shades of opinion. This being accomplished I think we should get into the habit of following a leader in the house of commons, and who the leader should be there can be no doubt, as there is only one capable of standing up manfully and constantly against Canning. I look to the dinner plan therefore as a beginning of something else.[1]

It is not clear whether the bond was altered to cater for these views, but Abercromby soon wrote to Brougham, in a letter which appears less than frank:

if you wish to be installed leader I have no doubt that you would be placed there by an unanimous vote. But it would entail upon you endless toil and vexation, and by keeping clear of the name you will in fact add to your real power, for on all material points you will have as much influence as you please, and on all minor questions you will be free and unshackled. I see some disadvantages in not having a nominal leader, but they are not to be put in competition with the trouble and endless vexation that would be imposed by accepting the title.[2]

Once again Brougham declined to countenance the idea and the whole scheme foundered. Macdonald reluctantly acknowledged that he was 'right in declining to be bothered with the command of our ragammuffin forces', but at the same time he pointed to the misfortune to the party, 'for a leader makes his party respected in debate as a good general does his army in a campaign, and you may be sure none of us young lords will attempt what we manifestly cannot succeed in'.[3] No new schemes were urged after 1823; as the political temperature fell there was less incentive to organize for a more cohesive or effective opposition. When pundits were claiming that party had ceased to exist, it was progressive to agree, reactionary to organize. The problem of the leadership was solved only when, in 1830, a revived party turned to Althorp, who was overcoming his diffidence and soon became the tortoise on whose back the Grey administration was to rest.

[1] Russell to Brougham, n.d. [March 1823] (Brougham).
[2] Abercromby to Brougham, 26 March 1823 (Brougham).
[3] Macdonald to Brougham, 1 April 1823 (Brougham).

Whether or not the party had the benefit of a defined leader in the commons, it needed a whip. Such a 'whipper in', in the person of the patronage secretary to the treasury, was already a recognized figure on the government side. His emergence among the opposition was slower, though a *de facto* whip existed by the beginning of this period. This appears to have been James Macdonald, who was in the unfortunate position of sitting for one of the Marquis of Stafford's seats at a time when Stafford was drifting away from the whig party. Possibly because of the difficulties this was causing, Macdonald decided at the end of the war to go on to the Continent and in 1816 resigned his seat. Ponsonby reported to Grey: 'Macdonald who used to make out our lists and attend to our musters in the house will I presume not be in England at our next meeting and we must think of some other person; does any one occur to you as fit to be applied to?'[1] Grey's reply does not survive, but shortly afterwards these functions were being fulfilled by Lord Duncannon, who continued to exercise them right up to the accession to power in 1830.

With the tact of a true whip Duncannon was self-effacing. His personality is difficult to describe; he was a political technician working behind the scenes rather than an expounder of principles. Yet he quickly established himself as a major influence in the party, being involved in most of the pre-session preparations, one of the most prominent managers of Brooks's club, and active in the whig efforts for the Westminster elections in 1818, 1819, and 1820. At a more prosaic level, there are occasional mentions of Duncannon sitting anxiously in the house, counting the numbers drifting in and out, and, most characteristically of all, compiling lists of names, both after election results were known and before major divisions.[2] His, too, was the responsibility for sending lists of opposition voters in parliamentary divisions to the press, though Joseph Hume began to supplement the official whip's own efforts in the 1820's, with the result that the number of divisions actually published greatly increased.[3]

[1] Ponsonby to Grey, 4 January 1815 (Grey).

[2] See Buckingham and Chandos, *Memoirs of the Court of England During the Regency*, London, 1856, ii. 245, for an example of Duncannon observing fluctuations in attendance.

[3] The interest in these lists is indicated by a note from Black, editor of the

Much of the activity of both commons, leader and whip centred on the party list, 140 or 150 strong in the first parliament of the period, about 170 after 1818, and 180 in the 1820's.[1] To be on the list and to receive notes based on it was to be enlisted in the whig party: to ask not to be sent the notes or to fail to receive them was tantamount to withdrawal, although J. W. Ward in 1812 declined to make any such formal notification, complaining that 'the whigs consider themselves as having a sort of vested interest in every man that has ever supported them'.[2]

The responsibility for sending out requests for attendance at the beginning of each session appears to have been Ponsonby's initially. He was never very energetic, and in 1814 he did not bother to write at all.[3] In later sessions Tierney appears to have written to the English members from London, while Ponsonby wrote to the Irish. On Ponsonby's death the whole task fell to Tierney; on his resignation to Duncannon.[4] Not every member was written to directly. Those in the Grenville group were not written to without prior permission from their leader, and members grouped round a patron appear to have been contacted by a blanket letter to the patron.[5]

The second use of the lists was to send out notes requesting attendance at party meetings and at major party clashes on motions placed by a major whig figure, or on pieces of government legislation which the party was particularly concerned to oppose.[6] More continuous attendance was left to the haphazard arrangements of individual goodwill. The leading figures in

Morning Chronicle, to Hume, n.d. 'Friday' (Hume Papers): 'I shall publish as many lists as you send to me. It keeps the thing before the public and does good.' See also *Spectator*, 23 October 1830.

[1] Buckingham and Chandos, *Regency*, ii. 267–8; Lambton to Grey, 26 March 1818 (Grey); Camden, p. 80.

[2] J. W. Ward to Brougham, n.d. [1812] (Brougham); Maxwell, pp. 121–2. In 1819 Sir H. Parnell asked Duncannon not to send him any more notes, since he disapproved of the 'management and proceedings' of the party. He never received any again, though he continued to vote fairly regularly with the whigs. H. Parnell to Huskisson, 18 September 1827 (Huskisson Papers, Add. MSS. 38751, f. 15).

[3] Ponsonby to Grey, 25 November 1814 (Grey).

[4] Duncannon to Lambton, n.d. [1825] (Lambton).

[5] Tierney to Grey, 14 January 1816 (Grey); Darlington to Grey, 12 November 1819 (Grey); Tierney to Grey, 4 January 1817 (Grey).

[6] Maxwell, p. 121. Lord J. Russell, *Recollections and suggestions, 1813 to 1873*, London 1875, p. 41, mentions that he was informed by Tierney that the notes usually sent out when a party motion was contemplated would not be allowed in the case of reform,

opposition were reasonably good attenders, and in a dull house it was always the government, with its larger and looser fringe of uncommitted members, that dropped most heavily in numbers. An attempt was made to give opposition attendance a more organized form at the beginning of 1819. Arbuthnot, a hostile witness, claimed that the opposition had signed a paper binding themselves never to quit the house without Tierney's permission.[1] There was in fact a bond, but its stipulations were rather more prosaic: 'We the undersigned agree to attend every night in the house of commons (Wednesdays excepted) during the continuance of the public business of the day.'[2] The surviving copy carries twenty-five names, nearly all of them stalwarts of the party. The expedient was apparently successful in 1819, but whether it was regarded as extending beyond the one year is doubtful.

The nature of party unity dictated the pattern of activity. Leaders had to manage an army of volunteers, not of conscripts. The inclinations of these volunteers ranged from a mild phobia, even, for skirmishing to advocacy of vigorous guerilla warfare. Keeping the army in step needed continuous consultation and negotiation with magnates, and, more important, with and between important individuals, such as Grey, Lansdowne, Holland, Brougham, Tierney, Romilly, Macdonald, and Mackintosh.

Consultation became a continuous process. Before sessions the central problems of the issues to be raised and the desirability of an amendment to the address were usually discussed in leisurely correspondence between the leading figures, though by the 1820's even this discussion was minimal. There were basic arguments for and against an amendment. Duncannon favoured the full early muster it would achieve, but warned that, unless an early decision was taken to do something on the first day, it was better to do nothing, for without summonses the party would be weak for the first fortnight.[3] On the other hand, some thought an amendment necessary only when ministers were expected to commit the house to some undesirable point of

[1] A. Aspinall, *The Correspondence of Charles Arbuthnot*, Camden Society, 3rd series, vol. lxv, London, 1941, p. 15; Wilson to Grey, 8 March 1819 (Wilson Papers, Add. MSS. 30123, f. 55).

[2] Declaration in Lambton Papers relating to reform.

[3] Holland to Grey, 4 December 1816 (Grey).

view; and still others regarded a fight on the first day as a stand on unknown and disadvantageous ground.[1] These arguments against amendment normally prevailed, and only three party amendments were moved in this period, those of 1816, 1819, and November 1819.

As the session approached, personal contact supplemented correspondence, and Holland and Tierney normally took soundings of those in the metropolis. The ideal of a full muster for consultation was rarely realized, but enough people were normally in London before the session for clear indications of the pattern of opinion to emerge. From this time consultation, normally through informal channels, was continuous, and strategy was planned by the leadership group. In addition, during the session party co-operation entailed some measure of allocation of speeches by the leader in the commons, and also some consultation with him by individuals about intended motions, though, as Tierney pointed out to Castlereagh in debate, the leader's actual powers were very limited:

did the noble lord think, that he (Mr. Tierney) could have the impudence, even if he had the inclination, to say to any honourable member that such a motion should or should not be made? . . . he felt flattered by the attention of any honourable member who consulted him as to whether any particular motion ought or ought not to be made. But he should feel ashamed of himself if he went one step further than simply giving his opinion upon the question. The person so consulting was of course master of his own actions.[2]

Thus, when in 1818 Lambton announced his intention of opposing an indemnity bill on first reading, Tierney remonstrated, but to no avail. Lambton duly opposed.[3] Such independence occasionally led to mismanagement. In May 1820, after the defeat of a motion of his on the appointment of a fourth baron of exchequer in Scotland, Lord A. Hamilton rose to move a second motion, only to have Brougham step in with an amendment and Tierney with a motion for the previous question. Opposition's advantage in driving the government hard on the earlier motion was completely lost.[4] This kind of difficulty was

[1] Grenville to Holland, 14 January 1817, copy (Grey); *Morning Chronicle*, 30 November 1812.

[2] *P.D.*, N.S. iv. 30.

[3] Lambton to Grey, 6 March 1818 (Grey).

[4] Wilson to Grey, 16 May 1820 (Wilson Papers, Add. MSS. 30123, f. 157).

amplified by the independent propensities of the radicals. Whitbread in his last years gave no notice of his motions and caused acute embarrassment, because it was never clear how many whigs he would syphon off.[1] Thus the number of divisions in a session became a measure not only of the bitterness of party conflict but also of the weakness of party discipline.

Much of the consultation could be carried out through informal contacts. Some, however, required the more formal expedient of a party meeting. It has been stated that such meetings were called by party leaders who intended to lay down the law and 'came simply to announce decisions that had already been taken in the drawing-rooms of Lansdowne House, Holland House, Fife House, or Apsley House, by the few great men of the party'.[2] This may be true of the government, but on the opposition side the meetings were held for consultation rather than command: to decide on a line, rather than to lay one down. Evidence is available for twenty-six party meetings up to 1828, the largest meeting being that held on 5 November 1819 to decide on whig policy for the new session, and was attended by eighty-five M.P.s and twenty-three peers.[3] The second largest was held in May 1815 at Devonshire House to consult on the war, and was attended by over seventy M.P.s.[4] Only two others are described as meetings of the members in both houses. The rest, presumably attended only by commoners, appear to have been smaller; some as small as five in the case of the meeting held at Ponsonby's house just before the 1815 session, and seven in the case of the meeting held, again at Ponsonby's, before the 1817 session. Though small, they were mostly representative, in that leading figures from the different sections of the party were present. The venues differ, the meetings in the earlier part of the period being mostly held at Ponsonby's, those in Tierney's period of office at Burlington House. Later still Lansdowne House and Althorp's chambers, and even Burdett's house, were used. Only two meetings were held at Brooks's club.

In nearly every case discussion centred on policy decisions

[1] Tierney to Grey, 28 November 1812 (Grey).

[2] A. Aspinall, 'English Party Organisation in the Early Nineteenth Century', *E.H.R.*, 1926, p. 393.

[3] Fitzwilliam to his wife(?), n.d. [1819] (Milton).

[4] Horner to Murray, 24 May 1815 (Horner Papers, British Library of Political and Economic Science).

about approaching sessions or motions. Only eight meetings differed from this general pattern. One was a small meeting held in October 1821 to discuss Sir Robert Wilson's dismissal, another the meeting held in July 1818 to elect Tierney as leader. Five meetings were held in 1827 to deal with the problems posed by the break-up of Liverpool's government, and at the remaining one Tierney explained a proposed motion to the assembled party.

Meetings were few because they were only a logical extension of a process of informal consultation and contact which normally allowed opinion within the party to be sounded without the formality of assembly. The whigs, and more particularly the leading figures in the party, were a closely knit group. They were almost a social entity as well as a party. Ties of blood and marriage supplemented political ties; at least fifty-one of the 113 M.P.s who signed the requisition to Tierney in 1818 were related *to each other*, and at least sixty-two were related to members of the aristocracy, mainly to the leading peers in the whig party.[1] Social ties strengthened the political bond still further. The leading members of the party in lords and commons were on close terms socially, visiting the great whig houses outside the session, and during it dining in small and large groups at Devonshire House, Lansdowne House, Burlington House, and Holland House.[2]

These bonds were strengthened by the existence of Brooks's club. This was the social centre for the whig party, just as White's club was for the tories and Boodle's for the country gentlemen and independents, and it was almost an informal political headquarters. The 300 to 400 members of Brooks's included most of the whig peers and M.P.s, so that to enrol in the club was tantamount to enlisting in the party. Its head-

[1] The Tierney papers are now lost and Professor Aspinall's copy of the list is the only surviving one. It includes three sets of fathers and sons, seven sets of brothers. Five members were related to Lord Dundas, four each to Grafton and Spencer, three each to Bedford, Yarborough, Bessborough, Darlington, and Devonshire.

[2] Tierney to Holland, 6 June 1807 (Holland): 'They tell me there are many of the new members who will not vote unless they are asked to dine at Holland House at least ten days before the meeting.' Tierney to Grey, 26 September 1814 (Grey): 'To all those who are anxious to keep up the show of party . . . the shutting up of Holland House will be a sad grievance.' Tierney to Grey, 5 December 1817 (Grey): 'The meeting of parliament and a few Holland House dinners may perhaps put some life into us.' Lambton to Grey, 23 May 1820 (Grey): 'The Duke of Devonshire is giving regular opposition dinners and also weekly parties.'

quarters in St. James's Street were open day and night, dinner being provided each evening during the session, supper when required. The club also boasted a coffee room as well as a newspaper and a card room.[1] All this provided the ideal venue for informal discussion of politics. The social bond was further developed by formal functions. A pre-session dinner for those whigs already in London was a regular institution by the end of the Napoleonic war and it was supplemented by occasional special dinners.[2] In 1819 Tierney was persuaded to agree to a large dinner during the session, and though he consented reluctantly, with an attendance of 146 members the experiment was a great success.[3] The pre-session dinner continued as a regular institution down to the break-up of the party.[4]

A second series of dinners was organized by the Fox club, to which many leading whigs, peers, and commoners, belonged. The only meetings on which evidence is available are the dinners held at large hotels in London on the anniversary of Fox's birthday and occasionally at other times, particularly at Greenwich in the summer.[5] The other functions of the club are obscure though there is some indication that political functions may have been performed. When James Perry, the editor of the *Morning Chronicle* and treasurer or secretary of the club, died in 1821 Holland wrote to Grey to suggest a replacement from outside the club, since it was essential to have someone 'who is in the habits of conversation and intimacy with persons in both houses of parliament, and not averse, nor unused to communicate with those connected with newspapers and agents in elections, in the place of secretary or treasurer of such a club'.[6]

[1] Printed rules, 1817 (Althorp).

[2] *H.M.C. Dropmore*, x. 337; *Morning Chronicle*, 11 June 1813; Tierney to Grey, 23 March 1814 (Grey); *H.M.C. Dropmore*, x. 403.

[3] *Morning Chronicle*, 4 February 1819; Tierney to Grey, 24 January, and n.d. [February 1819] (Grey).

[4] H. Brougham, *The Life and Times of Henry Lord Brougham*, Edinburgh, 1871, ii. 465; Duncannon to Lambton, n.d. [1825] (Lambton).

[5] *Morning Chronicle*, 26 January 1814, 25 January 1816, 9 July 1816, 25 January 1817, 26 January 1818, 29 January 1820, 29 January 1821, 25 February 1822; *The Times*, 12 June 1827. Lord Ilchester states that it was a dining club formed in 1813 but that no dining lists survive until 1829: *The Home of the Hollands 1605–1820*, London, 1937, pp. 285–6.

[6] Holland to Grey, 15 December 1821 (Holland). Lord Holland's suggestion was H. F. Stephenson, private secretary to the Duke of Sussex. He does not appear to have been given the position.

Social contact helped cement the party in lords and commons. There was, however, another bond between these two sections in the political influence of peers. This influence both held the two groups together and strengthened the position of the peers within the party. It also provided the whigs with a firm nucleus in the commons and a basis for electoral planning. Estimates of the total number of seats in the grip of aristocratic and other borough proprietors of all shades of political opinion range from 200 to 500, depending on the radical propensities of the author and the distinctions drawn between influence and control. The estimates of the whig share of these figures vary similarly, ranging between a fifth and a third of the total.[1] A list confined to seats small enough to be controlled, and allowing for the fluctuations both of individual influences and of attachments to the party, gives totals of 42 in 1812, 43 in 1818, the loss of the Grenville seats being compensated for by the growth in the Darlington influence, 42 in 1820, 40 in 1826, and 36 in 1830, when the accession of Lord Radnor's influence was insufficient to compensate for the loss of Calcraft and Darlington.

Magnates took on the expensive task of building up an influence for motives of family prestige, personal advancement, and party loyalty. The same motives influenced their choice of members. A member of the family would inevitably be preferred, but some influences were larger than families, and in any case eldest sons were normally expected to uphold family prestige by fighting the counties. A total of 106 members sat for whig close boroughs during this period. Of these just over two-fifths were related to the controller of the borough, indeed about an eighth of them were the proprietors themselves or their eldest sons.[2] Some of these family members were real acquisitions for

[1] T. H. B. Oldfield, *The Representative History of Great Britain and Ireland*, London, 1816, vi. 285–99, estimates that in 222 seats the members could be nominated by an individual patron, while in 280 others the return could be influenced; 18 per cent. of the former and 17 per cent. of the latter were in the orbit of whigs, both peers and commoners. *The Analysis of the British House of Commons as at Present Constituted*, London, 1823, more soberly lists 103 English constituencies under the control of an influence. Of the 203 members holding these sets 35 were nominated by whigs. Finally, J. W. Croker estimated that of 150 M.P.s returned by peers, 54 were nominated by whigs (L. J. Jennings, *Croker*, i. 367–72).

[2] In making the calculations a member is counted twice if he sat for more than one patron. The total of 106, however, is the actual one.

the party, but taken as a body they were one of its weakest sections, mainly because of their lax attendance. In the 1818–20 parliament members for close boroughs who were related to the proprietors and sat for the whole life of the parliament are listed for an average of sixteen votes, those who were not related are listed for an average figure of twenty. Because it was dragged down by the lax habits of relatives of proprietors the average number of published votes for members for close boroughs is very slightly below that for the whole party in this parliament.

Selection of the remaining members was inevitably influenced by what Grey described as 'all the circumstances of personal engagements, family connection, private friendship and local interest, by which most of them are more or less hampered'.[1] With all such obligations allowed for, the remainder of the seats could be used for party purposes. Here finance was probably a difficulty, for some of the magnates, particularly the smaller ones, appear to have expected a payment, often as high as the prevailing market rate, from their members.[2] In one case, that of George Philips, the Duke of Norfolk brought in a member in lieu of payment of a debt.[3] Used for party purposes, several seats thus became a home for middle-rank figures who were able to pay for them. They were, however, at times used to bring in up-and-coming young men such as Henry Brougham and also as a refuge for senior figures who had been defeated in contests: the party could not afford either the accusation of not looking after its own, or the loss of debating talent.[4] In these last two cases, payment would appear to have been waived or reduced to a minimum, though evidence is scarce. Finally, some superannuitants were also put out to grass in the seats: William Plumer, already 76, was offered a seat by Fitzwilliam in 1812 for his long service to the party. Despite bad health and 'gouty infirmity' he soldiered on to die as a member in 1822.[5]

With the odd exception such as Creevey, who disappeared to

[1] Grey to Lamb, 12 November 1812 (Grey).

[2] In 1807 Thanet required a candidate for Appleby, who was prepared to pay, and Tierney was able to send him the names of Lord Lismore and N. R. Colborne: Tierney to Holland, 20 May [1807] (Holland). Denman was brought in for Calcraft's seat in 1818, his expenses being paid by Lansdowne and Devonshire: J. Arnould, *Memoir of Thomas, First Lord Denman*, London, 1873, i. 118.

[3] Maxwell, pp. 274–5.

[4] Grey to Devonshire, 13 December 1812 (Devonshire).

[5] W. Plumer to Fitzwilliam, 7 August 1812 (Fitzwilliam).

Brussels for three years while sitting for Thetford, the seats when used for party purposes normally brought in active men, including several major figures, some of them as a result of direct suggestions from Grey or other leading whigs, as well as several promising younger men, most of whom were formally sounded on their opinions before selection.[1] The best illustration of the working of the system is provided by the 1812 election, when Romilly, Brougham, Horner, Tierney, and William Lamb all found themselves left standing in the electoral game of musical chairs. Buckingham made room for Horner by persuading one of his members for St. Mawes to go out, while Norfolk brought Romilly in for a vacant seat at Arundel. Tierney was offered a seat by Buckingham but declined it to avoid an unwelcome tie. Not until Grey had written urgently round the magnates was an arrangement arrived at whereby John Courtenay agreed to vacate Thanet's borough of Appleby in return for the payment of his debts, and the Duke of Devonshire and Lord George Cavendish agreed to pay the debts and the expenses of a new election, a total estimated at between £2,000 and £3,000.[2] No seat could be found for Brougham until 1815, when Darlington brought him in for Winchelsea at Grey's direct request. Lamb too was left out and bitterly asked of Grey 'whether those who afford so little mutual assistance can in any reasonable sense of the word be said to act together'.[3] Holland was able to offer him a seat at the end of 1815, on the condition that his views on the restoration of the Bourbons agreed with those of the party, but they did not, and the seat went instead to Sharp.[4] Even James Macdonald, who resigned his seat because he could no longer accept the Marquis of Stafford's political views, received more prompt attention than Lamb. He was brought in in 1816 for Lansdowne's seat at Calne, whose sitting member agreed to go out. The same year Lamb found a seat when Ponsonby's transfer to Wicklow freed Fitzwilliam's seat of Peterborough.

[1] Elliot to F. Lawrence, 8 December 1801 (Milton); Sir R. Heron to Fitzwilliam, 6 and 10 November 1819, and Heron to Milton, n.d. [1819] (Milton); Holland to Brougham, 2 January 1809 (Brougham).

[2] Tierney to Grey, 6 September 1812 (Grey); Holland to Grey, 7 November and 10 December 1812 (Holland).

[3] W. Lamb to Grey, 3 November 1812 (Grey).

[4] Tierney to Holland, 30 November 1815 (Holland); Tierney to Grey, 8 December 1815 (Grey).

The proprietary boroughs provided a nucleus of electoral organization, but inevitably they had to be supplemented by some way of securing seats for other party members, and candidates for favourable seats. An obvious broker was Duncannon, but many did not know him, a few even declined to use his services. Lady Warwick, controller of a strong interest in Lincoln, declined to contact him when she was searching for a candidate in 1817 because she was anxious that secrecy should be maintained.[1] Grey and the leader in the commons were other obvious figures, and Tierney wrote in 1820 that his room had become 'a sort of office for electioneering', adding 'I do nothing but write and talk about contested counties, cities and boroughs'.[2] Perry was also concerned as secretary to the whig club, and in 1820, and possibly at other elections, there was a committee sitting at Brooks's to mobilize the collective wisdom of the party for these purposes.[3] Even so, much remained to be done by informal contacts and by individuals with local knowledge. Much, too, fell to individual magnates who kept a superintending eye on seats where they had property. The compendious Fitzwilliam papers, for instance, show the earl providing candidates for East Retford, Hull, and York, and also putting up financial support for the campaigns of these men.

The main difficulty in electoral brokerage was the question of price. The type of seat, between the closed and the very large boroughs, which was open to outside candidates, was expensive to manage. Agents were inclined to hold out alluring prospects, but nearly always the cost was over, and often well over, £3,000.[4]

[1] Lady Warwick to Fitzwilliam, 12 September 1817 (Fitzwilliam, F. 49).

[2] Tierney to Devonshire, 16 February 1820 (Devonshire). In 1820, when Graham withdrew from Hull, he notified Tierney of his intention: Graham to Fitzwilliam, 9 February 1820 (Fitzwilliam, F. 49*b*). In 1815 Tierney was offered a seat at fair market value, this to be determined by himself and one other assessor, and estimated to be in the region of £3,000: Tierney to Holland, n.d. [1815], and 30 November 1815 (Holland). The seat appears to have been Portarlington.

[3] Perry to Grey, 21 October 1812 (Grey): 'as there appeared to be no arrangement made, nor any exertion desired, I thought it vain to trouble you with the applications that were made for candidates'. *Morning Chronicle*, 26 October 1812, stated that its editor had seen applications for candidates 'from every part of the kingdom'. The committee at Brooks's is mentioned in Graham to Fitzwilliam, 4 February 1820 (Fitzwilliam, F. 49*b*).

[4] Some examples will illustrate the scale of costs. Baring put the expense of Taunton at £3,000–4,000: A. Baring to Lansdowne, 16 September 1825 (Lansdowne). Fazakerly's first election in Hull cost £6,000–7,000: Yarborough to Fitzwilliam, 21 February 1820 (Fitzwilliam, F. 49*d*). Ellice's second for Coventry,

Candidates who matched suitable principles with suitable pockets were not common. Many more candidates were likely to be forthcoming in a lower price range, but their prospect was a difficult one. H. S. Fox was anxious to find a seat in 1812, but though Brougham made every effort on his behalf he failed, partly because he was a late starter, but mainly because he was unable to pay more than £2,000.[1] This imbalance of supply and demand produced frequent whig lamentations about want of candidates. These cries became even stronger in years like 1812 when zeal for the cause was low.[2]

Other election initiatives were few. On rare occasions there was some general concern about particular elections, especially when major figures were contesting large and prestigious seats. Brougham claimed that in fighting Westmorland he was fulfilling a party objective, for 'was there ever a case in which the *ministers* as such were more implicated than in an attack on Lonsdale's party influence? Does he not always use it in the most consistent and yet the *meanest* and *shabbiest* way against us?'[3] It is probable that he received financial aid from members of the party, though Devonshire, Darlington, and Carlisle all refused even to use their influence in the county against the Lowthers.[4] Romilly's candidature for Bristol in 1812 was sup-

£5,000–6,000: Ellice to Grey, 16 March 1820 (Grey). Birch's three contests in Nottingham cost nearly £11,000: P. Crompton to W. Roscoe, 30 January 1807 (Roscoe Papers). In York the 1818 election cost Dundas £7,000 and that of 1820 cost the two whig candidates £15,000, most of these sums being paid by Fitzwilliam: W. Hotham to Fitzwilliam, 2 November 1820 (Fitzwilliam, F. 49*d*). Even without a contest Hull cost 3,000 guineas: Graham to Fitzwilliam, 4 February 1820 (Fitzwilliam, F. 49*b*). In 1818 Lady Warwick agreed to limit any candidate on her interest at Lincoln to a maximum expenditure of £5,000, which she had been told was often spent for a 'common borough': Lady Warwick to Fitzwilliam, 14 February 1818 (Fitzwilliam, F. 49).

[1] H. S. Fox to Brougham, 4 October 1812 (Brougham).

[2] Tierney to Grey, 10 October 1812 (Grey): 'It is a singular thing but it is true that neither opposition nor government have been able to find candidates for places offered to them and in many towns the electors have been left entirely to themselves to manage their own concerns in their own way.' Tierney to Grey, 'Sunday night' [March 1820] (Grey): 'if we had good active candidates with some money we might very much increase the small number which, even as matters stand, we shall gain'. See also Wilson to Grey, 18 March 1820 (Wilson Papers, Add. MSS. 30123, f. 141).

[3] Brougham to Grey, 22 February 1818 (Brougham).

[4] Brougham to Wilson, n.d. [1818] (Wilson Papers, Add. MSS. 30115, f. 110): 'You may thro' some judicious friend set agoing the plan of raising a few hundreds at Brooks's'; Brougham to J. Brougham, 26 February 1818 (Brougham); Darlington to J. Atkinson, 23 January 1818 (Brougham).

ported by a subscription from prominent whigs reputed to have totalled £13,000.[1] Similarly, S. C. Whitbread's fight in Middlesex in 1820 was supported by leading whigs with money and effort.[2] The major example, however, is provided by the Westminster contests. In 1818, when Romilly was persuaded to stand for the constituency, a whig requisition was drawn up, a committee of leading party figures was arranged, a subscription levied, and whig hostesses like Lady Lansdowne and Lady Jersey were put out to canvass.[3] After Romilly's suicide later in the year a small group led by H. G. Bennet attempted to put up first Lord John Russell and then S. C. Whitbread.[4] They secured little support until the radical committee issued a bitter denunciation of both the whigs and Lord Grey. Asked by Lambton to disavow, Hobhouse, the radical candidate, declined.[5] Without awaiting Grey's inevitably angry reaction, Holland, Sefton, Duncannon, Macdonald, and Abercromby agreed to start a whig candidate to vindicate the party, and settled on George Lamb, who, as Abercromby pointed out, was 'in no respect obnoxious to the tories', and as Lambton urged, was 'not of sufficient consequence in the party to make his failure a party disgrace'.[6] The committee interviewed Lamb, made him disclaim his brother William's politics, and adopted him as the whig candidate.[7] His election became a party struggle between whigs and radicals, with the ministerialists throwing their weight on the whig scale.[8] Similar, though less spirited, arrangements were made for the election of 1820, but no ministerial support was forthcoming and whig efforts were also distracted by the simultaneous Middlesex election. Lamb was defeated.

[1] *Bristol Mirror*, 27 June 1812; *A Sketch of the Proceedings of the Bristol Election*, Bristol, 1812, under date 6 October.

[2] S. Whitbread to Grey, 5 May 1820 (Grey).

[3] *The Times*, 9 June 1818. Devonshire subscribed £100 in 1818 and in 1819: Abercromby to Devonshire, 16 February 1819 (Devonshire). So did Bedford, who also gave Holland permission to draw on him for any sum: Bedford to Holland, n.d. [1819] (Holland). Canvassing is mentioned in Lady Morpeth to Devonshire, 15 June 1818 (Devonshire).

[4] Tierney to Grey, 21 December 1818 (Grey).

[5] Ibid.

[6] Abercromby to Devonshire, 16 February 1819 (Devonshire); Lambton to Grey, 12 February 1819 (Grey).

[7] Lambton to Grey, 13 February 1819 (Grey).

[8] Tierney to Grey, 4 January 1819 (Grey), shows that it was known at an early stage that ministerial support would be available. Later soundings confirmed its availability: Rosslyn to Grey, 17 February 1819 (Grey).

The informality which characterized the electoral arrangements also typified the financial. In the late eighteenth century there had been a regular party fund based on six annual contributions of £200 from leading magnates and spent on pamphleteers and the press.[1] Temporary funds were revived after the reunion of the party, for in 1806 there was a fund into which party members wanting seats subscribed the market price and from which the magnates were paid, often at a lower rate. The surplus was presumably used to buy other seats.[2] There was also a party fund, possibly the same one, left over from the 1807 election, but no trace of such financial arrangements can be discovered at any later period.[3] Instead, the financial effort seems to have concentrated on subscriptions for particular purposes; the occasional election, one to pay off Tierney's debts in 1815 and described by Grey as a 'great party object', and another for Sir Robert Wilson when he lost his commission in September 1821.[4]

Regular party funds were the less necessary in this period because the press, previously a big drain on them, was less demanding. Liberal principles, at a discount in the war, rapidly became profitable in terms of expanding circulations. The *Morning Chronicle*, the leading whig newspaper, was of that persuasion not because of any subsidies (on the contrary it was a considerable commercial success), but because its editor, James Perry, was strongly whig in his sentiments, was on terms of intimacy with many of the leading figures in the party, and was prepared to accept written contributions and suggestions from them. Similarly the whig-radical evening paper, *The Traveller*, was so prosperous that its proprietor Colonel Torrens was anxious in

[1] W. Adam to Fitzwilliam, 4 July 1793 (Milton). Fitzwilliam to W. Adam, 2 August 1793 (Milton).

[2] Tierney to Holland, n.d. [October 1806] (Holland).

[3] S. Romilly, *Romilly*, ii. 237. Tierney reported to Grey, 22 January 1820 (Grey): 'if we had money, we might do a great deal. . . . In talking on this subject with Thanet the other day he offered to subscribe £2,000 if I could get a reasonable number of our other grandees to come forward.' There is no indication that the offer was followed up, perhaps because, as Holland commented, 'If others are like me I know there will be little or none of the sinews of war': Holland to Grey, 19 February 1820 (Holland). The only indication of an organized fund is that prepared for the 1831 election, to which Cleveland gave £10,000. C. C. F. Greville, *The Greville Memoirs*, London, 1874, ii. 143, entry for 29 April 1831.

[4] Grey to Holland, 12 August 1815 (Hickleton Papers); *Morning Chronicle*, 9 October 1821.

1821 to take over the *Chronicle* on condition that he could replace Perry in the confidence of the whig party.[1] His attempt was frustrated when the paper was purchased by William Clement, proprietor of the *Observer*, who installed Perry's assistant, John Black, as editor, after which the *Chronicle* began to move towards a more radical editorial line. Torrens, who collected papers like stamps, compensated by buying the *Globe*, the *Nation*, the *Evening Chronicle*, and the *Argus*, and amalgamating them with the *Traveller*, as a flourishing whig-radical periodical which took the name of the *Globe and Traveller*. Other journals, from *The Times* to the *Leeds Mercury*, that tended to back opposition, however independently, were equally self-supporting.

One other means of influence was more usual in this period, that of writing articles to be published in friendly papers. Brougham's efforts for the *Morning Chronicle* and *The Times* are well known, but others, including Lambton, Mackintosh, Tierney, Wilson, and Romilly appear to have written for the daily newspapers and, in the case of Lambton, for local papers too. Lambton at the beginning of 1819 was considering forming a committee to organize press support for the party, and hiring a room, as had been done in the 1807 election, at which communications could be received.[2] So far as is known this came to nothing, but Grey himself was suggesting a more co-ordinated effort by the end of the year.

> Daily articles exposing the whole policy of the government and particularly the exaggerations and falsehoods by which the alarm has been propagated will I hope be supplied to the papers which are friendly to us, for this purpose. The means of doing this I should hope might be found amongst our young friends out of parliament, assisted as they might be by others. If you, Tierney, Brougham and Co., could during the recess arrange and superintend the execution of a plan of this nature there seems to be good grounds for expecting in the present state of the public mind, the best effects from it.[3]

The only response seems to have been rare comments in the *Morning Chronicle* and *The Times*.

[1] Lambton to Grey, 10 December 1821 (Grey).

[2] Lambton to Grey, 15 January 1819 (Grey). C. W. New, *Lord Durham*, Oxford, 1929, p. 23, assumes that the suggestion was implemented. There is no indication that this was so.

[3] Grey to Holland, 26 December 1819 (Holland).

Propaganda through the press, supplemented by the occasional pamphlet from politicians such as Brougham, Erskine, or Creevey and the continuous whig barrage from the *Edinburgh Review*, indicates a recognition by the opposition that their struggle with tory principles and policies was being waged on a front much wider than parliament. The same issues and questions which had divided whig from tory on the parliamentary scene had also divided opinion in the political nation outside. There liberal and conservative attitudes also clashed, a conflict complicated by the greater strength of radical views outside parliament than in it. In the towns and counties the division of views was symbolized by the competition of newspapers. Many of the larger towns could support two, or in some cases more, papers of differing political persuasions. It was also brought out into the open by clashes of opinion at public meetings and discussions. In the counties and represented boroughs with a sizable electorate differences of opinion and political view were also the basis of some of the electoral conflict. Important as family influences were, they were usually mobilized as part of a party effort, and the clash of opposition and ministerial groups was a normal feature at most of these elections.[1]

There were no strictly organizational links between whigs in parliament and like-minded groups outside. The political nation was a small one, with the number of electors under half a million, and the social groups whose views were politically important may well have been but little more numerous. In a hierarchical society the aristocracy and gentry, their tenants and dependants, and the manufacturers and their associates and employees, were bound together without the intervention of political ties. Finally, the normal usage of county society and personal and business contacts naturally brought together different groups. These factors obviated the need for any mass party structure. They were supplemented by two sources of contact between parliamentary whigs and like-minded groups outside.

Less important were informal contacts of a personal nature. Brougham in organizing the campaign against the orders in council, in standing for Liverpool in 1812, and in his trips on the

[1] T. H. B. Oldfield estimates in his *Representative History*, iv. 132, that twenty-six counties were represented by a compromise between the parties.

northern circuit, had been brought into touch with leading middle-class whigs and radicals in the larger towns. H. G. Bennet and Whitbread were channels of contact with Westminster and Middlesex radicalism, Alderman Waithman with the City. George Philips and Joseph Birch, and a few other such members, though mellowed politically, were not divorced from their Manchester and Liverpool roots; while Rosslyn, Brougham, Mackintosh, and Lord Archibald Hamilton were links with the growing whig party in Scotland.

More important were local roots. Because of the shortness of the session, a mere ninety-six days in 1823, M.P.s were not professional politicians needing a machine to keep them in touch with constituents or home environment, particularly if they represented counties or big boroughs. This made the M.P.s and peers themselves the main bond of unity with opinion outside. They constituted the leaders of the whig party in their home areas and the nucleus of larger bodies similar in sentiment. They were also a channel for organizing outside pressure on parliament. When strongly aroused, or when presented with some popular issue, their normal recourse was to organize requisitions for county or town meetings, urge friends, supporters, tenants, and dependants to attend, and then secure the passage of resolutions and of petitions to parliament, or addresses to the crown. To organize the expression of 'public opinion' through these traditional channels was for the whigs a natural extension of the parliamentary struggle, and a means of appeal to a court less likely to be prejudiced against their case.

There was even some attempt to provide, on a small scale, something of the same social organization which was found in the parliamentary party. The central Fox club was duplicated by a series of similar institutions in different parts of the country, all of which brought local whigs, and in some cases M.P.s and peers, together. Newcastle Fox dinners occasionally provided a public platform for Grey.[1] The Norfolk Fox club dinner reached, in 1820, an attendance of 460, including the Duke of Sussex and the leaders of local whig society.[2] The first public Edinburgh Fox dinner was held in 1821 as a rallying point for Scottish

[1] *Morning Chronicle*, 25 September 1817 and 6 January 1819. Lambton to Wilson, 28 September 1821 (Wilson Papers, Add. MSS. 30109, f. 236).

[2] *Norfolk Chronicle*, 29 January 1820, 27 January 1821, 26 January 1822.

whigs.[1] Others are found in Glasgow, Suffolk, and Bristol.[2] Probably, too, they were held in other parts of the country, their proceedings preserved only in local newspapers, if at all.

Fox clubs and dinners were only part of a number of similar institutions. There were also whig clubs in some parts of the country, one of the most active of which was the 'whig club of Cheshire and the neighbouring counties', formed in 1821, and active throughout the 1820's. This club dined annually and brought together many prominent whigs from the area, as well as visitors from outside it.[3] Similar were the Devon county club,[4] the Essex whig club,[5] the Gloucester whig club,[6] the Colchester independent club,[7] and perhaps the Kent liberal dinner;[8] while the concentric societies of Liverpool and Bristol were similar bodies of urban middle-class reformers.[9] Increasingly, too, whigs began to imitate the practice of radicals and hold dinners to celebrate election victories and bind supporters in the constituencies together.[10]

All these clubs and functions were essentially social, their purposes perhaps best described in a speech of the Earl of Albemarle at the Suffolk Fox dinner:

[1] Cockburn, *Memorials*, p. 378; Lambton to Grey, 13 January 1821 (Grey); *Morning Chronicle*, 30 January 1822, 18 January 1823, 31 January 1824, 29 January 1825; Brougham to Grey, 23 September 1823 (Brougham).

[2] Place Papers, Add. MSS. 36627, f. 39; *Ipswich Journal*, 17 February 1821; *Bristol Mirror*, 25 January 1812; *Bristol Gazette*, 28 January 1813, 26 January 1814, 26 January 1815.

[3] *Manchester Guardian*, 16 October 1824; E. D. Davenport to Roscoe, 23 October 1821 (Roscoe Papers); accounts of the meetings are found in *Manchester Guardian*, 13 October 1821 (95 present), 12 October 1822 (100), 11 October 1823. Meetings were held right up to 1830. The club also had an offshoot in the Nantwich whig club: *Morning Chronicle*, 4 January 1823; *The Times*, 27 December 1823.

[4] *The Alfred*, 26 October 1819. *Morning Chronicle*, 6 August 1828, reveals that there was also a Devonshire whig club, though this may have been the same body.

[5] *Morning Chronicle*, 16 November 1821.

[6] *Morning Chronicle*, 3 October 1816; *Gloucester Journal*, 29 January 1821 and 28 January 1822.

[7] *The Times*, 15 October 1828.

[8] *Morning Chronicle*, 23 December 1828.

[9] Broughton Papers, Add. MSS. 36458, f. 3; *Liverpool Mercury*, 8 December 1820. For the Bristol society see *Bristol Gazette*, 22 September 1819, and for its involvement in the 1820 election *Bristol Mirror*, 25 March 1820.

[10] The Westminster dinner was the most long-standing, but there were others in Aylesbury: *The Times*, 28 June 1827; Reading: *The Times*, 18 January 1823; Southwark: *Morning Chronicle*, 23 June 1824; Nottingham: *The Times*, 26 November 1823; Norwich: *The Times*, 29 October 1818; Middlesex: Lambton to Grey, 17 May 1820; and Westmorland: *The Times*, 7 July 1818 and 5 October 1819.

The noble lord . . . declared Mr. Fox's name to be the rallying point of the constitution: he rejoiced in the utility of these meetings: in them, he said, there was an union of minds to discuss political subjects: they elicit liberal notions, and smooth the rough edges of our nature, so that men of different ranks, and with different degrees of information unite in the support of constitutional principles.[1]

They were also useful platforms and means of propaganda.[2] In a few cases, however, similar bodies can be discovered which did not confine their activities to such purposes. In York the whig club, as well as organizing dinners, appears to have been responsible on occasions for the calling of town meetings, and also for backing whig candidates for the seats.[3] The same was true in Malden of the independent club,[4] while in Bristol, where the tories of the town had long been organized in the steadfast society that had existed since 1737, the local whigs formed the independent constitutional club, which existed from 1802 to 1812 to fight elections.[5] These examples do appear to have been exceptional, though there can be no certainty that some of the other bodies did not engage in similar activities.

All the clubs and dinners appear to have been transient phenomena. By the late 1820's they were gradually ceasing to exist: partly because the rival bodies, the Pitt clubs, were dying away, partly because, as a report said of the Cheshire whig club,

[1] *Ipswich Journal*, 17 February 1821. The aims of the Cheshire whig club were 'to keep alive the old free spirit of the county and to collect the scattered friends of rational liberty under such a bond of social union as will encourage independent men to speak their minds freely upon public occasions, ensuring the toleration, if not propagation, of liberal principles': *Manchester Guardian*, 16 October 1824.

[2] Lambton comments on one that he expects 'true good from our Fox dinner, it will be a mode (and the only one now parliament is not sitting) of calling the public attention to the state of affairs abroad and at home'. Lambton to Wilson, 21 August 1824 (Wilson Papers, Add. MSS. 30111, f. 175).

[3] *The Poll for Members in Parliament to Represent the City of York*, York, 1830, Preface, v and vi. *Morning Chronicle*, 23 October 1821, 7 December 1821, 8 November 1822.

[4] *The Times*, 21 July 1830.

[5] The history of the club is given in *Bristol Mirror*, 11 July 1812. The club split in 1812 when it resolved by three to one to support the candidature of Sir Samuel Romilly for the seat. A minority split away and supported Protheroe. This brought it to an end. The tory club came to an end in the 1820's: *Bristol Gazette*, 5 October 1826. Having decided on candidates it had been the custom of both clubs to call meetings of their respective interest to raise money for them: *An Authentic Representation of the evidence produced before the Committee of the House of Commons to try the Bristol Election*, Bristol, 1813, p. 114.

'some . . . are supposed to entertain doubts as to the policy of continuing their meetings as whigs and thereby assenting to perpetuate party distinctions';[1] partly because the party splits divided whig from whig. The impermanence of these pre-reform bodies and the comparative smallness of their numbers should not conceal their importance. They helped to bring together whigs in parliament and out of it, and to increase contact between groups of like opinion throughout the country. Like the central organization they are part of social as well as political history, the outward and visible sign of ties that have little counterpart today.

[1] *Morning Chronicle*, 12 October 1827. See also James Macdonald to Lansdowne, 18 August 1822 (Lansdowne).

III

PARTY AND POWER

POLITICIANS in the seventeenth and eighteenth centuries looked to the crown for power and office, those of the mid nineteenth century looked to the fluctuations of support in the commons, while the twentieth-century leader looks to public opinion as voiced by the electorate. Early-nineteenth-century whigs were in the uncertain position of looking to all three. They could hope to bring the government down by breaking its control of the commons, they could try to force such a change by public pressure on the house, or they could hope for a call from the crown.

The king was the traditional source of office and still a real power in the constitution. However, this was the period of that prolonged decline in royal power from the successful dismissal of the 'talents' to the failure to get rid of Melbourne. Under George IV royal authority seemed to be running on prejudice and received impetus rather than on the high octane of real power which had fuelled it under his father. As king and prince regent, George's own powers were negative rather than positive: he could obstruct but not initiate, and even his obstruction could be overcome by a united cabinet. The only powers the crown retained undisputed were those of changing ministers and dissolving parliament; but then the new ministers had to be able to command a majority in the commons, for the king could no longer provide one through patronage, and the appeal to the country, so successful in 1784 and 1807, whether through patronage or public opinion, seemed likely now to be a declining asset. Each election after 1807 and up to 1831 left ministerial strength unchanged or produced a loss of support. Yet the whigs rarely got so far as considering a difficulty contingent on attaining office. Given George IV's dislike of the whigs there seemed little enough chance that the power of dismissal would be used in their favour.

Old hostilities were part of the explanation: prince and politicians, so long allies, each felt betrayed by the other. 'Prinny' was treated by his former party with all the bitterness normally accorded an apostate, and the Carlton House party, a dwindling band among whigs, had largely ceased to exist by 1815. Personal antagonisms played a part. Grey had never troubled to hide his contempt for a weak and vacillating ruler; hatred for Grey became one of George's standing irrationalities. Brougham, too, offended deeply by his part in the queen's trial. The result was a ban on office, against Grey for the whole period, and against Brougham after the trial. More important were differences of principle, for George had felt it incumbent on him to inherit his father's prejudices. His views on foreign politics were strongly conditioned by his preference for the continental allies. He was flatly opposed to catholic emancipation, on repression he was more alarmist than most of his ministers, his response to change was uniformly hostile. All this provided little incentive for an anxiety-ridden monarch to venture into uncertainty by breaking with ministers whose views he found congenial and some of whom were personal friends. Only intense frustrations and quarrels, usually centred on personal issues, prompted the king to pocket both pride and prejudice and consider change. Always his enthusiasm died as he contemplated the alternative. This situation had its constitutional importance, for George's freedom of choice was greatly circumscribed, and the strength of tory ministers *vis-à-vis* the king increased proportionately to his dislike of the whigs. This was no comfort to a whig party effectively excluded from office.

Even more slender was the hope of office through the reversionary interest. By the nineteenth century this was selling spot to buy, not futures, but irredeemable consols. Princess Charlotte was thought to be favourable to the whigs, some of whom had taken her part in the quarrels with her father in 1814. She died in 1817, but it was agreed by most whigs that the loss was hardly a serious one for the party. The next heir, the Duke of York, combined militant anti-catholicism with a marked distaste for whig politics. The Duke of Clarence, who became heir on York's death in 1827, was a less unlikely prospect, if only because he lacked the prejudices of his brothers, but even then the reversionary interest amounted to little more than an end to old hostilities.

There was, of course, the possibility that the prince's hand would be forced by the break-up of the existing ministry or that the whigs would be brought in by a partial reconstruction. Both looked unlikely. By 1815 a triumphant foreign policy had established the Liverpool administration in a strong position. The gradual reunification of the remaining fractions of Pitt's old party provided reserves of strength. Like a magnet of steadily growing power the ministry drew the scattered remnants together. Sidmouth, who had shown the way in 1812, was followed eventually by the Canningites, the Wellesleyites, and the Grenvillites. Only unusually severe differences on issue of principle, or deaths, could dislocate the government. Both seemed unlikely. The disagreements of its members with the whigs were always greater than their differences with each other, and the death which would disrupt the administration, that of Liverpool, whose geniality and conciliatory skill held the team together, was long unlikely. George was always more likely to reconstruct out of existing or similar materials than to call on the whigs, and the number of existing ministers with whom the whigs could have collaborated without real sacrifices of principle was always small.

If, therefore, whig hope sprang not eternal but intermittent, it did so because of the parliamentary struggle. There could be nurtured, not only hopes of 'doing good' by subjecting the government to the constant scrutiny of opposition, but also, though more rarely, prospects of bringing down the administration. The constitutional purist might have echoed Pitt's claim of 1784 that the choice of ministers was the king's and the house had no power to oblige them to resign. The realist saw that a minister who faced repeated defeats would be unable to carry on. In such a position the king would have been compelled to reconstruct or replace. With other avenues to power all blocked the whigs were sustained by this hope and it was by this route that they did eventually come to office.

In the decisive theatre of the commons all depended on numerical strength. Whig prospects did not appear hopeful, for few allocated the opposition as much as a third of the 658 members of the commons. Estimates before 1812 had tended to fluctuate at something over 150 members.[1] Estimates up to 1830

[1] The *Morning Chronicle*, 29 June 1807, estimates the whigs at 157. See also *Morning Chronicle*, 6 October 1812.

show gradual increases on these figures. In 1817 Tierney was talking of '161 in unequivocal, undisguised opposition, of which 21 are either abroad or from circumstances of illness are incapable of attending'.[1] Next year his estimate was very similar, embracing '149 who I am satisfied may every one of them be relied upon as far as relates to steady adherence to the principles they have professed'.[2] The 1818 election raised the total, for by 1819 Tierney's estimates had reached 175.[3] Subsequent estimates were higher still. After the 1820 election Brougham reported Duncannon as claiming 207 'thick and thin men' and some dozen or two voting generally with the whigs, and estimates during the 1820's tended to be in round figures of 200 whigs.[4] A final estimate, drawn up for the government after the 1830 election, tends to confirm this, since it lists 'foes', the members of the old opposition, as 188, to which can be added eight other members originally listed as 'bad doubtful' and then corrected to 'opposition'.[5]

All these estimates refer to the hard core of the opposition. There also existed a looser fringe with vaguer attachments. The only available indication of the size of this body is a government list, drawn up probably in 1813, which allocates both to ministers and to opposition their somewhat looser fringes.[6] This counts 222 members as opposition and 393 as government, with only sixteen doubtfuls and ten hopefuls in between. Whatever its size it was difficult to rally the members of this loose fringe, while the attendance and the loyalty of the hard core itself also fluctuated, though to a smaller extent. As a result opposition very rarely mustered its full numbers. In the eleven years from 1816 to 1826, if the catholic question and parliamentary reform be excluded, the opposition secured 150 or more votes on only just over a score of occasions.[7]

Extra support was required if the opposition was to defeat the government. Yet such defeats could be inflicted, and over a score

1 Tierney to Grey, 4 January 1817 (Grey).

2 Tierney to Grey, 11 April 1818 (Grey).

3 Tierney to Holland, 23 August 1818 (Holland); *H.M.C. Dropmore*, x. 442.

4 Brougham to Hutchinson, 'Monday', n.d. [1829] (Peel Papers, Add. MSS. 40344, f. 37).

5 Peel Papers, Add. MSS. 40401, ff. 182–95.

6 List in P.R.O., T 64–33.

7 It was estimated that in 1822 and 1823 more than 400 people had voted in only ten divisions, more than 300 in a further seventeen: *The Times*, 11 August 1823.

of reverses in the period from 1816 to 1826, three quarters of them on major issues, both demonstrated ministerial vulnerability and kept hopes alive. They were always dashed. The defeats were never frequent or serious enough to turn the government out; on each occasion when it appeared that a further push by the opposition must bring the government down, support returned and the opposition attacks were successfully beaten off.

Contemporaries themselves were prone to offer a series of over-lapping explanations for this paradoxical situation, which combined basic ministerial strength with superficial weakness. While accepting the existence of a two-party system they also discerned a third element, a neutral group between the two major parties and permanently committed to neither. Sir Samuel Romilly distinguished two component elements in this group: 'a considerable number were those who professed to be of no party, but to be neutral or independent. Other gentlemen did not object to party altogether, but were retiring from one party and approximating to another, they might be said to be, in the legal phrase, *in transitu*.'[1] Few others discerned a considerable number. The *Edinburgh Review* regarded such members as being few, and Tierney, in 1817, totted up only sixty-eight members unconnected with ministers or opposition, estimating that some twenty-five of these could be relied on to vote with the opposition on popular questions.[2] After the 1818 election he saw their numbers as much the same, sixteen to twenty-eight doubtful but with a strong leaning towards the government, and twenty-six doubtful but holding aloof from it.[3] Though they disagreed on its size, contemporaries were clear that the changing attitudes of this central group were one of the main reasons why government could occasionally be defeated.

Another element of their explanation was the fringe of loosely attached members on both sides of the house. Both whigs and ministers had frequently to consider the attitudes and alarms of this section. Tierney acknowledged that

[1] *P.D.* xxxvii. 970. See also C. W. Wynn to Southey, 22 February 1811 (Wynn, 4814): 'usually since I have been in the house there have been but three parties, the ins, the outs, and the independents': and Castlereagh in *P.D.* xxxv. 270.

[2] *Edinburgh Review*, no. lii, 1816, p. 377; Tierney to Grey, 7 January 1817 (Grey).

[3] Tierney to Holland, 23 August 1818 (Holland). See also *H.M.C. Dropmore*, x. 442.

There was, indeed, a considerable number of members in that house belonging to that class of persons who 'do good by stealth, and blush to find it fame'. This respectable body of representatives, though for the best of reasons doubtless they lent their aid to ministers, yet were not without their feelings: they had a sort of sense of decency, and it required sometimes a good deal of management to keep them in good humour. These scruples made them sometimes a little restive, and unless certain forms of decorum were preserved to satisfy their consciences a little, they were apt to say to a minister —'If you don't do so and so, we shan't vote for you.'[1]

A third element, never specifically distinguished from the other two, comprised the country gentlemen. Belonging to both sides of the house, these members were apparently most numerous on the ministerial side. They were regarded as being liable to act together as a body and accustomed, particularly where financial questions were involved, to acting independently of government. At times it seemed that they claimed a right to act in this way. Frankland Lewis told the house in 1816 that the proposal for a large standing army 'had been resisted on a principle wholly unconnected with any party feeling—it had been resisted by a body of men acting independently of any administration—he meant the country gentlemen of England; who had invariably united in their hostility to a measure of that nature'.[2] Opposition regularly threw out appeals to this section of the house, ministers attempted to propitiate it by meetings and concessions, and all agreed in attaching considerable importance to the opinions and attitudes of the country gentlemen.[3] Their views were frequently diagnosed at length at the beginning of sessions, and regarded as the main auguries for the course of hostilities.[4]

Later historians, in describing fluctuations in voting, have tended to hark back to this contemporary emphasis on the country gentlemen.[5] But neither the contemporaries nor their modern echoes have gone behind the image to give a clear picture of the country gentlemen. Nor did the country gentlemen themselves help to clarify the situation. Their views consisted of assump-

[1] *P.D.* xxxv. 277.
[2] *P.D.* xxxii. 846.
[3] For examples see Plunket in *P.D.* xxxiii. 650, and *The Times*, 3 March 1816.
[4] Lady Seymour, '*Pope*', pp. 195–6; Tierney to Grey, 23 January 1822; R. Russell, *Early Correspondence of Lord John Russell*, London, 1913, i. 190.
[5] W. R. Brock, *Liverpool*, pp. 81–82; *George IV*, ii. 162.

tions and prejudices rather than well-thought-out opinions, and those individuals to whom this label was most commonly attached rarely thought it necessary to explain, much less to describe themselves.[1] As one of them put it: 'he was only a plain country gentleman; but though he was not able to speak well, he had the courage to do his duty. Certainly, if there was anything which he detested doing, it was speaking.'[2] Lack of knowledge about these individuals and their role in parliament is one of the major gaps in early-nineteenth-century political history.

In default of any useful information from contemporary stereotypes the only way to explain the strength and weakness of the government and the position of the opposition is by an analysis of the house of commons. This can be carried out only by using the division lists published in *Hansard*.[3] To divide members into groups on the basis of their recorded votes is to superimpose a mechanical grid on the fine nuances of opinion and personal connexion in the house. It does have the justifications that the ultimate test of government or opposition was in terms of these same votes, and that at the same time it provides categories which help the historian to explain the pattern of politics.

If the parliament of 1820 to 1826 is taken as an example, eleven divisions can be taken as the basis of the analysis. These are the only ones in which government and opposition clashed and for which the votes of both sides of the house are recorded.[4] A total of 683 members voted in one or more of these divisions. Of these, 361 members voted only on the government side and 206 only for the opposition, their votes being distributed in the following manner:

[1] The obituary of one of these members, Sir Edward Knatchbull, stated that 'He did not want intuitive sense, which fixed on right results, though he might not have the skill to unravel the paths to it': H. Knatchbull-Hugesson, *Kentish Family*, London, 1960, p. 161.

[2] Sir Thomas Lethbridge in *P.D.*, N.S. xvii. 556.

[3] Professor Aspinall has stated that the lists are 'about 99% accurate': *Three Early Nineteenth Century Diaries*, London, 1952, p. xxiii. They may be less accurate than this, but correction from the newspapers and use in conjunction with a complete list of members probably bring them near this degree. In all the calculations in this and later chapters pairs and tellers are counted as voters. When people shut out from a division are listed they are counted as having voted.

[4] The divisions used here and later are those on political issues as defined in Chapter I, but not including either the catholic question or parliamentary reform.

	Number of votes											Total
	1	2	3	4	5	6	7	8	9	10	11	
Government only	57	48	61	42	45	39	30	13	13	12	1	361
Opposition only	26	22	29	14	31	24	23	22	10	3	2	206

Here are the indications of a two-party system drawing into its scope the bulk of the house. There are, however, a further 116 members who voted on both sides, sixty-one of them giving more government votes than opposition, forty more opposition than government, and fifteen dividing their favours evenly.

To bring into the analysis the other 'political' divisions in which government and opposition clashed, but for which only the names of the opposition voters are recorded, is to complicate the situation and display the looseness of the party system. A total of 250 of those who had voted only for the government on the earlier motions did not give any opposition votes on the 203 other divisions recorded in the debates. On the other hand, fifty-one cast one opposition vote, thirty-five gave two, and twenty-five gave more than two. Those who had voted only for the opposition on the earlier motions now cast the following further opposition votes:

None	1–10	11–20	21–30	31–40	41–50	More	Total
1	24	36	22	31	11	81	206

To consider only the motions with both sides listed is therefore to over-simplify. Outside these motions some government supporters were not absolutely reliable, some oppositionists were lazy.[1]

This suggests a method of analysis which, while it does not accord with vague contemporary classifications, does accord with voting habits and is reasonably comprehensive. The 250 members who supported the government on the eleven motions,

[1] Not all were lazy, for some of the members on both sides were not in the house for its full life. The number of members in this position, analysed in terms of the eleven fully listed motions, is:

	Number of votes								Total
	1	2	3	4	5	6	7	8	9	Total
Government	31	19	13	13	7	8	7	2	1	101
Opposition	12	5	4	2	5	2	2	..	..	32

and gave no opposition votes at all on the others, can be regarded as the supporters of the administration and are therefore classified as 'government'. Among those giving mixed votes on the eleven motions are thirteen who gave some government votes but only one opposition vote, an aberration which they did not repeat on any of the 203 other opportunities that presented themselves. These are added to the eighty-six government supporters who voted for opposition no more than twice on the 203 motions, to make a total of ninety-nine members described as 'government fringe', because they were prepared, very occasionally, to desert. On the other side of the house those members who, among the 206 voting for the opposition on the eleven motions, also voted for opposition on a tenth or more of the other divisions can fairly be classified as 'opposition'. They make up a total of 154.[1] Those among the 206 who fell below this arbitrary threshold are combined with fifteen of the members giving mixed votes on the eleven motions, to form an 'opposition fringe' of sixty-six members who were inclined to the whig side of the house but were not completely reliable.[2] All the remainder become an intermediate group, christened 'waverers', comprising 114 members.[3]

Applied not only to the 1820 parliament but also to the two preceding ones the method of analysis yields the following results:[4]

	Govt.	Govt. Fr.	Waverers	Oppn. Fr.	Oppn.	Totals
1812–18	253	78	102	83	149	665
1818–20	261	80	48	16	171	576
1820–6	250	99	114	66	154	683

Here is a picture of a house with a two-party system modified by the existence of unreliable groups on the fringes of both sides,

[1] In the case of members who were in parliament for less than half its life the threshold is reduced by half, in this case from twenty to ten.

[2] The fifteen are members who gave only one government vote on the eleven divisions but enough opposition votes on the 203 to cross the threshold of twenty votes. One member giving one opposition vote on the eleven but no others at all is grouped with the waverers.

[3] The title 'waverer' is used in a general sense and has to reference to the specialized meaning of 1831–2, when it was used to denote those peers who changed their votes on the reform bill.

[4] For the analysis, and general comments on the method used, see the Appendix.

and by a cushion group between the two, whose voting record indicates no attachment to either party. It is also a house in which the government could clearly count on a majority in normal circumstances. In order to shed further light on the pattern of politics and to discover whether any factors would predispose members to any one section of the house it is necessary to use these groups as the basis for further analysis. For this purpose the different parliaments have been added together, members who sat in more than one being counted afresh for each parliament. This method avoids the use of three sets of tables; the trends illustrated by the one table are the same for each separate parliament.

Using available biographical information from contemporary sources, and later compilations, it is possible to provide a comprehensive picture, albeit in general terms, of the occupational groupings among M.P.s. Those engaged in commerce or law, or having a navy or army background, are examined separately. The remaining group, 'land', is a more general one. While it is possible to discover who was actively engaged in other pursuits, information on landholding is more difficult to secure. Thus, while probably all the members of this group were landowners and only four doctors are known to have another occupation, in a small number of cases this is only a presumption made in the absence of information on alternative pursuits.

	Govt.		Govt. Fr.		Waverer		Oppn. Fr.		Oppn.	
Law	11·4%	(87)	10·5%	(27)	9·8%	(26)	3·0%	(5)	13·5%	(64)
Army and Navy	22·9%	(175)	12·8%	(33)	10·6%	(28)	13·9%	(23)	11·8%	(56)
Commerce	11·8%	(90)	17·1%	(44)	23·9%	(63)	26·1%	(43)	20·9%	(99)
Land	53·9%	(412)	59·6%	(153)	55·7%	(147)	57·0%	(94)	53·8%	(255)
Totals	100%	(764)	100%	(257)	100%	(264)	100%	(165)	100%	(474)

The tendency for men with a military or naval background to cluster round the fount of honour and promotion is understandable, though the magnet of office was less effective for lawyers, who are found in very similar proportions on government and opposition sides but are less numerous in the centre groups. More surprising is the marked tendency for those actively concerned in commerce or business to lean away from the government and towards independence or opposition.[1] The

[1] The figures in the table were tested for significance by Mr. J. S. Wabe of

phenomenon can be examined more closely if all those who had an interest, in the form of an investment or a previous involvement, are added to those actively concerned, and those involved in more than one aspect of affairs are separately counted in each different category. In this way rather sharper categories can be defined.

	Govt.	Govt. Fr.	Waverer	Oppn. Fr.	Oppn.
Bankers	40	24	29	26	46
Merchants	31	24	32	14	39
Manufacturers	10	5	4	6	21
East Indians	57	22	25	15	39
West Indians	37	17	12	5	26

Those with East and West Indian interests are the least likely to be against the government, presumably because of the close connexion between government and the East India Company and the association of whigs with anti-slavery attitudes. Similarly, the 'official' element, bank and East India directors and government contractors, are also pro-government. On the other hand the bankers, merchants, and manufacturers are clearly inclined to an opposition which was more liberal in its commercial as well as its political attitudes, and more likely to urge the views that accorded with those of commercial interests in foreign policy. Their inclinations weight the whole group of commercial men towards independence and opposition. As a result commercial men make up a quarter of the waverer category. This is a surprising discovery in view of the contemporary emphasis on the country gentlemen. Whatever weightings tradition might accord, one vote still had one value, and contemporaries would appear to have been mistaken in ignoring the independent propensities of this new element.

The table of occupational backgrounds sheds little light on the problem of the country gentlemen. Landed members are more strongly represented in the middle three groups than in the solid ranks of government and opposition, but the trend is far from overwhelming and the analysis is not specific. Information on wealth would be very useful, for in the minds of many

Nuffield College. The tendency for commercial members to be independent or against the government is significant at the 0·001 level. Such a relationship would occur by chance less than once in a thousand times.

the country gentlemen were the substantial landowners below the aristocracy. Their wealth was a guarantee of their independence, and Charles Chaplin told his Lincolnshire electorate that 'he did not vauntingly boast of his fortune, but its possession placed him beyond the necessity of asking favours; and if he supported the measures of the administration from a sense of their general correctness, he was nonetheless independent on that account'.[1] While there are some members of the waverer group like Mathew Russell, 'the richest commoner in England', who were obviously substantial citizens, to judge the whole by their standards would be wrong. The only guide, and it is a very rough one, is in terms of status. The publication of Burke's *History of the Commoners* in the 1830's does give a reasonable measuring stick for the gentry, the substantial landed or official families below the peerage. These gentry members were more numerous in the middle group: they made up only 9 per cent. of the government and 11 per cent. of the opposition members, but 16 per cent. of the government fringe, 17 per cent. of the waverers, and 21 per cent. of the opposition fringe. If the same classification is applied simply to the landowners, distinguishing at the same time those members whose families had been listed in Burke's peerage by the same period, then the following pattern emerges:[2]

	Govt.		Govt. Fr.		Waverer		Oppn. Fr.		Oppn.	
Peers, Barts.	54%	(221)	43%	(66)	45%	(67)	54%	(51)	55%	(140)
Gentry	8%	(35)	14%	(22)	18%	(27)	24%	(22)	13%	(34)
Others	38%	(156)	43%	(65)	36%	(53)	22%	(21)	32%	(81)
Totals	100%	(412)	100%	(153)	100%	(147)	100%	(94)	100%	(255)

The intermediate categories do include significantly higher proportions of members from the gentry. Yet though this indicates that the heavy emphasis on the country gentlemen has some justification it does not show that they had the overwhelming importance which contemporaries attributed to them. This

[1] *The Late Elections: An Impartial Statement of all the Proceedings Connected with the Progress and Result of the Late Elections*, London, 1818, p. 170.

[2] In this table only those who were brothers or sons of peers, baronets or 'commoners', have been included in the peerage and gentry. Members who were listed in the early volumes of Burke's *Commoners*, but were raised to the peerage or becoming baronets before 1838, are listed under gentry. The relation between membership of the gentry and voting in the government and opposition fringes and among the waverers is significant at the 0·001 level.

attribution is the product of tradition, and of the importance attached to landed wealth and membership for counties, rather than of any detailed study of the situation. Country gentlemen were a substantial proportion of those sections of the house least involved in the party system, but they were not the only section, nor the one most prone to independence.

Whigs took pride in regarding themselves as an aristocratic party. Radicals took pleasure in dismissing both whig and tory as aristocratic factions, the 'two battalions of the well paid regiment'.[1] The accuracy of these views is worth assessment, both for its own sake and because of the possibility, already suggested by the previous table, that waverers came from a less exalted social background. A first approach is to look at status as indicated by titles.[2]

	Govt.		Govt. Fr.		Waverer		Oppn. Fr.		Oppn.	
Title or courtesy title	13%	(100)	6%	(15)	7%	(18)	9%	(16)	16%	(75)
'Honourable'	13%	(103)	10%	(26)	6%	(16)	11%	(18)	12%	(57)
Baronet	13%	(97)	16%	(42)	12%	(31)	17%	(28)	10%	(48)
Knight	6%	(44)	2%	(5)	2%	(6)	1%	(1)	2%	(10)
No title	55%	(420)	66%	(169)	73%	(193)	62%	(102)	60%	(284)
Totals	100%	(764)	100%	(257)	100%	(264)	100%	(165)	100%	(474)

The waverers and the other central groups certainly include the highest proportions of unadorned members.[3] This might, however, be due to the fact that their independence removed them from the source of patronage, which even the whigs had visited, albeit briefly. It is necessary to examine connexions with the aristocracy.

Whatever its boasts, the whig party, in the shape of regular opposition voters in the commons, was no more aristocratic than the government ranks. It contained only slightly more elder sons and rather fewer sons and brothers of peers. By contrast, the

[1] The *Morning Chronicle* asserted in its radical phase, 14 July 1829, that 'one division of the aristocracy call themselves tories and another whigs. The difference is rather the result of hereditary connection than any intelligible diversity of principle.'

[2] The tendencies for the titled, and those with courtesy titles or described as 'honourable', not to be found among the waverers, and for those with no title to be concentrated there, are significant at the 0·001 level.

[3] The tendency for the government fringe and waverer categories to include higher proportions of those not related to the aristocracy is significant at the 0·001 level.

	Govt.		Govt. Fr.		Waverer		Oppn. Fr.		Oppn.	
Irish title	1·6%	(12)	0·4%	(1)	1·5%	(4)	0·6%	(1)	1·7%	(8)
Eldest sons	9·0%	(69)	6·2%	(16)	8·3%	(22)	4·9%	(8)	11·2%	(53)
Sons, brothers	17·4%	(133)	10·9%	(28)	5·3%	(14)	17·6%	(29)	14·1%	(67)
Other relatives	6·8%	(52)	4·7%	(12)	3·4%	(9)	3·6%	(6)	4·2%	(20)
Rel. by marriage	12·1%	(92)	10·5%	(27)	12·9%	(34)	11·5%	(19)	14·8%	(70)
Not related	53·1%	(406)	67·3%	(173)	68·6%	(181)	61·8%	(102)	54·0%	(256)
Totals	100%	(764)	100%	(257)	100%	(264)	100%	(165)	100%	(474)

waverers and the government fringe group include the lowest proportions of members connected with the aristocracy. Here at least the prototype of the country gentleman has some relevance, if it be interpreted as substantial commoners, independent of the aristocracy.

This fact also indicates a possibility that the waverers wavered because they lacked those connexions with the competing sections of the aristocracy which influenced the two opposing sections of the house. It is also clear that they lacked some of the other ties binding the two major sections, particularly ties of family. In the 1820 parliament just over a quarter of the government members were related to other members sitting at the same time as themselves in that parliament. Among the opposition and opposition fringe members the high proportion of two fifths were so related. Since most of these relationships were with members on the same side of the house, here is clearly part of the explanation of the ties which bound party together. By contrast, only a fifth of the waverers were so related, and almost the same proportion of the government fringe members.[1] There is, therefore, the possibility that the members in these two categories, like the floating voter of modern psephology, were less reliable because they lacked the ties which held other members.

Type of seat also merits examination, since most of the individuals commonly referred to as 'country gentlemen' are county members. This might point to an unreliability caused by a greater susceptibility to constituency pressures. For this purpose the seats have been divided into national groups and the English seats into four types according to their size.[2]

[1] The difference in this respect between the waverers, the government fringe, and the rest, is significant at the 0·001 level.

[2] The largest boroughs are those stated by T. H. B. Oldfield, *Representative History*, and *The Extraordinary Red Book*, London, 1817, to have 800 or more electors.

	Govt.		Govt. Fr.		Waverers		Oppn. Fr.		Oppn.		Whole Ho.	
English counties	8%	(57)	10%	(26)	17%	(46)	16%	(26)	17%	(80)	12%	(80)
Large boroughs	4%	(34)	8%	(20)	10%	(27)	9%	(15)	18%	(86)	12%	(78)
Medium boroughs	17%	(132)	21%	(53)	24%	(64)	30%	(49)	26%	(125)	19%	(128)
Small boroughs	44%	(337)	24%	(63)	28%	(74)	23%	(39)	14%	(67)	31%	(203)
Wales	2%	(18)	5%	(12)	6%	(12)	5%	(8)	4%	(18)	4%	(24)
Scotland	8%	(57)	9%	(24)	6%	(15)	6%	(10)	10%	(48)	7%	(45)
Irish counties	9%	(69)	14%	(37)	6%	(17)	8%	(13)	7%	(34)	10%	(64)
Irish boroughs	8%	(60)	9%	(22)	3%	(9)	3%	(5)	4%	(16)	5%	(36)
Totals	100%	(764)	100%	(257)	100%	(264)	100%	(165)	100%	(474)	100%	(658)

The opposition has a clear claim to be the most popular party. It includes among its ranks the largest proportion of the all important county M.P.s, as well as a surprisingly large proportion of the members from the very largest boroughs.[1] This, and the government's reliance on the smaller seats, indicate that the traditional type of court-versus-country conflicts still formed a real element in the clash between government and opposition in the house of commons. In this clash the waverers constitute something of an intermediate element, less 'popular', in this sense, than the opposition, but more so than the government. Their unreliability so far as the government was concerned may, therefore, have been partly due to constituency pressures. This was not so, however, in every case for a sizable proportion of them came from small and closed boroughs. These members could clearly be affected by the impact of distress on their own fortunes, whether as landowners through reductions in their rents, or as commercial men through the slowing of trade. They could also be influenced by political osmosis, their roots in the community making them intermittently, if not continuously, sensitive to its views and problems.

The net result of this detailed examination of the different types of members is not to contradict, but to modify the contemporary stereotypes. The section of the house not firmly attached to party was both more numerous and more diverse than

A large electorate is a reasonable indication that a borough is open, but small size does not always indicate that it is under control. For this purpose the small boroughs are those listed as under the control of an influence in the *Analysis of the British House of Commons*. The association between opposition and large boroughs and counties and between government and small boroughs is more significant even than the very high 0·001 level.

[1] These trends are confirmed by the pamphlet, *An Exposition of the British House of Commons as at Present Constituted*, London, 1823, p. 38. See also *The Times*, 12 April 1823.

contemporaries allowed. As these contemporaries thought, it did contain more substantial landed men than either the government or the opposition, but it also contained a substantial proportion of mercantile members. Its connexions with the aristocracy and with other members of the house were rather weaker and it was rather more liable to constituency pressures than government members, though less so than the opposition. All these differences are, however, tendencies rather than sharp contrasts. The waverers and the members of the fringes are far from being a completely distinct element in the house.

The categories also indicate why the government could be defeated. By a full muster of the opposition, a stiffening of the whig fringe, the attraction of a substantial proportion of waverers, and a number of government fringe members, the opposition could secure a majority, particularly if the government had also to combat abstentions in its own ranks. The division on the property tax, a major ministerial defeat of 1816, provides an effective illustration, for then the ministry attracted 63 per cent. of the government group, 44 per cent. of the government fringe, 30 per cent. of the waverers, and 4 per cent. of the opposition fringe. On the other hand, opposition secured the support of 88 per cent. of the opposition members, 76 per cent. of the opposition fringe, 52 per cent. of the waverers, and as many as 35 per cent. of the government fringe members. Occasionally, too, if attendance was rather low and many of the government and government fringe supporters were absent, it was possible for the opposition to defeat the government by securing a strong attendance of its own ranks and the votes of a few waverers.

These defeats were never followed up by further victories or by government collapse. Opposition speakers tended to put the blame for this on government patronage.[1] It is difficult to refute such claims completely, for much patronage was confined to the constituencies and is not susceptible to easy analysis. If, however, only patronage in the house is considered, then there is a ready test in the report on offices, reversions, and pensions held by M.P.s in 1821.[2] Excluding those M.P.s listed as king's coun-

[1] Tavistock in *P.D.*, N.S. v. 1418, and Graham in *P.D.* xxxix. 1064.

[2] *Report of the Select Committee on the Returns made by Members of the House of Commons to the Several Orders of the House, of the 8th day of June 1821*. 'Ordered by the House of Commons to be printed, 9 July 1822.'

sel, this shows that only sixty of the government members, thirteen of the government fringe, and five of the waverers came into these three categories.[1] The numbers involved are very small beside the exaggerated claims made by the opposition. It would seem that patronage did not extend very far. In any case it did not always impose a tie that was absolutely binding.[2] The real explanation of the whig inability to bring down the administration must be sought elsewhere.

One reason was the unwillingness of those who wandered from the government fold to travel far. The members of the government fringe group are in that category because they gave only one or two votes against the administration. The largest single number voting against the government on any one motion was the twenty-four who opposed renewal of the property tax. All the others were scattered over a series of divisions.[3] Sizable proportions of those classified as waverers or opposition fringe could hardly be said to be much more independent. Counting all their opposition votes, the following pattern emerges:

	Number of votes							
	1	2	3	4	5	6	More	Totals
1812–18								
Waverers	10	26	20	10	9	5	22	102
Oppn. Fr.		8	10	6	6	4	49	83
1818–20								
Waverers	3	1	16	6	7	3	12	48
Oppn. Fr.		1	2	3	5		5	16
1820–6								
Waverers	2	11	18	14	6	11	52	114
Oppn. Fr.				7	3	1	55	66

Substantial majorities of waverers in all three parliaments gave fewer than seven opposition votes on all the motions examined.

[1] Most of the five waverers with office are Grenvilles who had sown their wild votes before taking office. The report also lists one opposition fringe member and three oppositionists as holding office. The last three are clerk to the privy seal, clerk of the pipe, and A.d.C. to the king.

[2] C. S. Parker, *Sir Robert Peel*, London, 1899, i. 41–42, for Liverpool's views.

[3] In the parliament of 1820 to 1826 an examination of all those government fringe members who cast only one vote against the government reveals that the largest single concentration on any one division was fourteen on Sir M. W. Ridley's motion of 1 March 1822 on the navy estimates. The next was eight, then six.

Waverer is therefore a better title than 'neutral', for this was hardly a degree of independence sufficient to endanger the government over a long period. Even some members on the fringe of the opposition were hardly more energetic. It is worth noting in passing that those waverers who gave more than six opposition votes are similar in their characteristics to those who gave less. Further refinement does not produce any essence of 'country gentlemen'. Indeed the commercial members and those from the larger boroughs were the most likely to be more independent.

The whigs faced the further difficulty that it was only on a very narrow range of issues that they were able to attract substantial numbers of votes from outside their own ranks. To analyse the government majorities in terms of averages for any one session is to show that they were lowest on questions of economy, law reform, and Scottish reform, and highest on issues of foreign policy, repression, and on general party clashes. Indeed the waverers and government fringe members, whom the opposition would have to attract if it was to secure majorities, were often openly antipathetic to many of the causes urged by the whigs. Situations which in 1817 and 1819 led to repressive legislation found these groups openly alarmist. Catholic emancipation, always a basic principle for the opposition, was opposed by a majority in these groups. This is clear from an analysis of votes in the 1820 parliament.

	Govt.	Govt. Fr.	Waverer	Oppn. Fr.	Oppn.
For catholic emancipation	49	22	39	48	138
Against	163	66	63	9	9
Gave mixed votes	5	7	5	2	1
No votes	33	4	7	7	6

The same was true of parliamentary reform, which was not a party question with the whigs but was advocated by a sufficiently sizable proportion of them for it to be associated with the party in the minds of both government members and waverers. For the most part these latter were opposed to such reform. Their votes in the 1820 parliament were:[1]

[1] In this parliament the opposition vote is given for several motions on reform, but both sides are listed only on one. The figures in the table therefore tend to overestimate support for reform and underestimate the opposition to it.

	Govt.	Govt. Fr.	Waverer	Oppn. Fr.	Oppn.
For reform		2	14	50	151
Against	81	36	35	1	..
No votes	169	61	65	15	3

Finally, foreign policy also saw them antipathetic to whig views; more strenuous for dealing firmly with France and less welcoming to liberal departures.

Their disagreements with the whigs on such subjects as catholic emancipation, foreign policy, and parliamentary reform constituted one reason why the waverers preferred the existing administration to the alternative. Further illustrations of their views are supplied by the known attitudes and behaviour, and the public declarations, of many of the individual members who compose this central and important category.

In the amorphous mass defined as 'waverers' certain small groups do appear to be acting together with some consistency. These are the nineteenth-century counterparts of those factions which had been so important in the politics of the previous century. It is possible to identify, in the government and opposition fringes and among the waverers, fourteen members who can be described as Canningites, eleven Grenvillites, and four Wellesleyites. In addition, if the 'saints' be defined as a faction in the same sense, half a dozen of them can be picked out. Normally these saints went marching into the government lobbies. The whigs had little hope of receiving permanent support from any of these groups. The Grenvilles formed a section of the whig party until 1817, when they broke away because of continued disagreements and took up a separate bench of their own, intending to form the nucleus of a third party. They were thrown from their impartial perch by the alarm about radicalism in 1819 and their opposition to whig views on the queen in 1820. They voted occasionally with opposition in 1820 and 1821, though completely opposed to any new alliance, until in June 1821 overtures were received from the administration, which they finally joined in December of the same year. Canning and Wellesley had been loosely associated with each other in 1812 and at the end of that year Wellesley had made overtures to the whigs about the possibility of an alliance.[1] Though Grenville had been sympathetic, considering 'the acquisition of Canning almost a *sine qua non* to the hope of making a successful stand against the court in the house of commons', the rest of the party had trusted Canning too little to agree to any alliance.[2] Canning for his part was opposed to any understanding with the whigs, generally disposed to support the administration, and anxious only to reach some compromise with the government. His acceptance of the Lisbon embassy in 1814 and the entry of some of the others into office hardened their hostility to the whigs. Wellesley, left on his own with his tiny group of followers, co-operated with the whigs up to 1818, but the admission of his brother to the government and the alarms of 1819 caused him to break the association and accept office in 1821.

The whigs had as little hope of permanent support from the great mass of the waverers as they had from the factions who passed through the category. Richard Ellison claimed to act with 'perfect independence', a claim which would probably have been echoed by the great majority of the waverers.[3] Though Acland defined independence as 'that which is directly contrary to party spirit, be it ministerial or the opposite', so far as the opposition was concerned, the independence was very one-sided.[4] It meant a lack of overt dependence on government, combined with a preference for the men in office over their opponents.[5] The majority of them were not prepared to bring the government down.

Their comments and speeches bring out the reasons for their preference. One was a general admiration for the policies of the administration. 'It was not from obligation . . . that he spoke,' declared Sir Frederick Flood, 'for he stood where he was unplaced and unpensioned. . . . He approved of the conduct of the administration. . . . The country owed everything to his majesty's ministers; it was they who appointed the Duke of Wellington; and the Duke of Wellington saved the country.'[6] Others accepted the somewhat old-fashioned premise that the crown had

[1] Adair to Grey, 12 November 1812 (Grey).

[2] Grenville to Grey, 10 November 1812 (Grey).

[3] *P.D.* xxxviii. 101.

[4] *The Late Elections*, p. 100.

[5] An indication of this is provided by the treasury list of M.P.s in 1813. Of the eighty-seven waverers there classified, sixty-one were listed as government supporters, only thirteen as opposition.

[6] *P.D.* xxxvii. 998–9.

the right to appoint the ministers while M.P.s had the duty of supporting them. E. J. Curteis declared that 'ministers ought always to be watched and sometimes to be opposed; but that as the constitution of the country had given to the throne the power of choosing its ministers, to act in uniform hostility to them, right or wrong, at all times and on all occasions appeared to him an absurdity, and certainly not the duty of a member for a county'.[1]

Many others agreed generally with the principles supported by ministers. Richard Ellison stated: 'I have always supported the measures of his majesty's ministers, from a fair conviction of the soundness of the principles on which they have acted.'[2] They were willing, therefore, to support ministry so long, in Brougham's words, as 'they could at all support it' or so long as a due, or in some cases even a symbolic, deference was paid to opinion outside.[3] Albany Savile pointed out that

> So long as ministers attended to the voice of parliament, he would always give them his support. He wished to be considered as an independent man, and when he gave his support to ministers, he gave it on general grounds. He had never desired a place from ministers. . . . He had no wish to stand well with ministers. He wished to stand well with the respectable part of mankind in general, for he was not indifferent to the *vox populi*. . . .[4]

When ministers failed to defer, or when the waverers could convince themselves that some particular policy was not in the interests of the nation, desertions ensued. They were nearly always desertions without any intention of bringing the government down. Many believed, with Henry Bankes, that 'these occasional defeats neither shake nor endanger the ministers', some considered they were necessary to keep government on its toes.[5]

[1] *An Account of the Sussex Election*, Colchester, 1820, p. 120. See also the comment of Colonel Wilson: 'when I was first elected. . . . I made a declaration to the effect, that it was my determination to support the government of my royal master, without caring who composed it, when it was acting for the welfare of the country, and to oppose it when my conscience told me it was acting otherwise. . . . I do not care for ministers. I do not mind who they are. The appointment of my royal master is enough for me. Whether they are whigs or tories, it's all one to me. While they act conscientiously I'll support them. While they act otherwise I'll oppose them': *P.D.*, N.S. xx. 584–5.

[2] *P.D.* xxxviii. 100. [3] *P.D.* xxxviii. 42. [4] *P.D.* xxxvii. 189.

[5] Lord Colchester, *The Diary and Correspondence of Charles Abbot, Lord Colchester*, London, 1861, iii. 253.

For the most part the waverers were not prepared to take independence so far that it actually endangered the administration. They were mostly aware of the alternative sharply posed by Henry Bankes when talking of the six acts:

the opposition, he stated, were not only pledged to the repeal of those bills, but to a reform in parliament . . . they were pledged to a reform which the present circumstances of the country could not with safety allow, and he therefore viewed it with unqualified apprehension. Another question to which they were pledged was catholic emancipation . . . if the opposition came into power, that ruinous measure which he deprecated would inevitably pass. The honourable member then proceeded to remark, that the opposition were bound to a complete change of the system of government. . . . He concluded by expressing his firm reliance upon the councils of his majesty's government, and reiterating his opinion, that in the dangerous circumstances of the country no administration could be found so well entitled to his support as the one at present existing.[1]

More pithily T. S. Gooch declared on another occasion: 'as he would rather have the present ministers in place than their opponents, he would resist the motion'.[2] The remainder said little but their votes on crucial party motions echoed the voices of the outspoken few.

Here was the nub of whig difficulties in the commons. The situation had changed from the early and mid eighteenth century. Then defeat, or the prospect of defeat, caused a ministry to lose numbers through abstentions and desertions to the opposition.[3] When the conflict between ministry and opposition was also a conflict between tory and whig principles, danger tended to have the opposite effect. The possibility that the administration might collapse posed a straight choice between ministry and opposition and led to a resurgence of support for the government. It was a situation which ministers inevitably exploited by rumours of danger and threats of resignation. Taken with the fact that one defeat, or even a minor series of defeats in the course of one session, were not considered to entail the resignation of the government, this was a situation which made it almost impossible for the opposition to bring the ministry down

[1] *P.D.*, N.S. iv. 394. [2] *P.D.*, N.S. v. 1422.

[3] See J. H. Plumb, *Sir Robert Walpole*, London, 1960, ii. 263–7, and J. B. Owen, *The Rise of the Pelhams*, London, 1957, pp. 22–40.

through action in the house of commons.[1] Given the nature of the political system and of party loyalties in the house, the occasional success was possible to provide encouragement to the opposition and boost whig hopes. Given the attitudes and prejudices of the important waverers, and the basic loyalty of the government fringe members, nothing more was possible, until the situation changed radically in 1830.

[1] Urged, in 1821, that the government should resign, Wellington replied: 'it would certainly not do to go on if a *system* of not supporting the government was acted upon, but that it would not do to refuse to carry on the business when our general line of policy was approved of merely because an office or two had been objected to': F. Bamford and the Duke of Wellington, *The Journal of Mrs. Arbuthnot, 1820–1832*, London, 1950, i. 150.

IV

WAR AND PEACE · 1815–1816

THE story of the whig party from the fall of the 'talents' to the end of the war is a chronicle of decline. Growing frustration resulted from an inability to make any impression on the government, a failure to discover a practical alternative policy, and the dwindling prospect of an offer of place from the regent. Heavy losses in the 1812 election were avoided only because of the general lack of interest and the comparatively small number of contests and changes in that year. Even so, a tiny handful of votes in the commons was lost and several prominent whigs found themselves temporarily out of parliament.[1] After 1812 the situation deteriorated further. During the final succession of victories criticism of the government was at a discount, and the existing disagreements with Whitbread and his followers were soon supplemented by emerging differences between the Grenvilles and the Foxite section of the party. The former were anxious to crush France completely and drive Napoleon from the throne, the latter were prepared to offer favourable terms of peace. Only the adjournment of parliament from December 1813 to March 1814 prevented whig differences coming into the open.

With the return of peace, ministers basked in the glow of their new prestige. Consequently Tierney's prognostications for the meeting of parliament in November 1814 were gloomy: 'we shall be regarded as a party discomfited and broken up. The attendance on our side of the house will, as far as I can learn, be very small indeed, and I must say that, if so, the figure we shall make will not be very creditable to us.'[2]

He ignored the new issues provided by peace: demands for

[1] Tierney calculated a loss of two or three: Tierney to Grey, 30 October 1812 (Grey). Other calculations, mostly indicating no change, are found in Grenville to Newport, 28 December 1812 (Grenville–Newport Correspondence, Bodleian Library, Oxford); *H.M.C. Dropmore*, x. 298; G. Ponsonby to Devonshire, 4 October 1812 (Devonshire).

[2] Tierney to Grey, 15 October 1814 (Grey).

economy and disarmament and criticisms of the continental allies and of the Vienna proceedings all gave the opposition a series of new weapons. The result was a successful session in which ministers were strongly opposed. This taste of success stimulated high hopes and new activity for the next session in 1815.[1] Tierney, Grey, and Ponsonby all agreed that the party should exploit hostility to the war-time taxation by encouraging a popular agitation against the property tax.[2] Distress was the cause of this popular pressure, but wherever possible the whigs encouraged and guided it in proper directions. The result was thirteen county meetings to petition against the property tax and over 150 petitions to the commons.

With such popular encouragement, Ponsonby sent out a circular for full attendance in the 1815 session and excitedly anticipated that a few weeks of hard work would bring down the ministers.[3] The first review of troops was equally encouraging. Tierney comments that they

> appear to be in very good humour and apparently want nothing but to be well led and to be satisfied that we are all pulling together. There is a great attendance . . . with a very trifling exertion we could divide 153, including none but steady partisans. Add to this the variety of important business which must be brought forward by ministers and might be brought forward by ourselves, and it cannot be denied that for an opposition prospect, that before us is rather encouraging. . . . I might with truth brighten the colours by adding that the government is very low in popular estimation and that there exists in the house of commons a more than usual proportion of persons unconnected with it.[4]

The prospect was dimmed when ministers announced on 20 February that they would surrender the property tax. Hope vanished entirely on 10 March. Castlereagh then announced that Napoleon had landed in France. Attention was immediately exported to the Continent.

Within two weeks it was clear that Napoleon would control France, and the question of peace or war was posed for Britain.

[1] Tierney to Grey, 25 November 1814 (Grey).

[2] Tierney to Grey, 7 December 1814 (Grey); Ponsonby to Grey, 25 December 1814 (Grey).

[3] Ponsonby to Grey, 3 February 1815 (Grey).

[4] Tierney to Holland, 16 February 1815 (Holland).

Just as they had in a similar situation in December 1792, Grenvillite and Foxite now took opposing views.[1] To Grenville and his followers peace with Napoleon was impossible. The emperor's personal character, the military nature of his régime, and his dependence on the army, all made him inevitably aggressive. The duty of the allies was clearly to strike promptly and effectively before Napoleon entrenched himself and discouragement affected the coalition.[2] As in 1792, Fitzwilliam took a similar view. Indeed, Grey believed that Fitzwilliam and his member William Elliot 'were the persons most active and efficient in urging Grenville to adopt the part he took'.[3]

The case for war was straightforward. The case put by the Foxites against it was less clear-cut, partly because it sprang from deep-seated attitudes. Most basic of these was the concept of non-intervention in the affairs of other countries. The rapid collapse of the Bourbons and the welcome given to Napoleon constituted, for the whigs, a free choice of ruler by the French people. That ruler now had the support of the great majority of the population and the property of the country, and the allies had no right to oppose this choice. Some whigs were sympathetic towards Napoleon; others were prepared to trust him. Even those little inclined to either of these views opposed war until Napoleon had had time to demonstrate his intentions, feeling that if a war were then forced on the allies it would be more successful, because more just.

Interrupting as it did the whig campaign against the terms of the peace settlement, the threat of war was hardly likely to find the party enthusiastic to fight for a system they opposed, with allies they distrusted and whose strength they doubted. A final group of arguments brought the whigs on to weaker ground. It

[1] Grey commented on Grenville that 'to bring him to listen to arguments which impeach in the slightest degree the original policy of the wars which have sprung from the French revolution I know to be impossible. It is the only point on which during my connection with him I have inclined to think him a little unfair': Grey to Holland, 14 January 1816 (Grey).

[2] Grenville's views are taken from Grenville to Grey, 28 and 31 March 1815 (Grey).

[3] Grey to Holland, 26 June 1815 (Grey). Elliot would appear to have been a key link between these two groups, for he was in the habit of consultation with Grenville: Elliot to Fitzwilliam, 22 January 1817 (Milton). On this occasion he was keeping Fitzwilliam closely informed of Grenville's views: Elliot to Fitzwilliam, 1 April 1815 (Fitzwilliam, F. 32 f.).

savoured of defeatism to emphasize the weakness of the country after a long war, the difficulty of raising further taxation, and the strength of France. To attack France, it was argued, would be to rally the country behind Napoleon and to allow him to unleash again the spectre of revolution throughout Europe. Tierney declared on 14 June:

it was probable that the war on which we were entering would be a protracted war, as it was engendered in a degree of animosity, which had not been witnessed since 1793. Did the right honourable gentleman think that there was any possibility that this war would be a short one? . . . he saw no probability of anything of the kind; the war could be determined by nothing but the overthrow of the people of France.[1]

This was four days before Waterloo.

Both sections of the party were formulating and discussing their views privately, except for an early protest against intervention by Whitbread. Nevertheless, Horner, who held Foxite views but sat for one of Buckingham's seats, was convinced by the beginning of April that nothing could stop the disclosure of the fundamental differences, and Lord George Cavendish anticipated an end to the Grenville connexion.[2] Both Grenville and Grey, after a lengthy correspondence, appeared inured to a divergence, though both were anxious to postpone it. Grey stated: 'viewing the dissolution of the party in opposition (independently of all personal considerations) as the dissolution of our best hope, in the event of a new war, of averting a revolution, there is nothing that I would not do, short of a sacrifice of fundamental principles, and opinions, to avoid so great an evil'.[3] He was prepared therefore to agree to immediate defensive preparations in case of attack, and to accept negotiations with the allies in order to renew their concert, though on a defensive basis.[4] This was sufficient to provide a temporary bridge between the two camps.

On 6 April a message from the prince regent urged the

[1] *P.D.* xxxi. 815.

[2] Horner to Grey, 2 April 1815 (Grey); Lord G. Cavendish to Fitzwilliam, 31 March 1815 (Fitzwilliam, F. 32 f.).

[3] Grey to Grenville, 1 April 1815, copy (Grey). Grenville's views are mentioned in Elliot to Fitzwilliam, 1 April 1815 (Fitzwilliam, F. 32 f.).

[4] Grey to Grenville, 30 March 1815, copy (Grey).

strengthening of the armed forces and closer concert with the continental allies. That night a meeting, which included men from both whig groups, was held at Ponsonby's house. This produced an agreement not to oppose the address, and as a result the whig peers were able to avoid broaching their differences in the lords.[1] In the commons, however, when Ponsonby followed the official line, Whitbread rose to protest against giving a blank cheque to ministers. His own amendment asked for exertions to maintain peace. It was supported not only by the radicals but also by senior figures such as Tierney and Abercromby. The bulk of the party followed the official line of supporting the address. The amendment secured only thirty-seven votes.

In the next few weeks the failure to provide any official lead, beyond the increasingly untenable compromise, allowed the more radical in the commons to keep the initiative. The renewal of the property tax to provide the sinews of war also went through the commons like a beater driving whig grouse from cover. On the first reading, on 17 April, Brand moved for a two-week adjournment, winning the support of Ponsonby and fifty-eight whig votes. Later seventeen whigs opposed the tax unconditionally, but Grenfell, Baring, Wynn, Methuen, and Plunket all came out in favour of renewal of a tax many of them had earlier opposed. Whitbread himself forced the issue still further on 28 April by moving an address to the regent asking him to prevent the country's being involved in war. Ponsonby, Tierney, and Althorp were among seventy-two supporters of this address. It was strongly opposed by William Elliot and by Newport, and was defeated by a majority of 201.

In the lords both Grey and Grenville maintained an austere silence until, on 22 May, the announcement of the renewed coalition against France made declarations imminent. The same day a meeting was held at Devonshire House and over seventy M.P.s attended to discuss the opposition's attitude.[2] The decision was taken to move an amendment urging concert with the powers on a defensive basis and condemning a war for proscribing the ruler of France. When this was moved by Grey the next

[1] Grey to Wellesley, 6 April 1815 (Wellesley Papers, Add. MSS. 37297, f. 238).
[2] Lord Colchester, *Diary*, ii. 544; Horner to Murray, 24 May 1815 (Horner Papers).

day, he and Grenville both outlined their positions, Grenville announcing his support for ministerial policy, while Grey emphasized the right of nations to choose their own government. Each echoed the other in lamenting their differences. In the division the opposition lost the support of Grenville, Erskine, Ossory, Stafford, Carrington, Cassilis, Bulkeley, and St. Vincent.[1] In the commons only ninety-two votes rallied to the official amendment when it was moved by Lord George Cavendish. This was a mere twenty more than Whitbread had secured the month before. It was defeated by 239 votes, for the opposition had lost the support of all the waverers, much of its loose fringe, and all of the Grenvilles and Fitzwilliams. Only Nugent and Ebrington remained loyal, and even they had not voted. The amendment was opposed by several of the leading opposition spokesmen, such as Grattan and Plunket, and received no support from many others, through accidental or deliberate absence.[2]

At no other time were the whigs so weak. The only hopeful feature was that all regarded the disagreement as affecting only the issue on which it had originated. Co-operation between the different groups continued on other issues, and on one it was even successful. When ministers introduced the Duke of Cumberland's establishment bill to provide for his marriage, their majorities dropped, and then finally disappeared on an amendment moved by C. C. Western to postpone consideration for six months. Yet this was the only cheering prospect in an otherwise disastrous session.

Despite Grey's easy optimism that, as he says, 'our concert may be renewed with the same cordiality as before this interruption', the rapid defeat of Napoleon and the quick peace with France brought not a whig *rapprochement* but more serious disagreement.[3] Whigs, who had opposed a war to turn Napoleon off the throne, now opposed a peace which imposed the Bour-

[1] Horner to Murray, op. cit.

[2] An indication of the support lost by the whigs is given by comparing the vote on Tierney's motion for a committee on the civil list with that on the address: forty-eight members voted for the one and not for the other. They include Aubrey, Elliot, Fazakerly, Frankland, Fremantle, Grattan, Grenfell, Methuen, Milton, Pelham, Plunket, Protheroe, Warre, and Wynn as well as prominent waverers such as T. D. Acland, Bankes, and Wilberforce.

[3] Grey to Holland, 26 June 1815 (Grey).

bons on France. They objected both to the doctrine of legitimacy and to the violation of national self-determination. The Bourbons, they argued, were an unpopular and even a dangerous family, which could be kept on the throne only by foreign bayonets. Grenville was inclined to condemn the occupation almost as strongly as the whigs, but neither he nor his closest associates could agree either that the allies had no right to interfere in France when European security was at stake, or about the Bourbons.[1] Holland reported that Grenville

considers the support of Louis 18th both in policy and justice a right measure and that . . . no government in France would be satisfactory to him which *descended from the revolution* and the Duke of Orleans for instance would be as objectionable as a republic or Napoleon. He holds very cheap the arguments of our having violated our promises to the French, and departed from the declarations of confining our hostility to one obnoxious man and his family.[2]

Mackintosh, after seeing Grenville, feared that the peer would not be able to allow the occasion to pass without 'asserting his consistency and claiming his share in the triumph over the French revolution'.[3] Approval of the Bourbons did not prevent the Grenvilles from urging that defeat should have been used to weaken France by reducing her territory.[4] The point was not one at issue with the rest of the party, for Grey and Holland were prepared, reluctantly, to agree to it.[5] It was Elliot who disagreed, urging that a reduction of territory was not only difficult to execute but probably unnecessary. He also differed from the Grenvilles in thinking the army of occupation a necessary evil.[6]

The differences between Foxite and Grenvillite, clear and sharp only on the issue of legitimacy and self-determination, were magnified by rumour and a breakdown of communication. Correspondence between Grey and Grenville was resumed only

[1] Grenville to Lansdowne, 18 January 1816 (Lansdowne); Grenville to Grey, 10 February 1816 (Grey).

[2] Holland to Grey, 6 February 1816 (Grey).

[3] Mackintosh to Lansdowne, 19 January 1816 (Lansdowne); Grenville to Lansdowne, 18 January 1816 (Lansdowne).

[4] Wynn to Southey, 3 July 1815 (Wynn, 4814); Grenville to Grey, 10 February 1816 (Grey).

[5] Holland to Grey, 5 January 1816 (Grey).

[6] *P.D.* xxxii. 763–8.

in February 1816, and up to January, when Mackintosh saw him and he wrote to Lansdowne, Grenville's views were known only through rumours, indirect reports, and correspondence between Holland and Thomas Grenville that soon reached deadlock.[1] As early as August 1815 Grey lamented that prospects of agreement were slight, and by October Tierney considered that the Stafford connexion was lost to the party.[2] In December Rosslyn was evaluating the difficulties that would be caused by the loss of the Grenvilles:

in the present state of political party, considered with any view to the possible success of opposition, I don't think it signifies one farthing, or places you one half hour further from the possession of the government. . . . When numbers cease to be of the least importance, and when you have nothing to restrain the free indulgence of your own opinions, without the fear or consideration of the varying sentiments or prejudices of your allies: opposition becomes if not a more profitable speculation, at least a more agreeable occupation. I think that happy period of despair is near at hand, and I hail it with some satisfaction.[3]

So, he reported, did other sections of the party.[4] By January Tierney considered the connexion was at an end.[5]

It was generally recognized that the differences of opinion would appear on the discussion of the peace treaties. As the session approached there developed a fear that they would appear in the debate on the address.[6] Grey feared that the address would be so framed as to provoke controversy, Holland that the more militant sections of the party would not be satisfied without an amendment, and Tierney that unless some united policy were agreed a chaotic discussion would ensue.[7] Grey and Holland were prepared to agree to an amendment, provided that it did not touch on the treaties, and in the middle

[1] Holland to T. Grenville, 8, 15, and 18 September 1815; T. Grenville to Holland, 9 September 1816 (Grenville Papers, Add. MSS. 41858, ff. 218–30 and 235–8).

[2] Grey to Holland, 12 August 1815 (Hickleton Papers); Tierney to Grey, 21 October 1815 (Grey).

[3] Rosslyn to Grey, 11 December 1815 (Grey).

[4] Rosslyn to Grey, 30 January 1816 (Grey).

[5] Tierney to Grey, 24 and 29 January 1816 (Grey).

[6] Grey to Holland, 14 January 1816 (Grey).

[7] Grey to Brougham, 16 December 1815, copy (Brougham); Holland to Morpeth, n.d. [December 1815] and 18 December 1815 (Carlisle); Tierney to Grey, 29 January 1815 (Grey).

of January such of the whigs as were in London met and agreed unanimously that the usual letters should be written to procure a full attendance for an amendment, its subject being left open.[1]

In view of approaching difficulties there was strong pressure on Grey to come to London in person. He obstinately refused, pleading illness and feeling 'unequal to . . . any discussions with the Grenvilles'.[2] His advice was to be given from afar, and the gist of it was to propose an amendment that would hold back the subjects of difference by concentrating on 'a strong recommendation of economy and retrenchment which ought to be the great cause of the session'.[3] The hope that the party could be united in this way was dashed almost as soon as suggested. Milton announced that any amendment carried a greater appearance of hostility than he was prepared to manifest.[4] Thomas Grenville expressed the wish that his friends would vote against one.[5] Grenville himself stressed to Holland that he was anxious to avoid 'any appearance of a desire to lessen by the introduction of topics, not of absolute necessity, the effect of the general expressions of the satisfaction of parliament in the accomplishment of what I consider as the primary object in this moment of all British and European policy';[6] and to Lansdowne that his general opinions were too strong to yield to any one.

The intention to propose an amendment remained, but even here difficulties appeared. George Ponsonby was delayed in Ireland by family business and Duncannon got himself shot in the foot. Tierney and Abercromby were therefore obliged to send out the notes calling members to a meeting on the Wednesday before the session.

A puzzled body of whigs began to arrive in London at the end of January, but the meeting the night before the session was very badly attended with only twenty-eight present.[7] Among them

[1] Grey to Holland, 14 January 1816 (Grey); Holland to Morpeth, n.d. [December 1815] (Carlisle); Tierney to Fitzwilliam, 26 January 1816 (Milton); Tierney to Grey, 22 January 1816 (Grey).

[2] Grey to Holland, 14 January 1816 (Grey).

[3] Ibid.

[4] Tierney to Fitzwilliam, 26 January 1816 (Milton).

[5] *H.M.C. Dropmore*, x. 412.

[6] Quoted in Lady Holland to Grey, 30 January 1816 (Grey); Grenville to Horner, 25 January 1816 (Horner Papers); Grenville to Lansdowne, 18 January 1816 (Lansdowne).

[7] Lambton to Wilson, 30 January 1816 (Wilson Papers, Add. MSS. 30108, ff. 108–9).

were Nugent, Ebrington, and Bernard of the Grenville group, Fremantle having refused to come, as had Elliot. Tierney had prepared an amendment designed to maintain unity: this now being impossible, Brougham and Romilly took the amendment home to rewrite it and infuse rather more spirit.[1] The next day Holland decided not to move any amendment in the lords, 'partly for peace sake and partly for personal convenience'.[2] When Grenville announced his hearty concurrence with the address, the most that was said on the other side was Lansdowne's attempt to point out that his own approval was confined within limits.[3] In the commons the amendment was proposed by Brand and Lord John Russell and opposed by Milton. The decision was taken, apparently on the spot, not to divide. With this understanding many whigs went away, only to have Sir Gilbert Heathcote step forward and force the amendment to a division. It rallied a pathetic twenty-three votes. As Tierney commented, 'it was bad enough to have brought up many from the country who when they came into the house were told there would be no division, but it made it a good deal worse when, after they were gone . . . they found that one had taken place'.[4] This fiasco was followed by others. Brougham's motion for a copy of the holy alliance treaty between Russia, Austria, and Prussia rallied only thirty votes a week later, and a motion on Spain secured only forty-two.

Behind the scenes Holland was carrying on the attempt to reach agreement with Grenville and Fitzwilliam. He found both immovable and was gloomy: 'I am much afraid that the persuasion which must grow on Grenville that Louis XVIII cannot be maintained without large armies and expense rather reconciles him more than he expected to armies and expenses than convinces him of the impracticability of the object.'[5] Two days later Lauderdale reported that 'Holland and Tierney both speak of separation as nearly inevitable'.[6]

[1] See Lady Holland to Grey, 1 February 1816 (Grey) and Tierney to Grey, 1 February 1816 (Grey).

[2] Holland to Morpeth, 31 January 1816 (Carlisle).

[3] *P.D.* xxxii. 9–11.

[4] Tierney to Grey, 2 February 1816 (Grey); *P.D.* xxxii. 63; Rosslyn to Grey, 2 February 1816 (Grey).

[5] Holland to Grey, 3 February 1816 (Grey).

[6] Lauderdale to Grey, 5 February 1816 (Grey).

The situation was saved by a new approach. After his discussions with Grenville in January Sir James Mackintosh had suggested that the best way to avoid a break was for both sides to express their views without bringing forward any motion which might compel them to vote on opposite sides. Since the treaties could not be changed he suggested that the party should confine itself to opposition to the military occupation of France.[1] Lansdowne now put this scheme before Grenville, who agreed to think the idea over for a couple of days.[2] Whig hopes immediately began to rise. They were justified when Grenville produced an amendment which made no mention of legitimacy or Bourbons, but deplored the maintenance of a large army and the occupation of France. 'My object is', he told Grey, 'without compromising or even suppressing my own opinions, in a case where it is my duty to express them fully, yet to use such a form of words as may be least exceptionable to friends who I am confident know, without my giving fresh assurance of it, that it is always most unwillingly that I am seen in any shape differing from them.'[3] The draft was well received by Grey, Holland, and probably by a meeting of M.P.s held on the 11th.[4] All that remained was for both groups in the party to place their views on record, a thing they could do while appearing to be expressing different reasons for the same amendment. In the lords Grenville urged the abridgement of French territory, but placed his main emphasis on the good whig ground of opposition to standing armies, and Holland brought out his distrust of the Bourbons, but stressed the cost of the peace establishments.[5] The only note of disagreement in either house was struck by an ailing Elliot, who argued the case for hereditary succession in France as the best guarantee of a return to moral order.[6] The debate, so long dreaded, had come off with such success that few were worried by the low vote of seventy-seven in the commons. 'On the whole,' thought Tierney, 'we have got through

[1] Mackintosh to Lansdowne, 19 January 1816 (Lansdowne).

[2] Lady Holland to Grey, 6 February 1816 (Grey); Rosslyn to Grey, 6 February 1816 (Grey).

[3] Grenville to Grey, 7 February 1816 (Grey).

[4] Grey to Grenville, 14 February 1816, copy (Grey); Holland to Grey, 7 February 1816 (Grey); Tierney to Grey, 10 February 1816 (Grey).

[5] *P.D.* xxxii. 653–64; 664–5.

[6] *P.D.* xxxii. 763–8.

our differences of opinion better than we had any reason to expect.'[1]

With this source of difference out of the way the party could look forward to what Grey described as 'a cordial and vigorous cooperation during the remainder of the session on those points on which we agree; to enforce a system of economy, to reduce unnecessary and expensive and dangerous establishments, and to bring back the government to the true principles of the constitution'.[2] Grenville was reported to be eager, and the prospects in the commons looked good, for Tierney reported: 'every day confirms me in the notion that the temper of the house of commons is not favourable to ministers, and if we play our game well and do not go too fast they will have a sour time of it'.[3] Popular pressure for retrenchment and reduction of taxation was a major feature, owing to the serious distress, the worst of the post-war period. This affected all sectors of the economy, agriculture, trade, and industry. The resulting search for solutions inevitably centred on the property tax, and ministers realized that it was likely to prove the major issue of the session.[4] Several whigs had already urged an active campaign: Fitzwilliam was for rousing every town, village, and county; and in December Grey was lamenting 'that a fire has not been already opened and steadily kept up from this battery, the only one from which our artillery can be expected to produce any real effect'.[5] This fire was opened through the *Morning Chronicle*, and rather later through the *Edinburgh Review*, but further action to rouse the public was precluded by ignorance of the government's intentions, made clear only at the opening of parliament, and by the differences on the treaties.

In the face of the consequent whig indecision the campaign against the property tax appears to have sprung not from an organized effort but out of spontaneous splutterings in the country, and, much more important, from pressure in the City of London. Tierney commented: 'The city of London have set a good example as to the property tax and I hope it will be followed up by the country, but I must confess I have my doubts.

[1] Tierney to Grey, 21 February 1816 (Grey).

[2] Grey to Fitzwilliam, 25 February 1816 (Milton).

[3] Bedford to Grey, 24 February 1816 (Grey); Tierney to Grey, 21 February 1816 (Grey).

[4] C. D. Yonge, *Liverpool*, ii. 251.

[5] Grey to Brougham, 16 December 1815, copy (Brougham).

Vansittart is to state to us on Monday the amount of the peace establishment and if that be as high as report states it it may produce an effect on the public'.[1] With the bandwaggon already moving, the *Morning Chronicle* and other papers promptly demanded that all steps should be taken to assemble public meetings.[2] From within parliament the whigs now did their best to encourage public pressure and meetings, using the supply committee of 12 February as a platform for a series of harangues against the property tax, and an appeal to the nation at large.

The campaign quickly gathered pace. A trickle of petitions began to reach the commons on 7 February, becoming a flood two weeks later: over eighty were presented on 28 February alone. The government became anxious that the division on the tax should be taken as soon as possible, while the opposition bent all their efforts to delay. The army estimates were opposed at length, and the presentation of petitions provided a pretext for daily declamations against the property tax and the size of the establishments it was to support. On 26 February, when Vansittart proposed to bring the matter to a decision in two days, Baring announced his intention to employ parliamentary obstruction, and other members asked for delay to allow scheduled meetings of their constituents. Vansittart changed the date to 1 March, but then agreed to two further delays because of pressure of business. This helped to seal the fate of the tax by allowing a long series of debates on the presentation of petitions, the holding of most of the county meetings, and the presentation of half of the petitions received. Nearly 400 petitions were presented to parliament, and at least eighteen county meetings were held, nearly all of them large and virtually unanimous.[3]

[1] Tierney to Grey, 10 February 1816 (Grey).

[2] *Morning Chronicle*, 9 February; *The Times*, 13 February 1816; *Norfolk Chronicle*, 17 February 1816.

[3] Somerset: *Bristol Mirror*, 9 March 1816. Hertfordshire: *The Times*, 4 March. Surrey: *The Times*, 11 March. Yorkshire: *The Times*, 18 March. Norfolk: *Norfolk Chronicle*, 16 and 30 March. Devonshire: *The Alfred*, 26 March. Lincolnshire: *Newcastle Chronicle*, 9 March. Northamptonshire: *Northampton Mercury*, 17 and 24 February. Berkshire: *The Times*, 24 February. Hampshire: *Political Register*, 24 February. Cambridgeshire: *The Times*, 28 February. Essex: *The Times*, 29 February. Middlesex: *The Times*, 6 March. Staffordshire: *The Times*, 15 March. Kent: *Political Register*, 23 March. Monmouthshire, Suffolk, and Gloucestershire: *Commons Journals*, 1816, pp. 123, 188, 211.

The efforts of the previous year had been greatly improved upon.

It is extremely difficult to assess the whig share in this massive campaign. There is no evidence of any central planning or co-ordination, nor of any direct stimulus beyond the efforts of individual whigs in their own localities. In certain areas whig influence was very slight indeed. In London, which provided almost a sixth of the petitions, this was so. The body of discontent among the merchants was beyond the dimensions of party, and it is significant that the three leading speakers at the common hall meeting were Sir William Curtis, Sir James Shaw, and Alderman Atkins, all M.P.s and all normally ministerialist in their sympathies. These three were also active in the wards. In Southwark and Westminster the drive came from radicals, but they were anxious for whig support. Brand, Brougham, Lambton, Bennet, and Maddocks agreed to take an active part, but when they attended the Westminster meeting a violent attack on the whigs by Hunt provoked them all to leave the platform in protest.[1]

In other large centres the whig role may have been as slight as it was in London. The impetus behind the meetings held or attempted in places like Manchester, Liverpool, and Bristol came from both middle-class radicals and the mercantile community, but there is no evidence that these were anything other than self-interested initiatives, and support from other elements of opinion, even from those normally ministerialist, was widespread.[2] Among the smaller towns and the villages inspiration is impossible to attribute, though it is difficult to believe that when Higham Ferrers, Calne, Horsham, Wareham, and Chester petitioned, Fitzwilliam, Lansdowne, Norfolk, Calcraft, and Grosvenor bore no responsibility. Elsewhere local magnates who were whigs would almost certainly use their influence to produce petitions. Responsibility can be clearly brought out only for the county meetings. In some counties, such as Somerset and Gloucester, ministerialist country gentlemen appear to have worked in coalition with whigs, but in the case of eleven meetings the whigs appear to have been largely responsible. Here

[1] *Political Register*, 24 February 1816.

[2] Manchester was one of the few places where the issue became one of party strife: *Manchester Mercury*, 27 February 1816.

alone the main impetus, many of the signatures on the requisitions, and most of the speeches at the meetings, came from whigs.[1]

It is difficult to find clear support for the views of those historians who have portrayed the campaign against the property tax as a triumph for the whigs, and particularly for Brougham.[2] Preaching and propaganda do not necessarily create meetings, and the main impetus for these came from the marked distress affecting all sections of the community. In the urban areas, which provided a large proportion of the petitions, this produced apparently spontaneous protests against the only effective taxation on non-landed wealth. In the counties and rural areas the whigs appear to have been more directly responsible for the initiation and organization of meetings, but even here they received support far wider than the boundaries of party, largely because of the prevailing distress. In part, therefore, Tierney's verdict on the 1815 agitation seems relevant to that of 1816: 'it has resulted entirely from the impatience of the country at large, and cannot be attributed in any degree to the exertions of the opposition.'[3]

Even before the campaign ministers had been worried about property tax renewal. As agitation gathered pace they attempted countermoves. A meeting of country gentlemen mustered few and accomplished little.[4] Ministerial speakers began to turn the

[1] As an example, the Northamptonshire requisition included among its nineteen signatories Bedford, Sondes, Fitzwilliam, Milton, and Tavistock, as well as some local whigs: *Northampton Mercury*, 7 February. The Surrey requisition, with fifteen signatures, included Spencer, Bessborough, King, Bulkeley, Althorp, Duncannon, W. J. Denison, Robert Hurst, W. H. Fremantle, C. Calvert, C. Palmer, and H. Howarth: *The Alfred*, 18 March 1816. In Norfolk 37 of the 105 signatories also signed a requisition for a county meeting in October 1819 to protest against the Peterloo massacre. The latter was a largely whig campaign, and the extent of the overlap, given the time in between and the somewhat haphazard nature of canvassing, is surprising: *Norfolk Chronicle*, 16 March 1816 and 23 October 1819.

[2] See E. Halevy, *The Liberal Awakening, 1815–1830*, London, 1949, p. 7; A. Aspinall, *Brougham*, p. 59; C. New, *The Life of Henry Brougham to 1830*, Oxford, 1961, p. 165; F. Shehab, *Progressive Taxation*, Oxford, 1953, pp. 60–69. The dissentient is A. H. Jones, *Income Tax in the Napoleonic Wars*, Cambridge, 1939, who lays the emphasis largely on public reaction against war taxation.

[3] Tierney to Grey, 28 January 1815 (Grey).

[4] *Morning Chronicle*, 23 February 1816. Ossulston reported that only thirty-five were present and that only two M.P.s declared in favour of the tax, while the two Burrells and Ruthven came out against it: Ossulston to Grey, 24 February 1816 (Grey).

daily declamations from the other side into debates, but they were too heavily outnumbered. Attempts were made to secure support from individual country gentlemen, but at the same time others were coming out against the tax in parliament and at public meetings. Nevertheless ministers remained confident of a majority of about forty.[1] The whigs, for their part, fluctuated between hope and despair.[2] The uncertainty was ended on 18 March when the property tax was defeated by 238 votes to 201.

The regular opposition voters who made up the core of this majority were joined by half of the waverers and a third of the government fringe members. At the same time the government had to face difficulties not only with these two groups, but also from heavy abstentions among its own supporters, under two-thirds of whom voted. While the distribution of opposition to the tax is clear, the reasons producing it are not. The direct operation of public pressure is too simple an explanation. Members from small boroughs among the waverers and government fringe swung against the tax almost as heavily as any, county members in these two groups were but slightly more likely than the average to vote against it, and, among government supporters, members from counties and large boroughs were more likely than the average to turn up and vote for it. The government's main abstentions were found among the Irish members, who were unaffected by either tax or agitation.[3] The figures are small and therefore inconclusive, but the indications are that it was these abstentions, combined with a greater-than-average swing against the government among members from large and medium boroughs and those with commercial backgrounds, which helped to decide the issue.[4] The discontents of the towns

[1] *George IV*, ii. 160.

[2] J. Gore, *Creevey*, p. 100; L. Horner, *Horner*, ii. 346; Holland commented, 'opinions vary so much about the lot of the property tax that one hardly knows what to believe', Holland to Grey, 2 March 1816 (Grey).

[3] Among those county M.P.s coming into the categories of waverer and government fringe nearly six out of ten of those who voted were against the tax. Among government M.P.s in the house at the time 63 per cent. voted for the tax, but further analysis of this group shows that as many as 79 per cent. of the county M.P.s coming into it voted for the tax, compared with only 46 per cent. of the Irish group among government members.

[4] Among the waverers and government fringe members, 61 per cent. of the medium and large-town members who voted were against the tax, and 70 per cent of the commercial members.

and the merchants appear more important than those of the counties.

Victory naturally stimulated whig hopes. If the government was to be brought down by further defeats it was imperative that the coalition of 18 March should be kept up. Two days later it broke. Methuen moved for papers on the increase in the salary of the secretaries of the admiralty, contending that these salaries should be reduced in peace-time. In the course of the debate Brougham made a violent personal attack on the regent. This was heard with great enthusiasm by the opposition, but then the motion was defeated by 159 votes to 130. Government and opposition members both agreed in attributing the result to Brougham's performance, and Brougham himself, though blustering to others, was sufficiently abject to write to Grey: 'If you think my going out of parliament would in the smallest degree tend to relieve the party from the injury they think I have brought upon them, I am ready and desirous to do so and authorise you to take the steps necessary for this purpose.'[1]

Modern historians have tended to echo this contemporary chorus.[2] Indeed, scapegoats were in fashion at the time. On 25 March, when an attack on the navy estimates failed, this was blamed by many on a blunder of Tierney's in forgetting that estimates normally rose in the year after every war. Croker made a powerful reply and opinion is stated to have swung against the whigs.[3] Shortly afterwards a further government victory in committee was attributed to another powerful speech by Croker.[4]

For the first time the whigs had stumbled over the difficulty which was to preoccupy them for several years. A successful attack was followed neither by government collapse nor by further victories. The reasons are numerous and the scapegoats singled out at the time are not pre-eminent among them. The administration was taking steps to strengthen its support. Liverpool wrote to the magnates and to prominent government

[1] Brougham to Grey, 21 March 1816 (Brougham); C. W. Wynn to Southey, 4 April 1816 (Wynn 4814): 'five members professed to have altered their vote and 27 to have gone away in consequence of Brougham's intemperate and indecent speech.' See also *George IV*, ii. 161; Heron, p. 67; and S. Romilly, *Romilly*, iii. 236–7.

[2] C. New, *Brougham*, p. 170; A. Aspinall, *Brougham*, pp. 61–2 and 66; H. K. Olphin, *Tierney*, p. 172.

[3] L. J. Jennings, *Croker*, i .81–85; *P.D.* xxxiii. 567–91.

[4] Ibid. 80 and 84. This reference has been understood to refer to two incidents.

supporters to stiffen their backing, secured a declaration of support from the regent, and held a meeting of those country gentlemen known to be government supporters.[1] In addition, concessions were made to the state of feeling in the house by giving up the war malt tax as well as the property tax, agreeing to reduce the salary of the treasurer of the navy, and reintroducing the army estimates with some reductions.

The pressures which had led to ministerial defeat over the property tax were clearly confined to that issue. Whatever the influence of the public campaign, it came to an end almost immediately after 18 March. The division itself was clearly an exceptional one. For fifty of the waverers and government fringe members who voted against the property tax it was their only opposition vote on any of the major motions in the session. Indeed, three-fifths of the waverers had voted for the army estimates earlier in the same month, prepared, apparently, to will the end if not to vote the means. Even that minority of waverers prepared to cast other votes against the government did not concentrate them on any one issue: the largest number voting for any motion after the property tax was nine on Methuen's motion on the admiralty salaries. This was less than had been secured earlier in the month on the attempt to reduce the army estimates.[2] There was, indeed, little incentive to stray further from the fold. Great gains had been made, public demand had been satisfied, and to do more would have been to endanger a government which to many, and to Liverpool himself, seemed to be hanging by a thread. This was something the waverers were reluctant to do, and Marryat probably spoke for others as well as himself when he commented 'that there was a certain point beyond which violent and intemperate zeal would defeat its own object. A pretty large dose had already been given to ministers, and he was anxious to see how that dose worked before the house proceeded further.'[3]

[1] *Morning Chronicle*, 30 March 1816.

[2] Considering only the waverers who had voted against the property tax, twenty-six did not vote on any of the other ten motions which secured 100 votes or more in the course of the session. Of the twenty-four who did, ten voted to reduce the army estimates, on 8 March, nine to cut the household troops, on 11 March, and nine on the admiralty salaries. The next largest really was six on Althorp's motion of 7 May for a committee on public offices, and then five for Tierney's motion on the secretary of state.

[3] *P.D.* xxxiv. 360.

As it became clear that the government was not to be brought down, and as the opposition cast around for explanations, the pace slackened. Attention was diverted to Western's committee on agricultural distress. Attack was resumed with five major motions for economy in the course of April and May, some very general, like Lord George Cavendish's motion for a reduction of public expenditure, others relating to a particular office, like Tierney's motion to abolish the third secretaryship of state. All were beaten, some with the help of ministerial concessions. Thereupon the house turned its attention to questions of principle and other topics with little attraction to waverers—the alien bill, the continuation of the bank restriction, and the catholic question. Not until the last few days of the session did the possibility of a further attack on economy present itself. The whigs were able to defeat the government on 12 June in its attempt to claim that the treasurership of Greenwich was a commission, so that appointment did not require re-election, and on 17 June by securing a majority for Ponsonby's motion to reduce the salary of the vice-treasurer. In neither case did the numbers involved in the divisions rise above 200, and in both whig victory was mainly due to keeping up their own attendance at a time when the government's was inevitably falling.

These were the last issues of the 1816 session, which came to a close on 27 June, after a prolonged whimper and a very minor bang had already concluded the economy campaign. It had been a major testing time for both government and opposition. The reversion to the politics of peace had, as a distant observer commented, 'been a most perilous session for the government, and one in which it has now suffered very severely. All seems right now—but the escape has been a narrow one.'[1] Yet the government had learnt lessons. It had decided to strengthen itself by bringing Canning into the cabinet, and it had learnt the value of tactical concessions. Opposition, after its high hopes, had failed. Even with the support of a massive agitation outside parliament it had proved unable to bring the government down. The very real difficulty of holding the support of the waverers had been encountered, though not quite understood, for the first time in the new post-war situation.

[1] Charles Bagot to Huskisson, 4 July 1816 (Huskisson Papers, Add. MSS. 38741, f. 83).

V

REPRESSION · 1817–1818

THOUGH the high hopes of 1816 had been disappointed, the distress and recession which had helped produce them lifted only slowly in agriculture, not at all in industry. The whigs were naturally optimistic for the coming session. Holland even asked Grey to consider whether they could form a government, and the leader responded with a full review of policy and a brief consideration of personnel, so as to demonstrate that the whigs were an effective alternative, and 'that we can and will form a ministry and that we are prepared both with a first lord of the treasury and a leader in the house of commons'.[1] Tierney, too, considered that ministers had little hold on public opinion, and that 'so many of their great supporters will hang back from the fear of hazarding, and so many will, upon particular questions, vote against them with a view to securing their elections, that if our real strength is fairly brought into the field I do not see how they are to maintain themselves'. Ministers, he reported, were expecting defeats.[2] With such optimism reigning, Grey wrote to ask Ponsonby to secure a full attendance for the first day, only to find that he had already begun to write round.[3]

Consensus for action was not matched by agreement on the subjects to be agitated. Holland urged emphasis on foreign policy, since to give up all interference in France and the Continent would save more money than any possible reform, but such a policy could only open up the differences of the previous year. The same dangers attended reform. Over 600 petitions for reform came in in 1817, and, though these were mostly from the manufacturing areas and the petitioners of low social status, Tierney found the clamour for reform more serious than he had

[1] Grey to Holland, 17 January 1817 (Grey); Holland to Grey, 10 January 1817 (Grey).

[2] Tierney to Grey, 19 December 1816 and 10 January 1817 (Grey).

[3] Ponsonby to Grey, 8 December 1816 (Grey).

ever expected.[1] Bedford and Albemarle, therefore, urged their fellow whigs to capitalize on the demand.[2] In these circumstances Grey was prepared to bring into the campaign a declaration similar to his vague stipulation for reform in 1810, Holland was ready to follow, and Tierney became rather more enthusiastic when a group of moderate reformers in Westminster, which included Alderman Waithman and the Lord Mayor, sent a deputation along to approach him.[3] Though damping the enthusiasm of the Westminster group, Tierney began to urge that the party should attempt to convince people both that it had the will to come into office and that it would do something on reform when it did.[4] Thomas Grenville and William Elliot were seen reporting in alarm to their respective leaders that Tierney intended to place the whigs at the head of the moderate reformers.[5] They opposed any such plan and found that Ponsonby, too, had grave doubts.[6]

Even the old standby of economy was not without difficulty. Holland reported that retrenchment and economy were in the mouths of all the Pittite and tory country gentlemen.[7] They were, too, in the thoughts of Grey, but close to the heart neither of Elliot, who regarded the size of the military establishment as a small price to pay for avoiding European revolution, nor of Grenville, who was prepared to trust to the good intentions of the ministry and regarded the distress as purely temporary.[8] These reservations might have melted under discussion, for Grey had arranged to come up early. Unfortunately he had got no further south than Milton in Northamptonshire when Lady Grey fell ill with scarlet fever. Grey declined to leave her.

[1] Tierney to Grey, 24 December 1816 (Grey); *Morning Chronicle*, 22 January 1817.

[2] Holland to Grey, 10 January 1817 (Grey); Allen to Horner, 20 November and 28 December 1816 (Horner Papers, British Library of Political and Economic Science).

[3] Grey to Holland, 23 November 1816 (Grey); Tierney to Grey, 19 and 24 December 1816 (Grey); *Independent Whig*, 1 December 1816, 19 January 1817.

[4] Tierney to Grey, 19 December 1816 (Grey); *The Times*, 18 January 1817; Holland to Grey, 15 and 17 January 1817 (Grey).

[5] Elliot to Fitzwilliam, 20 January 1817 (Milton); *H.M.C. Dropmore*, x. 421–2.

[6] Elliot to Fitzwilliam, 20 and 22 January 1817 (Milton); Wynn to Southey, 1 December 1816 (Wynn, 4814).

[7] Holland to Grey, 4 December 1816 (Grey).

[8] Grey to Holland, 8 December 1816 (Grey); Elliot to Fitzwilliam, 25 December 1816 (Milton); Grenville to Holland, 14 January 1817, copy (Grey); Grenville to Lansdowne, 31 January 1817 (Lansdowne).

As Ponsonby had not yet arrived, Tierney thus became responsible for planning. He favoured an amendment to the address, preferably one which should be a manifesto to the country, and Grey, Duncannon, and Macdonald also favoured a division on the first day.[1] On the other hand, Holland, consulting Morpeth, Abercromby, and Lord George Cavendish, had found them less sympathetic, while Lord Grenville urged a waiting policy, and Tierney found that Thomas Grenville preferred an early motion on revenue and expenditure.[2] Tierney, therefore, began to envisage a complex compromise, by which a motion would be moved for a committee on the state of the country as soon as the address had passed. This, as Lambton pointed out, presupposed more discipline than the whigs possessed, and also that Burdett would not step into the gap so obligingly left.[3] Grey brought Tierney back to his senses by urging that the party should

> introduce some general clause, lamenting the distresses of the country, deprecating the fallacious and mischevious view which is taken of them when they are represented as being of a temporary character and like those which have occurred upon the termination of former wars, expressing our regret that the ministers did not sooner feel the necessity of reverting to the measures of retrenchment which they now seem inclined to adopt for their relief, and pledging ourselves to a strict and solemn enquiry into the causes which have produced them, and generally into the state of the country.[4]

These views were communicated to Tierney and the newly arrived Ponsonby.

This firm opinion tipped the scale. A meeting was arranged at Ponsonby's on 21 January, and attended by Ponsonby, Morpeth, Tierney, Abercromby, Piggott, Romilly, and a reluctant Elliot, who 'appeared to be in a state of more than usual alarm'.[5] Elliot launched into a long denunciation of reform, only to find that the issue was not raised: Grey had already decided against making it a subject of party discussion, and preferred to leave it

[1] Tierney to Grey, 7 January 1817 (Grey); Grey to Holland, 23 November 1816 (Grey); Tierney to Grey, 12 December 1816 (Grey).

[2] Holland to Grey, 4 December 1816 (Grey); Grenville to Holland, 14 January 1817, copy (Grey); *H.M.C. Dropmore*, x. 418–19.

[3] Lambton to Grey, 15 January 1817 (Grey).

[4] Grey to Lambton, 17 January 1817 (Grey).

[5] Tierney to Grey, 22 January 1817 (Grey).

to individual initiatives and declarations, of which a few were later made, one by Grey himself.[1] Instead, the meeting agreed to an amendment drawn up by Tierney from Grey's suggestions. Later soundings brought out the fact that Thomas Grenville found the amendment unexceptionable, Grenville considered it harmless, though unnecessary.[2] Everything appeared to be going well when, three days later, Grey arrived for final consultations and a meeting of the party (from both houses) at Burlington House the night before the opening.[3]

The campaign went ahead exactly as planned. In the commons Ponsonby moved the amendment with a strong attack on ministerial extravagance, while the next day in the lords Grey made a wider-reaching attack, which embraced foreign policy but emphasized exactly the same demand for 'rigid, unsparing economy'.[4] Yet, though it was supported by speech and vote from all sections of the party, the amendment secured only 112 votes, hardly any of them from 'out of the holy brotherhood itself'.[5] The reason was clear. Some whigs, such as Derby and Grenville, had already been worried lest the agitation produced by distress should get out of hand, and Tierney had anticipated that it would take some managing.[6] None had foreseen the magnitude of the difficulty. Early in the year agitation in the northern industrial areas assumed intimidating proportions, and on his way to open parliament the regent was hooted by an angry crowd and attacked. On 5 February secret committees were set up to consider documents illustrating a conspiracy against the constitution. Support for the government hardened among alarmed waverers, and the whigs despaired, Thanet commenting 'the attack upon the regent seems to have made a very serious impression upon our friends as though it had made all opposition useless'.[7] Brougham recognized that all thoughts

[1] Elliot to Fitzwilliam, 22 January 1817 (Milton); Grey to Holland, 17 January 1817 (Grey); *P.D.* xxxv. 426.

[2] Grenville to T. Grenville, 23 January 1817 (Grenville papers, Add. MSS. 41853, f. 348).

[3] Lord John Russell, *Recollections*, p. 30; Tierney to Grey, 19 December 1816 (Grey).

[4] *P.D.* xxxv. 19 and 54.

[5] *Letters of the Earl of Dudley to the Bishop of Llandaff*, edited by the Bishop of Llandaff, London, 1840, p. 159.

[6] Derby to Grey, 19 October and 15 December 1816 (Grey); Grenville to Lansdowne, 31 January 1817 (Lansdowne); Tierney to Grey, 12 December 1816 (Grey).

[7] Thanet to Grey, 7 February 1817 (Grey).

of turning out the government had vanished, and Whishaw's surmise that the fate of the session was already decided proved to be more than justified.[1] Though the planned campaign on economy went ahead, attention was concentrated on the looming crisis over repression, with a split between Foxite and Grenvillite widely anticipated.[2]

In any case ministers had skilfully undercut the opposition by offering concessions. On 7 February Castlereagh moved to set up a committee on public income and expenditure, described by whigs as 'the humbug committee'. Since it was chosen by ballot, this body was under ministerial control, but at the same time its creation appeared to justify claims that something was being done.[3] In addition, the regent agreed to reduce his own expenses and the cabinet decided to surrender unnecessary offices and sinecures, a decision which was shortly announced to a meeting of country gentlemen.[4] The combined effect of concessions and alarms led to the failure of a series of whig motions. Milton's motion to cut back the war salary of the secretaries of the admiralty to peace-time level went down on 17 February by fifty-five votes. Ridley's attempt to reduce the number of admiralty commissioners, which some whigs had expected to be carried, attracted only 152 votes, while in the lords Grosvenor's motion on sinecures secured only five votes. Still more striking was the defeat of Brougham's attempt to capitalize on the distress with a motion on trade and manufactures: this secured only sixty-three votes.

The whigs, like the nation, were awaiting the deliberations of the committee of secrecy. Only three opposition members, Bedford, Fitzwilliam, and Grenville, had been nominated to the committee in the lords. Since it was anticipated that the last two would be alarmist, Grey persuaded Bedford to stay away.[5] In the commons the committee included three whigs likely to be alarmist, Milton, Elliot, and Lamb, and two, Sir Arthur Piggott and Ponsonby himself, who were more orthodox. A similar

[1] A. Aspinall, *Brougham*, p. 74; Seymour, *Pope*, p. 165.

[2] Holland to Horner, 11 February 1817; Grey to Horner, 3 February 1817 (Horner Papers).

[3] Since ministers normally circulated identical lists of names to their supporters, they dominated the choice. See *P.D.* xxxvii. 203 for an illustration.

[4] R. Russell, *Russell*, i. 190; C. S. Parker, *Peel*, i. 238.

[5] Bedford to Grey, 6 and 9 February 1817 (Grey).

attempt to urge abstention was made by Dudley North in a long conversation with the last two, but it met with no success.[1]

The crisis, and a whig break already foreshadowed by rumour, were brought out into the open with the presentation of the reports of the committees and the introduction of a bill to suspend habeas corpus. Grey's stand was clear from the first:

the inclination of my mind is still very strongly against any alteration of the law upon a case which, as far as I can at present form an opinion on it, seems to have required nothing more than a vigilant and resolute exercise of the ordinary powers of the government, and which in point of fact appears to have been sufficiently provided against by those means. At all events, it seems too much to require of us to enact any new laws of a severe and coercive character, upon the mere recommendation of the committee . . . without a single tittle of evidence in support of that recommendation.[2]

He therefore called to his house a meeting of those members of the opposition in both houses who were likely to be against any interference with habeas corpus.[3] This appears to have decided to oppose the suspension, but to show some willingness to compromise on any other proposed legislation.

The subsequent debates in lords and commons revealed the extent of the split. Grey, with strong support from Wellesley, opposed suspension in the lords, as did Ponsonby and the majority of the party in the commons. On the other side, Grenville stated his belief that the case had been completely made out; Fitzwilliam gave a silent vote for suspension; Elliot, Grenville, Lamb, and Wynn spoke for it in the commons; and Carlisle's sons, Morpeth and William Howard, dropped quietly into abstention. These losses were serious, but they did not embrace the entire personnel of the Grenville and Fitzwilliam groups. Nugent and Ebrington adhered to the main body of the party, and Milton and Charles Pelham, though reluctant to diverge from their respective fathers, Lord Fitzwilliam and Lord Yarborough, considered that the case for suspension had not been fully made out, and that a conspiracy which had

[1] Described in C. Pelham to Yarborough, 28 February 1817. Sent by Yarborough to Fitzwilliam with endorsement 'Pray burn this' (Milton).

[2] Grey to Wellesley, 19 February 1817 (Wellesley Papers, Add. MSS. 37297, f. 248).

[3] Grey to Fitzwilliam, 'Saturday night', n.d. [February 1817] (Milton).

received no sanction from the higher orders could not be as dangerous as it had been portrayed.[1] Both voted against a suspension of which their fathers approved. Even so, the whig total of 103 votes on the third reading was enough to indicate that only the hard core of the party remained stout.[2]

Whig difficulties were not confined to disagreements with Grenville and Fitzwilliam and their supporters, for when Grey and Ponsonby announced their willingness to agree to other measures after modification, Auckland, Erskine, and Grosvenor still opposed the seditious meetings bill in the lords, and Ponsonby was defied by the more radical section of the party in the commons; fourteen opposed even the introduction of the bill. Already partly compromised through his inability to reveal the proceedings of the secret committee, Ponsonby was thus obliged 'not only to combat the gentlemen opposite, but also the charge of imbecility brought against him by his honourable friends around and behind him'.[3] He adhered obstinately to his course but was unable to prevent forty-four whigs from voting against the bill.

Whig fortunes had reached a new low. Little support was received from outside the house, and less had been forthcoming from the waverers and independent groups inside. There were hopes that the weakness would not be permanent, for both Grenville and Fitzwilliam had emphasized their desire for future co-operation, and there were real hopes that economy would provide a meeting ground.[4] Grey regarded ministers as far from impregnable, and hoped for some success after Easter

[1] *P.D.* xxxv. 730–3 and C. Pelham to Yarborough, 28 February 1817 (Milton).

[2] A comparison of the votes on the first and third readings of suspension with that on Ridley's motion for a reduction in the number of the lords of the admiralty shows that fifty-four members voted for economy but not against suspension. Of these one is classified as government fringe, and fifteen as waverers, the loss of their support representing the inevitable swing away on non-financial motions. However, nineteen are opposition fringe and nineteen opposition, their loss indicating the split within the ranks of the opposition itself. Of these thirty-eight members, fifteen had behaved in a similar fashion in 1815, voting for Tierney's motion on the civil list on 8 May but not for the amendment on the message relating to France on 25 May. This illustrates the degree of continuity between the warlike of 1815 and the alarmists of two years later.

[3] *P.D.* xxxv. 755.

[4] Grey to Fitzwilliam, 'Saturday night', n.d. [February 1817] (Milton); Fitzwilliam to Grey, 23 February 1817 (Grey); Grenville to Grey, 23 February 1817 (Grey).

on economy, but in fact only one motion, Calcraft's for a committee on the salt tax, came anywhere near success, being defeated by only nine votes.[1] On seven other motions the whigs rallied less than a hundred votes, while on one, Brougham's motion on the state of the nation, a direct censure of ministers, discipline broke down completely. The motion was supported only by the radical section which had initiated it; the more cautious went away. It provoked a powerful reply from Canning and was allowed to be negatived without division. The party had lost its momentum. Its plight was clearly shown on a straight party division, Lambton's motion on Canning's embassy to Lisbon, when only ninety-seven votes were rallied for the motion and 270 mustered against it. The only large vote was on the question of the speakership, when a full house turned out and 150 opposition members supported the candidature of Charles Williams-Wynn. They were defeated by a majority of 162.

The situation was made worse by the recurrence of subjects which divided the two sections of the party. On 20 May Burdett moved for a committee on the representation and seventy-seven whigs felt obliged to vote for it, while William Lamb and W. C. Plunket felt equally obliged to denounce it.[2] Equally dangerous were issues relating to repression. A circular sent out by Sidmouth, advising J.P.s that they could hold to bail or commit a person accused of publishing blasphemous and seditious libels, produced another debate and yet another demonstration of disunity. Spirits were extremely low in large sections of the party, Grey's speech in the lords was gloomy, and Albemarle even suggested a secession: 'I am for a complete secession from parliament. The crown is all powerful. The people servile. . . . We shall either have an established military despotism or a revolution. Our efforts can be of no avail.'[3] Then on 3 June a further message was brought down from the regent announcing the continuation of seditious practices and requesting a new secret committee to examine further papers. Ponsonby and Piggott attended the earlier stages, but when it became clear that the

[1] Grey to Lambton, 16 March 1817 (Lambton).

[2] *P.D.* xxxvi. 791, 811.

[3] Albemarle to Grey, 28 May 1817 (Grey); Wellesley to Grey, 9 May 1817 (Grey).

committee was going to recommend the continuation of the suspension, Ponsonby declared his opposition to such a move and absented himself. Piggott fell victim to a diplomatic illness.[1]

Yet, while Grenville and Elliot were as alarmist as they had been earlier, Fitzwilliam had become convinced that Yorkshire was peaceful.[2] When on 14 June the *Leeds Mercury* carried a major story about the activities of Oliver the spy, he seized on these as the cause of the existing unrest in Yorkshire.[3] Milton therefore announced that the differences with his father which had weighed so heavily on him earlier in the year were now at an end. Both he and Fitzwilliam were convinced that there was no ground for the extension of the suspension.[4] Grenville and Fitzwilliam, so often agreed in the past, were now divided.[5]

Oliver also became a major weapon in the ensuing campaign on the continuation of the suspension. On 16 June Burdett brought the subject up in the commons, and Grey in the lords, the latter using the information from the *Mercury* to throw doubts on the whole report of the committee of secrecy. 'He asked, whether it did not shake to the foundation the report of the committee, and convey strong suspicions that the secret conspiracies to which these unhappy men seemed prone, from the want of employment, and the distress consequent on the cessation of a long war, were not produced, fostered, and supported by the agents of government itself?'[6] Thus encouraged the whigs waged a much more energetic campaign against renewal. Three county meetings were arranged at short notice to protest against it.[7] Every stage was strongly opposed and support was forthcoming from a small number of members, including Deerhurst, Warre, and Protheroe, all of whom had voted for the earlier suspension, and all of whom now announced their intention of opposing the renewal.[8] Except on the first reading, the divisions

[1] Piggott to Grey, 2 June 1817 (Grey).

[2] Mentioned in Elliot to Fitzwilliam, 28 May 1817 (Milton).

[3] Fitzwilliam to Milton, 18 June 1817 (Milton).

[4] *P.D.* xxxvi. 1129–32; Fitzwilliam to Milton, 19 June 1817 (Milton).

[5] Grenville to Fitzwilliam, 23 June 1817 (Milton).

[6] *P.D.* xxxvi. 1003–4.

[7] Herefordshire, where Brand spoke, Essex to Wilson, 8 June 1817 (Wilson Papers, Add. MSS. 30108, ff. 327–8); Kent, where Thanet spoke, and Middlesex, where Bedford, Holland, and Burdett spoke, *Independent Whig*, 22 June 1817.

[8] Of the fifty-four M.P.s mentioned earlier as having voted for Ridley but not for suspension, eight now voted against renewal.

on both sides of the house were smaller than earlier in the year; it was the end of the session and members were going home, but the ministerial vote fell off more than the opposition. The average majority dropped from 159 to 81.

This was the only consolation. In the lords, Grey announced that 'he felt himself declining in years and strength, and that this might perhaps be the last duty he should perform for his country', a declaration which was quickly followed by Grenville's, to the effect that 'although it would only be with life itself that he would entirely abandon pursuits, and desert a cause in which he had been engaged for five and thirty years, yet it was not improbable that this might be almost the last occasion on which he should have to claim the attention of their lordships'.[1] Both statements were probably intended, as they were certainly taken to be, as public retirements.

The rupture with the Grenvilles was beginning to take on an appearance of finality, and Grey later dated the break from the end of the 1817 session.[2] There was no formal separation, but the war which had originally produced the co-operation was over and disagreements in peace-time had proved difficult to avoid.[3] In 1792 and 1795, with Fox in opposition and Grenville in power, the two groups had differed widely, first over war with France and then on repression at home. Now in similar circumstances they had slipped into conditioned postures.[4] The differences of 1817 had followed too quickly on the earlier ones, and they were followed by a breakdown of communication between the two groups which helped make future co-operation more difficult. Correspondence between Grenville and Grey appears to have come to an end, and future political contacts were rare. Changes of personnel helped widen the gulf. Horner, an important link between the two groups, since he sat for a seat controlled by Buckingham but sympathized with the rest of the party, died in 1817. Ponsonby, the only leader sympathetic to the Grenvilles, died in July of the same year. William Elliot,

[1] *P.D.* xxxvi. 1005 and 1013.

[2] Grey to Holland, 28 January 1818 (Holland).

[3] The dating of this break provides an illustration of the many minor inaccuracies in studies of the period. C. Grey, *Grey*, p. 370, claims that there was no political intercourse between Grenville and Grey after 1815. Donald Read, *Peterloo*, p. 200, and H. W. C. Davis, *The Age of Grey and Peel*, Oxford, 1929, p. 113, claim that the break occurred in 1819.

[4] *H.M.C. Dropmore*, x. 423–4.

a channel of communication between the Grenville and Fitzwilliam groups, died in 1818. Grenville, whose personal friendship with Grey had been strong, was withdrawing gradually from politics, as was Thomas Grenville, long associated with the whig party. Their place was taken by Buckingham, bound by none of the same personal ties, driven by his own powerful ambition, and reported, as early as June 1817, to be 'heartily sick of opposition'.[1]

These changes prevented any resurrection of the alliance. Perhaps there was no real desire for its revival. Some on the whig side were quite clear that the loss of numbers was negligible, others may have realized that a new freedom of action would follow from the break, and even Grey soon thought that 'except with respect to Grenville himself I do not think it greatly to be regretted'.[2] On the other side preparations were making for independent action. In April Thomas Grenville had visualized a body independent both of weak ministers and extremist opposition, and such a group was coming into being by the end of the session when Wynn observed:

> I find myself obliged to act entirely for myself in concert with a few friends only and without connection with either of the great parties. We are, to be sure, a little like the army of the republic of San Marino, which takes the field consisting of a general, five men, and a drummer of great experience, but when we cannot lodge in either of the two great camps, nothing remains but to pitch a tent of our own or to retire from the field altogether.[3]

For the time being the little knot kept its place on the opposition benches, but by September Buckingham was encouraging them to take a separate bench.[4] This they did at the beginning of the 1818 session, when Phillimore, the Wynns, Colonel Stanhope, and Fremantle moved to the front opposition bench below the gangway as an avowed third party. In this position they set out to lure support away from the opposition, and did succeed in attracting a few from the opposition fringe, such as Saxton and John and James Cocks.[5] Tierney noted that 'The Grenvilles

[1] *Letters of Dudley to Llandaff*, p. 168.

[2] Grey to Holland, 28 January 1818 (Holland); Tierney to Grey, 12 March 1818 (Grey).

[3] *H.M.C. Dropmore*, x. 425–6; Wynn to Southey, 'Wednesday' n.d. [1817] (Wynn 4814).

[4] *H.M.C. Dropmore*, x. 432.

[5] Buckingham and Chandos, *Regency*, ii. 237–8, 238–9, 244.

seem now to have openly quitted all connection with us', and shortly afterwards he was counting them as strangers in his calculations of divisions.[1] Thirteen years of co-operation were at an end.

The note of gloom on which the 1817 session thus ended was soon deepened. When Grey, in a brief moment of optimism, began to consider possible activity he was crushed by Tierney:

When you say that opposition may start next session with great advantages if they are not thrown away, I no more comprehend you than if you wrote in Hebrew . . . I confess I see nothing in the prospect before us to make me sanguine. . . . As for a good attendance, after what happened at the beginning of last session when everything appeared to be in our favour, I quite despair of it.[2]

Holland's reactions were similar, and even Brougham confessed himself to be 'sick to the heart of politics'.[3] Though Tierney was ready in London to do anything he was instructed in the line of preparing for the coming session, Grey relapsed into plaintive querulousness and, pleading illness, delayed his arrival in London until the session had begun. Nor was Holland eager to give a lead, while Brougham urged a waiting game.[4] As a result only the minimum of consultation and preparation took place. Romilly, Lord A. Hamilton, and Brougham met and decided to ask ministers before the address was moved whether they intended to repeal the suspension of habeas corpus. If the answer was in the negative then the repeal was to be moved in both houses. Duncannon was persuaded to send out the letters of summons.[5] When, however, the question put by Holland in the lords and Althorp in the commons, was answered in the affirmative all that could be done was to concur in the address. No alternative plan of attack had been worked out. For the first few days, Tierney pointed out to Grey, 'town is still very empty and the attendance in the house extremely slack'.[6] He therefore contented himself with endeavouring to put off major divisions and discussions for as long as possible.

[1] Tierney to Grey, 3 February 1818 and 11 February 1818 (Grey).

[2] Tierney to Grey, 1 November 1817 (Grey).

[3] Brougham to Lambton, 'Monday' n.d. [December 1817] (Brougham).

[4] Tierney to Grey, 20 January 1818 (Grey); Brougham to Grey, n.d. [October 1817] (Brougham).

[5] Brougham to Lambton n.d. [1818] (Brougham).

[6] Tierney to Grey, 3 February 1818 (Grey).

Despite this weak beginning, hope soon rose. Brougham wrote: 'there will be a great deal of sport after all notwithstanding the number of absentees and the dull appearance things have been wearing. The truth is we have many strong cases and even if we had not—an inactive dispirited session must be avoided in justice to our friends who are contesting everywhere.'[1]

Grey, too, was for action: 'I am convinced it ought to be the policy of our friends in the house of commons to debate and *to divide* constantly; without any regard to numbers. This in general, both to procure an attendance of your friends and to harass the government ought to be the tactic of an opposition'.[2]

The opportunity came on 5 February when the government moved for a secret committee on the state of the country, the intention being to justify the suspension of habeas corpus and provide indemnity for actions of magistrates in the period of suspension. Tierney led a spirited attack on the proposal and on the selection of the committee by ballot. No longer beholden to Grenville sensibilities, the whig party was free to launch into a series of criticisms of the suspension, concentrating its attack on the question of informers. Fazakerly moved for an instruction to the committee of secrecy to inquire into the activities of those 'who by their language and conduct have encouraged those designs it was their object to detect'. He rallied only fifty-two votes. Lord Folkestone moved for a committee to inquire into the truth of the allegations about imprisonments under the suspension act, and got a mere six more votes. Finally, Philips moved for an inquiry into the conduct of spies and informers, enunciating clearly his suspicion of ministers:

> He did not believe them capable of making a plot entirely themselves, when none of the elements of one were previously in existence. But he could not help remarking, that the plot had been most useful to them, in withdrawing the attention of the public, and of some of their wavering friends in the house, from the demand so generally made at that time for economy and retrenchment. . . . He would not say that ministers had made the plot, but he would say that they had made the most of it.[3]

The vote rose only to sixty-nine.

[1] Brougham to Lambton, n.d. [1818] (Brougham).
[2] Grey to Holland, 15 February 1818 (Grey).
[3] *P.D.* xxxvii. 825.

Even before Philips's motion was discussed, the report of the committee had been presented, on 23 February. Two days later an indemnity bill based on it was introduced into the lords. Opposing it, the whigs urged the need for full inquiry into the state of the country before and after the suspension, and indeed into the use that had been made of the extraordinary powers entrusted to the government. This argument received its main emphasis from Lansdowne and Erskine. Holland in the lords, and a vocal section of the party in the commons, tended to argue rather that the main object of the bill was to extend protection to spies and informers and prevent those arrested securing any legal redress against such individuals. The Grenvilles voted, inevitably, in favour of the bill, but so too did Fitzwilliam and Hereford in the lords.[1] In the commons a number of whigs and members on the fringe of the party were prepared to support it, including Powlett, Grenfell, Protheroe, and William Lamb, who even went on to justify the use of spies.[2] On no occasion did the opposition vote rise above sixty-five, and their weakness was such that an opponent, Sir Frederick Flood, could claim: 'The ranks of the other (the opposition) side of the house were broken and the arguments of a great part of that side of the house, militating one against the other, showed most clearly that the party whence they came was nearly dissolved.'[3] In Holland's view the party had never been more dispirited or more disorganized.[4]

The whigs were rescued only when the commons moved on to discuss economy. The contrast thus produced between their weakness on a major issue of principle, and success on one of finance, goes far to illustrate the whig dilemma of this period. On 12 March, between debates on the indemnity bill, Althorp moved for leave to bring in a bill to repeal the leather tax, and, receiving support from waverers such as General Gascoyne, carried his motion in a small house. This decision was reversed on second reading of the bill, though only narrowly.[5] An even

[1] Lambton to Grey, 10 March 1818 (Grey); Rosslyn to Grey, 6 March 1818 (Grey).

[2] *P.D.* xxxvii. 956, 922, 999–1009, 902. Powlett and Barnard eventually abstained: Darlington to Brougham, 15 March 1818 (Brougham).

[3] *P.D.* xxxvii. 998.

[4] Holland to Grey, 18 March 1818 (Holland).

[5] Wynn considered that the government would have been defeated had the debate ended earlier: Buckingham and Chandos, *Regency*, ii. 245–6.

more hopeful issue came up the next month when, on 13 April, the government brought down a message from the regent announcing the marriages of the royal dukes of Cambridge and Clarence. The same morning Liverpool had called a meeting of fifty to sixty 'country gentlemen' and explained to them, in advance of parliament, that the government intended to make a grant of £19,500 to Clarence, one of £12,000 to Cambridge, and the same sum to Cumberland, who had been refused a grant by parliament earlier but in the view of the ministers should now be treated like his brothers. The sounding-board thus chosen echoed discontent. Littleton later stated in the commons that 'he had been one of the meeting at Lord Liverpool's and had found a great many others like himself, friends to the measures of administration but who could not agree to the proposal made by Lord Liverpool'.[1] Forewarned by this useful barometer of storms to come, the government first delayed the discussion and then reduced the grants. This was not enough to satisfy Holme Sumner, who claimed that 'if the public necessity interposed, the royal dukes, in common with every other description of persons in the country, must yield to the pressure of the times'.[2] Supported by Ellison and Acland, he moved to cut the grant to the Duke of Clarence by half, a motion which was carried by the combined votes of opposition and waverers. The resultant majority of nine could well have been larger had not some of the opposition already gone away, thinking that Castlereagh would give way without a vote.[3]

Wisely the whigs had left the campaign on this issue to others. The next day, however, when Cambridge's grant came up for discussion the whigs themselves took the lead. They failed completely, receiving practically no outside support and rallying only ninety-five votes. Only on the grant to the unpopular Cumberland, which the house had already declined to make in 1815, did support return; then a majority of seven was achieved. The success of this campaign acted as a fillip to whig fortunes, and the *Morning Chronicle* triumphantly argued that no set of ministers had been so disgraced, defeated, or ridiculed.[4] Further

[1] *P.D.* xxxviii. 9. Others who admitted to having been present were C. W. Wynn (xxxviii. 42) and Holme Sumner (xxxviii. 97).

[2] *P.D.* xxxviii. 98.

[3] Lambton to Grey, 17 April 1818 (Grey).

[4] *Morning Chronicle*, 5 May 1818.

developments brought the whigs down from these clouds. On 1 May Tierney moved for a committee on the circulating medium and secured only ninety-nine votes, nearly all of them whig. On 15 May the party split on the question of a grant to the Duke of Kent on his marriage, Brougham supporting it for unexplained reasons, and Curwen, Althorp, and fifty-one others opposing it.[1]

But this time it was too late to expect any further successes, for the session was entering its dog days, and many members had left London, some through laziness, others because of the forthcoming elections. A small number of minor motions on economy were moved with very little success, and on the issue of principle raised by the renewal of the alien act the depleted state of the opposition was fully revealed; thirty votes was their average on the eight divisions on this question, fifteen less than the average in March on the indemnity bill. On balance, therefore, the session had been a very bad one for the whigs. Perhaps it was an achievement to have acted together at all, in view of the dismay and disillusionment with which the session had been ushered in, but the parliamentary campaign had hardly been a good preparation for successful effort in the election which ministers had decided to hold in 1818, somewhat before the deadline fixed by the septennial act.

[1] It was suspected by Althorp that Brougham was influenced by the leaders of the various charitable bodies on which the Duke of Kent sat: Althorp to Milton, 17 May 1818 (Milton).

VI

PARTY WARFARE · 1819

THE election of 1812 had been a 'holding' election, with little popular interest, a paucity of issues, and comparatively few changes. The first peace-time election in 1818 was very different. The only effective gauges of interest and activity for an election of this period are the number of contests and the number of new M.P.s returned to parliament. Both increased substantially on the 1812 figures.[1] Indeed, this was the most active election up to the introduction of the reform bill, with the possible exception only of 1830. Despite the comparatively minor role normally attributed by historians to national issues and to public opinion in pre-reform elections, the changes, as reflected in the allegiances of the new members, favoured the opposition. Most observers on both sides of the house considered that opposition had gained, and the following session was soon to make it clear that the whig vote had, indeed, increased.[2]

[1] The number of contested elections, calculated from H. S. Smith, *The Parliaments of England*, London, 1844–50 (3 vols.), shows the following trends:

	1812	1818	1820	1826	1830
England	50	86	69	84	78
Ireland	16	14	10	16	29
Scotland and Wales	19	9	10	1	4
	85	109	89	101	111

The numbers of members without previous parliamentary service, listed in G. P. Judd, *Members of Parliament 1734 to 1832*, New Haven, 1955, p. 28, is: 1812, 127; 1818, 157; 1820, 90; 1826, 144; 1830, 143.

[2] According to Thomas Grenville, Arbuthnot, in making calculations of his own side's standing, admitted a ministerial loss of ten: *H.M.C. Dropmore*, x. 441–2. Fremantle stated that ministers admitted a loss of fourteen in England, and estimated that the government's numbers would be reduced by twenty: Buckingham and Chandos, *Regency*, ii. 265. Other estimates are: an opposition gain of seventeen: Lady Morpeth to Devonshire, 22 June 1818 (Devonshire); a ministerial loss of twenty-five: C. W. Wynn to Southey, 27 June 1818 (Wynn 4814); an opposition gain of forty: *Leeds Mercury*, 18 July 1818; an opposition gain of forty-five: *Dublin Evening Post*, 1 August 1818; thirty-seven new supporters of retrenchment and

Appearances, too, were against the government, an important development in a period when impressions of the mood of the country carried by incoming members were almost as important as their political commitments. In the City of London three opposition members, including Alderman Waithman, a long-standing whig supporter on the City Council, had been elected, to only one ministerialist. In Devonshire Lord Ebrington had pushed Acland into third place. In Leicestershire Phillipps had driven out Keck, and in Southwark Sir Robert Wilson had beaten Barclay.

The widespread belief in opposition gains was in itself enough to encourage greater whig efforts. Grey announced his hopes that the effect of the popular enthusiasm for retrenchment, economy, and reform would be seen in the new parliament, and the *Morning Chronicle* rejoiced in the prospect before the whig party.[1] This stimulus was supplemented by the new unity produced by Tierney's formal election, and by rumours of ministerial disagreements.[2] As the session approached Grey's letters were unusually hopeful, and Wilson reported that Tierney was 'full of confidence, not merely in his cause, but in the accounts of his numbers. With attendance he flatters himself victory is certain'.[3]

These castles of easy optimism were not erected on firm foundations of concerted planning and consultation. Responsibility for preparations was simply left to Tierney, who elaborated his own plans, intending to reach final agreement in discussions with Grey.[4] Tierney was, however, prepared to shoulder responsibility: even a delay in Grey's arrival, caused by a new illness of Lady Grey's, was no set-back. Tierney's reaction was almost offhand: though still able to consult by post, he did not do so, but simply formulated strategy on his

reform: *Morning Chronicle*, 30 June and 13 July 1818. Lord Liverpool hoped that despite 'untoward circumstances' the balance of loss and gain would be fairly equal: Liverpool to Huskisson, 2 July 1818 (Huskisson Papers, Add. MSS. 38741, f. 226). Duncannon and Tierney were reported to be counting on an opposition gain of twenty to twenty-five: *H.M.C. Dropmore*, x. 441–2.

[1] *Morning Chronicle*, 13 July 1818; Grey's speech is in *Morning Chronicle*, 6 January 1819.

[2] Tierney to Grey, 21 December 1818 (Grey); *The Times*, 6 January 1819.

[3] Wilson to Grey, 4 January 1819 (Wilson Papers, Add. MSS. 30123, f. 3). This is confirmed by Lambton to Grey, 14 January 1819 (Grey).

[4] Tierney to Grey, n.d. [1818] (Grey).

own.[1] His intention was to avoid an amendment and concentrate on a motion for inquiry into the state of the public credit, with especial reference to resumption of cash payments. Since ministers were expected to announce the continuation of bank restriction, Tierney expected his motion to be a very popular one, and calculated:

we shall have for instance the Grenvilles to a man, and, if we can make a powerful muster of our own friends, many of the neutrals, and probably, because they voted with me last year, some from the ministerial ranks. I verily believe that a full attendance of opposition would enable us to divide not much if any less than two hundred. If we can accomplish this it must have considerable effect on our after operations.[2]

Having decided on his plan, Tierney initiated and supervised the sending out of letters of notification; the replies soon gave a favourable picture of numbers and zeal.[3] A small preliminary meeting of leading M.P.s took place on 20 January and a full party meeting, at which Tierney explained his plan of campaign and his motion, was held, after the opening of the session, at Devonshire House.[4]

The session began with no great urgency. Macdonald was put up on the address to state the opposition case against the government. He made a fighting speech, but the house lost interest when it became clear that no amendment was to be moved. Reports multiplied that ministers were worried by the temper of the commons, but Tierney managed to avoid any formal clash until 2 February, when his motion for inquiry into the effects of the bank restriction came up.[5] After a powerful speech against both the continuation of restriction and the whole of Vansittart's financial policy, Tierney found his motion undercut by the ministerial counter-proposal of a secret committee on the bank, with special reference to cash payments. This reduced the issue to a straightforward one of confidence between ministers and opposition, and withdrew much of the support which Tierney

[1] Tierney to Grey, 29 December 1818 (Grey).

[2] Tierney to Grey, 4 January 1819 (Grey). The extension of bank restriction was announced later, *Morning Chronicle*, 23 January 1819.

[3] Tierney to Grey, 24 January 1819 (Grey).

[4] Lambton to Grey, 21 January 1819 (Grey); Tierney to Grey, 24 January 1819 (Grey); Lambton to Grey, 16 January 1819 (Grey).

[5] Wilson to Grey, n.d. [January 1819]. (Wilson Papers, Add. MSS. 30123, F.23). Also *Morning Chronicle*, 26 January 1819.

had hoped to win from waverers. A vote of 168 to 277 was good in the light of this situation, but poor in that of earlier expectation, though some consolation was forthcoming when a motion to add Brougham to the committee was lost by only forty-two votes.[1] Nevertheless, spirits remained high, and the party dinner, held the day after the bank motion, was large and enthusiastic.[2]

Tierney declined to allow the high pitch of enthusiasm to divert him from his chosen policy of waiting on events. Grey, for once an uncharacteristic activist, urged a more aggressive policy, being anxious for something 'that may distinctly mark the line of division between the parties and in which the country may take an interest'.[3] Tierney clung obstinately to his own strategy.

> I should quite agree with you on the advantage of a constitutional question if one would come to us, but we should do no good by *making* one for our own purposes. We must wait for circumstances. As it is we are going on as well as possible. Everybody is in good humour and ready to do what they are desired. The impression too on the ministerial side of the house as well as outdoors is daily becoming more favourable.[4]

He appears to have persuaded his leader. To force the pace was to run the dangers of driving the newly elected members, many of them still uncertain in their allegiances, to a premature decision, and also of losing the support of the waverers, and particularly of the Grenvilles. In the prevailing uncertainty this latter group were looked to as being particularly important, as both votes and omens: they themselves were estimating their voting strength at a score and Tierney was inclined to a similar inflation.[5] The success of Tierney's policy is, indeed, indicated by the reactions of the Grenville group. They were increasingly convinced of the weakness of government and the growing strength of opposition.[6]

The waiting opposition was duly provided with an issue in the

[1] Tierney to Grey, 'Wednesday' n.d. [February 1819] (Grey). See also Lambton to Grey, 3 February 1819 (Grey).

[2] Lambton to Grey, 5 February 1819 (Grey).

[3] Grey to Wilson, 8 February 1819 (Grey).

[4] Tierney to Grey, 18 February 1819 (Grey).

[5] Buckingham and Chandos, *Regency*, ii. 317; Tierney to Grey, 18 February 1819 (Grey).

[6] Buckingham and Chandos, *Regency*, ii. 300–4.

questions of the Windsor establishment, and the grant to the Duke of York, who had inherited the care of George III's mad person on the queen's death. Doubtful of popular support on the Windsor establishment, Tierney decided to concentrate discussion on the grant to the Duke of York, arguing that it was not possible to deny to him the same sums as custodian of the king that the late queen had enjoyed, but that these sums should be charged to the privy purse, not the consolidated fund. So (he expresses his hopes)

> I shall save £10,000 a year to the country and quiet such of our friends as are indisposed to give the Duke anything. The true reason of the battle which government are obliged to fight is that the savings on the king's privy purse would upon his decease (he having made no will) vest in the regent, so that you see whatever the duke gains the prince loses.... I reckon we shall divide from 170 to 180 at least.[1]

Though lacking the clarity of a direct opposition this strategy placed ministers in the difficult position of defending a case which was the prince's and not their own. That they were prepared to do so was indicated by the circulation of rumours that they would resign if beaten.[2]

On 22 February Tierney moved his amendment. This won good support from outside the confines of the party, attracting Bankes, many of the Grenville group, some of the new members, and several waverers. Unfortunately the whig turn-out proved disappointing, partly, Tierney suggests, because 'many of our friends have no stomach for opposing the duke in anything by which he is to be personally a gainer'. Thus the losses cancelled the gains and the total of 186 was only what Tierney had anticipated.[3] Three days later Tierney, reluctant in any case to take an active part in this type of warfare, was unable to hold back the section of the party which was completely opposed to the grant. Williams proposed an amendment to cut it by half, Tierney felt obliged to support this, and the motion was pushed to a division when support appeared from waverers.[4] Since no muster had been made the vote dropped to 137, and the government majority rose from 95 to 110.

[1] Tierney to Grey, 18 February 1819 (Grey).
[2] Rosslyn to Grey, 18 February 1819 (Grey).
[3] Tierney to Grey, 28 February 1819 (Grey).
[4] Buckingham and Chandos, *Regency*, ii. 314–15.

Early March saw attention partially diverted to the final stages of the Westminster election, but, nevertheless, on 2 March Mackintosh's motion for a committee on capital felonies, though opposed by ministers, was carried by a majority of nineteen. Then on 18 March came Ridley's motion for an address asking the Prince Regent to give directions to reduce the number of junior lords of the admiralty. Ridley justified this mainly on its contribution—symbolic rather than real—to economy. The motion only received 164 votes, but the *Morning Chronicle* claimed that thirty regular opposition voters had been shut out, and the ministerial majority of eight-one was not large in view of the extent of the muster that had been made for it.[1] Success was closer on 1 April, when Hamilton's motion for papers on the Royal Burgh of Aberdeen was defeated by a mere five votes.

Up to the Easter recess the whigs were well satisfied with their efforts as a disciplined party. The team was pulling cordially together, and differences between the radical wing and the rest were submerged. The main difficulty arose from the strategy. The newly invigorated party was anxious for action and a trial of strength, desires which accorded ill with the policy of waiting for issues rather than forcing the pace. Careful choice of issues produced an appearance of strength, but the stronger the whigs seemed, the greater was the pressure for attack. Tierney still clung to his policy:

> It is to be sure very provoking that while we are so united and so numerous we cannot find many good questions. . . . but anything I am certain is better than that we should manifest an impatience to attack ministers. Whenever any event occurs which calls us naturally into action we shall find the advantage of not having been previously too eager.[2]

That the policy was promoting the desired objective is again indicated by the reaction of the Grenvilles, who continued to expect that changes would be forced on the ministers.[3] This was hopeful, and radical discontent with inactivity could be staved off as long as ministers seemed to be tottering. This did in fact appear to be the case, for government attendances were low, their debating inept, their supporters and the waverers both

[1] *Morning Chronicle*, 22 March 1819.

[2] Tierney to Grey, 'Wednesday Morn.' n.d. [March 1819] (Grey).

[3] Buckingham and Chandos, *Regency*, ii. 317.

disgruntled.[1] A policy that seemed to promise success was not one against which there could be legitimate complaints. Many expected intermittently that ministers would be brought down, and Lambton wrote to Grey on 9 March: 'people are anxious that you should be here in the event of any extraordinary occurrence which is looked forward to by a great many as likely to happen. In fact I do consider it impossible for ministers to go on as they are now, and in the present temper of the house.'[2] It was difficult in these circumstances for Tierney to put a foot wrong.

The turning-point came in the second half of the session. It was not immediately apparent, for on 6 May Hamilton's motion for referring the petitions from the royal burghs of Scotland to a committee was carried by five votes in a small house by dint of a strong muster of whigs and a low government rally. The turn was not even clear to ministers, who were particularly anxious early in May, partly because of the disinclination of ministerial supporters to attend, partly because of dangers anticipated from the decision reached on 8 May to impose £3 million of extra taxation. Liverpool himself thought that to remain in office after the defeats sustained was a positive evil unless a strong and decisive effort could be made to redeem the situation.[3] On the same day that his words were written the house settled down to discuss Tierney's motion on the state of the nation.

Such a general indictment of the government was a complete abandonment of the policy of caution. It was an attempt to separate sheep from goats and count them, which drew a flock of record size. Whether Tierney had been carried away by the *élan* of the earlier days, whether he believed the government to be so weakened as to be unable to carry on, or whether his judgement had been swayed by the urgings of the militants, is not known. For whatever reason he does not appear to have been completely happy with his lot, for there ran through his

[1] A. Aspinall, *Charles Arbuthnot*, pp. 14–15.

[2] Lambton to Grey, 9 March 1819 (Grey). See also, Wilson to Grey, 4 March 1819 (Wilson Papers, Add. MSS. 30123, f. 53): 'ministers will have great difficulty in preserving their power through the session. Many think it impossible.' J. R. G. Graham to Fitzwilliam, 9 February 1819 (Fitzwilliam, F. 36 c.): 'It is the opinion of much better judges than I am that the [government] must fall.'

[3] H. Twiss, *The Public and Private Life of Lord Chancellor Eldon*, London, 1844, ii. 329. See also *George IV*, ii. 288–91.

speech an ambiguity which indicates that he may have been in two minds about forcing the issue. The speech covered the whole spectrum of government from foreign policy to commerce and finance, and posed an indictment of government policy in each field. It began with a surprising admission: 'he was not so dull as not to perceive, that in bringing the question before the house in point of mere party, he was giving up many advantages'. It went on with a direct onslaught constituting a clear statement that 'the motion he was about to submit did go to produce a change of administration'. Nevertheless, shortly after, he brought in the reservation that anyone voting for the motion, 'merely admitted the necessity of inquiry, and marked his sense of the state of national affairs. He might support it, although he would rather see the opposition hanged than admitted to office.' Similar alternations went on throughout the speech, though the conclusion was a strong one and urged the dismissal of ministers by the regent.[1]

The subsequent debate indicated that doubts, if Tierney had had them, were justified. Three of the six waverers who spoke opposed the motion; another, Marryat, favoured the previous question; and a fifth, Wynn, proposed to abstain. The division rammed the lesson home: 178 voted for the motion, 357 against it. The whig party mustered well, but, foreseeing storms, the independents and waverers scuttled for a safe ministerial harbour. If the attitudes of those who gave opposition votes on other motions in the course of the whole session are considered then the following pattern emerges:[2]

	Number of opposition votes			
	1–5	6–10	11–15	16 and over
Voting for Tierney	18	43	61	59
Voting against	95	9	1	..
Not voting	40	13	3	..
Totals	153	65	65	59

Those who voted very occasionally with opposition had been frightened into supporting the government by a considerable

[1] *P.D.* xl. 474–94.

[2] The total along line one is not the actual total of votes and pairs. The difference is made up by those who voted for Tierney but do not appear to have cast any other opposition votes.

majority. The motion had received its only substantial support from those to whom opposition voting was almost second nature.[1]

Tierney had made two mistakes. He had placed his motion at a time when, because of the discussion of the catholic question earlier in the month, attendance was high.[2] Since opposition had made a full muster early in the session the new influx was certain to be more favourable to ministers. Secondly, he had forced the waverers and new M.P.s to a choice, and at a time when Liverpool was prepared to stake the existence of the government on acceptance of its measures.[3] Sir Robert Heron provides the best summing-up:

> Nothing ever appeared to me so imprudent, nothing ever was less successful. The floating party were, in fact, men unconnected with, and unknown to, each other: who had few of them any other intention than that of espousing the strongest side. Being driven to a premature decision, they joined the government, and, contrary to the expectations of both sides, gave them a triumphant majority.[4]

Heron regarded the decision of the floating party as premature. Probably it was predestined, but either way all the high hopes were dashed and the issue of the session was decided.

The government now took steps to strengthen itself by a circular to its supporters and a meeting addressed by Castlereagh.[5] Whig cohesion began to weaken, restraint to disappear. In addition the whigs met with real difficulties in two of the three topics which remained to be discussed. Currency, which Tierney had used as an issue to attack the government in February, soon boomeranged. Being on the committee curtailed Tierney's power to speak out when the extension of the suspension was agreed to in April, and neither he nor Grey fully approved of the payments resumption finally agreed.[6]

The second difficulty was on the question of economy. On 2 June Calcraft spoke out on the navy estimates and criticized the small number of men granted for the navy; 'a departure from our long established policy which he most sincerely de-

[1] The Grenville group split. Four went away, but Sir W. W. Wynn voted for the motion: Lord Colchester, *Diary*, iii. 76.

[2] *Morning Chronicle*, 6 May 1819, estimated that 574 M.P.s were in London.

[3] *George IV*, ii. 289–90 and 292–3.

[4] Heron, p. 102.

[5] *Morning Chronicle*, 3 June 1819.

[6] *P.D.* xxxix. 1407.

plored, as it implied a disposition to abandon our old system of defence, and rather to look for protection through the power of an army, than to rely upon those good old wooden walls, which had for ages proved our best and safest guardian'.[1] He was promptly followed by Ridley with a motion to cut the navy estimates by £200,000. This motion secured ninety-seven votes, exactly the same as a resolution against the malt tax on 9 June which won the support of some country gentlemen but of only a reduced number of whigs. The next day, when opposition attempted to recoup the situation by bringing more supporters in on Milton's motion to reduce the tax, only seventy-five votes were secured.

The third preoccupation of this part of the session was the rather more successful struggle against the foreign enlistment bill. Designed to prevent British subjects enlisting overseas without permission, it was essentially a foreign-policy measure, placating Spain by curtailing the supply of troops to South America. Many traders, however, feared lest this intervention should affect the growing trade with South America, so that several petitions were forthcoming from trading ports. It was opposed on the same combination of grounds, and a severe fight was put up on all stages. Though the bill passed, it did so with relatively narrow majorities, one being as low as thirteen on the second reading.

A session of bitter disappointment closed on 12 July. The *Morning Chronicle* had already written the obituary by claiming that ministers had frustrated the national demand for economy, with the result that discontent was beginning to burst into clamour in the manufacturing areas.[2] This discontent formed the preoccupation of the rest of the year. Government newspapers were soon stressing the dangers from militant radicalism in the north, while the *Morning Chronicle* was claiming that these dangers were unreal, being trumpeted only to sanction repression.[3] Thus when, on 16 August, the yeomanry rode into the crowd on St. Peter's field, Manchester, differences between government and opposition, alarmist and concessionary, were already becoming clear.

A united whig party condemned the 'Manchester massacre'.

1 *P.D.* xl. 825.
2 *Morning Chronicle*, 26 June 1819.
3 *Morning Chronicle*, 10 July 1819.

Within three days the *Morning Chronicle* had printed a strong criticism, and Grey, Lambton, and Brougham exchanged a mutual indignation.[1] Even the normally cautious wing of the party held no brief for the Manchester magistrates, Devonshire writing to his wife, 'with every disposition to excuse the magistrates for what they did, I think they were hasty and ill judged in employing yeomanry and people of the place in seizing Hunt &c. instead of regular soldiers who have no private and local enmities and who are in the habit of being calm'.[2] The Earl of Carlisle criticized both the magistrates and the government which had praised their conduct.[3] Even the Lancashire whigs, influenced as they were by local alarms, still criticized in subdued tones. Brougham reported that George Philips, the cotton-manufacturing M.P., was blaming the magistrates, though cautiously.[4] Derby wrote at length to Grey:

though I cannot entirely agree with you in thinking the conduct of the magistrates in Manchester in the whole of the late business *totally inexcusable* . . . yet I have certainly from my first acquaintance with the business been of opinion that to interrupt the meeting of the 16th at all, and much more to do so in the manner and time they chose for that purpose was a step of great rashness and has never been justified by any documents or arguments which I have hitherto heard advanced in its behalf.[5]

A unity of sentiment on the massacre was not enough to push the whigs to action. This was left to the extreme radicals, whose reaction was as prompt as it was predictable. They began to demand meetings to protest and press for reform: a campaign, begun in Westminster on 2 September and in the London common council a week later, rapidly radiated out to the large cities. The whig reaction was slower and more ambiguous. Tierney came out for organizing protest:

I cannot help thinking we ought to avail ourselves of the first opportunity to mark our opinions on the recent conduct of government, and to contribute our share towards stirring up the country

[1] *Morning Chronicle*, 19 August 1819.

[2] Duke of Devonshire to Duchess, 9 September 1819 (Devonshire).

[3] *Historical Manuscripts Commission, Fifteenth Report*, Appendix, Part VI. *The Manuscripts of the Earl of Carlisle*, London, 1897, pp. 741–2.

[4] Brougham to Grey, 'Tuesday' n.d. [1819] (Brougham).

[5] Derby to Grey, 8 September 1819 (Grey).

to address the regent or to petition both houses on the subject of the late measures. I take it to be our duty to do so, but putting that aside it seems to be our interest for if everything is left to the radicals as they are called, they will be sure to spoil a good cause and by the time it comes to our turn to take it up in parliament, they will have managed to disgust or alarm all those from whom we might hope to derive countenance or assistance.[1]

He therefore began to take soundings through Waithman about the possibility of a Middlesex meeting, and encouraged Calcraft to organize one in Kent.[2] Similar reasoning, natural indignation, and more radical propensities, influenced several others, particularly those M.P.s sitting for the larger boroughs. On 9 September Lord Rancliffe published an open letter to his Nottingham constituents, offering to return from Paris and support any measure they thought necessary. When a town meeting was called he attended together with Birch and Thomas Denman.[3] On 16 September R. H. Gurney addressed a meeting in Norwich and four days later Lawrence Dundas spoke at a mass meeting in York.[4] Coke and General Walpole set to work to follow up these beginnings by a Norfolk county meeting.

Holland, after weighing up the pros and cons, came down half-heartedly in favour of meetings, though announcing himself as 'disposed to follow what our friends decide'.[5] The majority of these friends appeared averse to exertion. A cautious Brougham merely urged the expression of a 'guarded opinion' as opportunity offered.[6] Mackintosh thought that radicals would outbid the whigs in the auction-yard of a public meeting; Derby warned Grey against the dangers.[7] More important, Grey himself had decided against meetings. He announced that he would have agreed to them if the party had been united, if discussion could have been confined to Manchester, and if there had been no threat of radical intervention, but since none of these conditions could be met, action could only reveal disunity and

[1] Tierney to Grey, 6 September 1819 (Grey).

[2] Tierney to Holland, 14 September 1819 (Holland).

[3] *Morning Chronicle*, 9 September 1819; *Independent Whig*, 3 October 1819.

[4] *Independent Whig*, 19 September 1819; *The Times*, 23 September 1819.

[5] Holland to Brougham, 19 September 1819 (Brougham).

[6] Brougham to Grey, 'Tuesday' n.d. [September 1819] (Grey).

[7] Mackintosh to Devonshire, 21 September 1819 (Devonshire); Derby to Grey, n.d. [September 1819] (Grey).

embarrass Derby and Fitzwilliam, lords lieutenant of the disturbed districts. His conclusion was that expression of whig views should be confined to such opportunities as Fox club dinners might provide.[1]

This lack of enthusiasm chilled both Holland's tepid and Tierney's warmer inclinations. The latter abandoned his efforts to rouse the party, complaining that the whigs were throwing away a great opportunity.[2] Even where efforts had begun they mostly ended in disappointment. In Norfolk a preparatory meeting decided not to call out the county.[3] In Essex Braybrooke found his plans checked by the opposition of C. C. Western, while in Liverpool Sefton declined to take the chair at a meeting organized by the concentric society.[4] The consensus of opinion among whigs in London was that the meetings should be abandoned.[5]

Reluctance and rebuffs combined to prevent or checkmate all whig activity except in Yorkshire. Before the crisis Earl Fitzwilliam had announced his conviction that the mass of the population in the West Riding was loyal and subversive characters few.[6] Influenced by this conviction, and by the good whig argument that the party could not be silent if the lower orders were to regard them as guardians of their rights, Fitzwilliam threw his weight behind preparations for a Yorkshire meeting. A requisition was drawn up for a meeting to call for inquiry, an astute choice of ground, since, whatever their other views, most whigs could muster on it.

This Yorkshire requisition and Fitzwilliam's respectable support forced whig hands elsewhere. Grey announced that it had put an end to his doubts and the party should follow the example: he now restarted the abandoned preparations for a Northumberland meeting.[7] Lambton began work in Durham, and Brougham, who viewed Fitzwilliam's lead as quite decisive, organized Westmorland.[8] He also threw his energy behind the

[1] Grey to Holland, 10 and 11 September 1819 (Holland).

[2] Tierney to Holland, 15 September 1819 (Holland).

[3] General Walpole to Grey, 30 September 1819 (Grey).

[4] *The Times*, 8 October 1819; Sefton to Brougham, 19 September 1819 (Brougham).

[5] Holland to Brougham, 24 September 1819 (Brougham).

[6] *Morning Chronicle*, 2 August 1819.

[7] Grey to Holland, 21 September 1819 (Grey).

[8] Brougham to Grey, 21 September 1819 (Brougham).

stagnating efforts to hold a Cumberland meeting, writing to Milton that the news from Yorkshire had enabled them to surmount most of their difficulties and boosted their requisition.[1] The effect was the same in Norfolk.[2]

Holland too began work for a Middlesex meeting, where Burdett obligingly hung back so as to allow the whigs to take the lead.[3] Carnarvon, hitherto alarmist and opposed to any meeting in Hampshire, began to make preparations.[4] In Essex and Hertfordshire requisitions went out; Tierney, after going to Hampshire to encourage the local whigs, organized a meeting to discuss a Surrey requisition, and Sefton changed his mind about the Liverpool meeting.[5]

Though the columns were marching there were significant gaps in the ranks. Carlisle and his son Morpeth refused to sign any requisitions, arguing that parliamentary inquiry would be premature while the issue was already *sub judice* in the forthcoming trials of Hunt and his supporters.[6] Devonshire and the Cavendishes also declined to sign, disliking any association with the radicals.[7] Darlington argued that county meetings were liable to get out of control, and Lord Carrington, C. C. Western, and Brand all refused to participate.[8] Grey wrote to most of the laggards urging that a united whig party should take up its post in defence of the people. Only with Jersey was persuasion effective.[9]

The campaign was opened by the Cumberland county meeting on 13 October. This was followed the next day by the most significant of the meetings, that in Yorkshire, where 20,000 freeholders assembled, and then by seven other county meetings while five attempts foundered and two planned meetings were

[1] Brougham to Milton, 3 October 1819 (Milton).
[2] General Walpole to Grey, 22 October 1819 (Grey).
[3] Holland to Brougham, 5 October 1819, copy (Brougham).
[4] Tierney to Grey, 25 September and 7 October 1819 (Grey).
[5] Tierney to Grey, 7 October 1819 (Grey); Tierney to Holland, 28 September 1819 (Holland).
[6] *H.M.C. Carlisle*, pp. 741–2; *Morning Chronicle*, 26 October 1819; Morpeth to Brougham, 3 and 9 October 1819 (Brougham); 'A Note on County Meeting, 1819' (Carlisle).
[7] Devonshire to Brougham, 6 October 1819 (Brougham); Lord G. Cavendish to Milton, 2 October 1819 (Milton).
[8] Darlington to Grey, 24 September 1819 (Grey); *H.M.C. Dropmore*, x. 450; *The Times*, 8 October 1819; Brougham to Grey, 18 October 1819 (Grey).
[9] Jersey to Grey, 'Tuesday' n.d. [1819] (Grey).

abandoned with suspicious readiness when the meeting of parliament was announced.[1] Everywhere the whig case was argued in similar terms. Lord Albemarle told the Norfolk meeting that the question they were concerned with was

> whether the people of England are to continue to enjoy, in security, their ancient rights and liberties—whether, under the written law of the land, they are to be any longer permitted, when lawfully and peaceably assembled, without riot or tumult, to exercise the sacred right of petition for removal of grievances; or whether they are to be subject to be dispersed by force, at the will of any set of magistrates. . . . During 26 years of my political life. . . . I never saw danger so imminent to the country as at the moment . . . never before did I see revolution so near . . . nothing can save the country, nothing can prevent revolution, anarchy, and bloodshed, but the union of men of character, talent, and respectability throughout the kingdom—of men like those who have come forward to sign the requisition. . . . Of men who are at all times ready to attend to the distresses, and, as far as is consistent with the security of the state, to the wishes of the people.[2]

One of the major achievements of the campaign was to put this case extensively before the public through meetings, press, and pamphlets. Another was to decide the ministers to summon parliament to an extraordinary session.[3] For the rest, though it was hardly an overwhelming demonstration of public opinion, the campaign was still a considerable success in view of prevailing alarms. It had brought the bulk of the whig party into a public and active stand in support of threatened freedoms, it had demonstrated that this stand had substantial backing, and

[1] Cumberland: *Morning Chronicle*, 18 October 1819. Yorkshire: *Morning Chronicle*, 16 October 1819. Hertfordshire: *London Gazette*, 20 November 1819. Durham: *Newcastle Chronicle*, 23 October 1819. Westmorland: *Morning Chronicle*, 26 October 1819. Norfolk: *Norfolk Chronicle*, 6 November 1819. Berkshire: *Morning Chronicle*, 17 November 1819. Cornwall: *The Times*, 29 November 1819. Herefordshire: *Morning Chronicle*, 20 November 1819. The failures were: Northamptonshire: Tierney to Grey, 25 September 1819 (Grey). Wiltshire: Thanet to Milton, 20 October 1819 (Milton). Northumberland: Ridley to Grey, 8 October 1819 (Grey). Surrey: Tierney to Fitzwilliam, 26 October 1819 (Milton). Essex: *Traveller*, 12 October 1819. Hampshire was called off when the meeting of parliament was announced: *Hampshire Chronicle*, 16 October. So was Middlesex: Tierney to Fitzwilliam, 26 October 1819 (Milton). However, a radical rump went ahead with a small meeting in the last county: *Independent Whig*, 14 November 1819.

[2] *Norfolk Chronicle*, 6 November 1819.

[3] C. D. Yonge, *Liverpool*, ii. 412–13.

it had given a real boost to party morale for the coming session: Brougham considered that 'we never had so few divisions among ourselves nor the country so much with us'.[1] It had not, in fact, united the party, but ministers themselves came near to remedying this by dismissing Lord Fitzwilliam from his lord-lieutenancy for his part in the Yorkshire meeting. This angered whigs of all shades of opinion, a reaction so unanimous that Althorp owned himself frankly delighted at the dismissal.[2]

Thus encouraged, and viewing the situation in apocalyptical terms as a 'race between anarchy and despotism', party opinion favoured active exertion in the forthcoming session.[3] Grey, more energetic than he had been for several years, began to write round to his leading associates to encourage attendance. Only from two did he meet with an unfavourable response. Derby was not prepared to press severe censure on the Manchester magistrates, and Wellesley viewed the crisis as much more alarming than that of 1817.[4] As the whigs began to assemble in London, it became clear that a considerable degree of unanimity prevailed on the need for parliamentary inquiry into the Manchester events. There was, however, more disunity on the repressive measures anticipated, and Holland for one thought the achievement of a nice blend of conciliation and coercion almost impossible.[5] For the present, opposition to the address was considered imperative, and it was decided to concentrate on the point of maximum unity. A three-point amendment was drawn up, condemning radical reform and pledging the maintenance of the constitution, but at the same time committing the house

[1] Brougham to Devonshire, 29 October 1819 (Devonshire).

[2] Althorp to Spencer, 24 October 1819 (Althorp); General Walpole to Grey, 1 November 1819 (Grey), 'the dismissal of Lord Fitzwilliam has had a great effect here and did us much service at the meeting'. Scarlet to Fitzwilliam, n.d. [1819] (Milton), says of Tierney: 'he hoped as I do that this attack upon you would bring all the whigs together.' It certainly healed the difference with Devonshire: Grey to Devonshire, 23 October 1819 (Devonshire).

[3] Graham to Fitzwilliam, 29 October 1819 (Milton); Holland to Grey, 16 October 1819 (Holland).

[4] Derby to Grey, 21 November 1819 (Grey); Wellesley to Grey, 17 November 1819 (Grey).

[5] Brougham to Lambton, n.d. [1819] (Brougham): 'The alarmists among us are few and no difference exists on enquiry—only as to precautionary measures—which indeed is the most important of all but don't arise at first.' See also: Lady Seymour, *Pope*, p. 208; R. Russell, *Russell*, i. 210–12; H. Brougham, *Life and Times*, ii. 347–50; Abercromby to Devonshire, 20 November 1819 (Devonshire). Holland to Grey, 16 October 1819 (Holland).

to inquire into the Manchester events and to attend to the complaints of the people. This was heartily approved by a large meeting attended by members of the party from both houses.

The session allowed the full amplification of whig arguments. On 23 November Grey and Tierney argued for concession and conciliation in reply to ministerial warnings about the extent of danger. Anxious to keep the initiative, the opposition followed its amendment with motions, moved in similar terms by Lansdowne in the lords and Althorp in the commons, for a committee to inquire into the state of the country. Here, again, was a wise choice of ground, for the great body of the whigs could agree in urging that both the grievances of the people and the state of the country should be fully investigated before any action was taken.

Another initiative was the act of an individual. At the end of September H. G. Bennet had visited George Philips in Manchester to gather information. The information he secured and the contacts he made were supplemented by correspondence with John Shuttleworth, a cotton dealer and a leading figure in Manchester's group of middle-class radicals. Bennet was therefore in a strong position to deal with the question. His first effort was disappointing. His speech on the address, though well informed, seems an unimpressive performance, though he himself complained of bad reporting.[1] Bennet also presented a petition for the Manchester radicals praying for inquiry into the massacre, but his main effort was reserved for 9 December, when he requested a committee to inquire into the state of the manufacturing districts. In a powerful speech he went into considerable detail concerning the poverty produced by unemployment and falling wages, and into the state of the local government machinery in Manchester and Lancashire generally. His arguments on the basis of local information were strong, but his more general points were weak, particularly since he mounted the currency reform hobby-horse he was to ride at hectic speed later in his career. Prominent waverers such as Wilberforce and Davenport made sympathetic though non-committal noises, but Bennet had achieved his purpose by deploying his information and drawing attention to the situation. The motion was withdrawn without division.

[1] Bennet to Shuttleworth, 25 November 1819 (John Shuttleworth Scrapbook, Manchester Central Reference Library).

The final whig attempt to maintain the offensive was on parliamentary reform. Even before the Peterloo massacre sections of the party had begun to toy with the subject, and a scheme had been discussed for transferring seats from boroughs disfranchised for corruption to unrepresented towns. Holland reported:

the idea seems to take on in the house of commons, and it will be a good answer to those who abuse us for not accomplishing or binding ourselves to accomplish impracticalities, to show that we never neglect the opportunity of doing what can be done with safety and without exciting alarm towards the extension of the elective franchise.[1]

Grey, though more doubtful, approved the device for tactical purposes, his main concern being to avoid anything of a more general nature and to prevent the opposition's pledging itself.[2] Lord John Russell, then casting about for a subject of which he could become the exponent, therefore came forward with such a plan, which promptly received accolades from the *Morning Chronicle* and the *Edinburgh Review*.[3]

The gathering support was stampeded by the massacre. Now a clear whig alternative to the radicals was imperative and many saw reform as an indispensable part of this alternative, Brougham arguing that it would be a means of confirming the whig popularity built up by the campaign of meetings.[4] Reform was also seen as an answer to the tumult in industrial areas, one which would give them more weight in the community and a safety valve to ventilate discontent.[5] At the opening of the session the leaders of the party declared for reform, Tierney boldly, Grey cautiously, and they were followed by a number of others in the next few days.[6] This paved the way for Russell's proposals on 14 December. He moved four resolutions putting the general case for transfers and urging specifically that the borough of

[1] Holland to Grey, 11 March 1819 (Grey).

[2] Grey to Holland, 19 March 1819 (Holland).

[3] *Morning Chronicle*, 6 and 17 July 1819; *Edinburgh Review*, no. lxviii, 1820, pp. 461–501; 1538–9.

[4] Brougham to Grey, 18 October 1819 (Brougham); Holland to Grey, 16 October 1819 (Holland).

[5] Holland to Grey, 6 September 1819 (Holland); *Edinburgh Review*, no. lxviii, 1820, p. 482.

[6] *P.D.* xli. 9 and 71–72. G. Philips: *P.D.* xli. 165. Lamb: *P.D.* xli. 555. Smyth: *P.D.* xli. 637. Waithman: *P.D.* xli. 775.

Grampound be disfranchised. The bulk of the party was prepared to fight on this very favourable ground, when, to the surprise of nearly all concerned, Castlereagh rose to announce that he would agree to a transfer of the Grampound seats.[1] Russell withdrew his motion and began to consider the problem of possible franchises for Leeds, his proposal for the new borough.[2]

The success of the initial opposition campaign was demonstrated by the size of the votes secured on the various motions involved: 150 on the amendment and on Althorp's motion, both larger than votes on similar issues in 1817. Equally important, taking the initiative had helped to conceal the differences in the ranks of the party. It had not, however, obscured them completely. Discussion on the Manchester meeting had brought out varying whig views on its legality. Two fairly consistent opposition voters, Sir John Sebright and W. H. Lyttelton, had both spoken against the amendment, Pascoe Grenfell had abstained, and two Lancashire whigs, George Philips and Lord Stanley, had supported it in such terms as to indicate their own alarm. Stanley admitted that the situation

> called for some measures to meet what the present laws were not sufficient to put down, what he confessed existed in his own country, atheism, blasphemy, and disaffection, to the greatest degree—he had almost said, to the borders of rebellion; but till the case should be fully made out, he could not pledge himself to any particular measure.[3]

Such attitudes boded ill for future agreement and the introduction of the government measures saw the whigs fighting on much more difficult ground. So far as their views can be gathered from letters and comments in the debates, they fell, broadly summed up, into three main schools of thought. The first was composed mainly of the more radical section of the party, Hutchinson, Donoughmore, and Bennet, but it also included Milton, and some senior figures like Grey. All these were inclined to deny that the measures were necessary at all, if only by asserting that the danger had been exaggerated beyond all proportion.[4] The second and probably the most numerous

[1] Althorp to Spencer, 21 December 1819 (Althorp).

[2] Lord J. Russell to Bedford, 9 January 1820 (Grey—sent on by Bedford).

[3] *P.D.* xli. 323.

[4] See Donoughmore in *P.D.* xli. 1250; Milton in *P.D.* xli. 654; Bennet in *P.D.* xli. 1352–60. Grey to Holland, 24 October 1819 (Holland).

group, comprising the moderate majority of the party, was prepared to admit some danger and the necessity for some measures, but argued that the ones actually proposed were not satisfactory.[1] The third group, the alarmists, was prepared to support some or all of the measures of government, feeling that the state of the country was too dangerous to trifle with. No compromise could hold these three groups together, and the debates saw a series of declarations from men like Darlington and his second son, from Morpeth, Protheroe, Grenfell, Dickinson, and Hamilton, of their differences with their fellow whigs. It was, however, possible to hold the first two groups together, and to invoke the occasional support of some in the third, by a plan of campaign which involved giving no opposition to the training prevention bill, concentrating opposition to the seizure of arms bill on one clause, that allowing right of search by night, suggesting modifications to the misdemeanours bill, and opposing the remaining measures. This was a plan energetically supported by the great majority of the party, though with some inevitable differences of emphasis. In the resulting debates nearly all the discussion was carried on by the opposition side of the house and the whigs were able to force sixteen divisions in the commons before the legislation was carried.[2] They were also able to secure one effective modification of the legislation, an amendment by Holland to limit delays in bringing *ex-officio* informations.

If whig votes were higher than on any other comparable occasion, this was because of a really thorough muster on the opposition side. On only two divisions was support forthcoming from outside the party. On the seditious meetings bill complaints from waverers decided Castlereagh to make the legislation temporary, but this decision failed to check all defections; Buxton moved to give the bill a life of three years instead of the ministerial proposal of five, and received some non-whig support. The attempt to delete the right of search by night from the arms bill also drew the support of so strong a ministerialist as Sir Joseph Yorke and a few other waverers. In both cases the reinforcements were very few in number.

[1] See, for example, Curwen in *P.D.* xli. 760–1; Lansdowne in *P.D.* xli. 1293–4; Abercromby in *P.D.* xli. 1350–1; Ebrington in *P.D.* xli. 1414. Holland to Grey, 16 October 1819 (Holland): Lauderdale to Grey, November 1819 (Grey).

[2] e.g. Davies, *P.D.* xli. 1416–17.

The political scene during this short session was the nearest approach to an effective two-party system which can be found in this period. Both sides had made their fullest possible musters, so that both opposition votes and government majorities were higher than in most previous sessions. The Grenvilles and the waverers, whose support the opposition had set out to secure in the earlier session, were too alarmist to be won. As Sir Robert Heron pointed out, 'there is no third body, of any weight or numbers to turn the scale on any occasion'.[1] This can be clearly seen by an analysis of the opposition voters on the twelve motions listed in the sessions:

Votes given	1	2	3	4	5	6	7	8	9	10–12
Number of voters	18	17	24	21	19	18	26	15	15	23

A substantial majority of opposition votes on any one motion came from those who were voting regularly; 137 people voted more than three times, and only fifty-nine voted three or less. Not only are occasional voters less numerous than usual, but their characteristics are also different. Normally a high proportion would consist of waverers deserting the government on one particular motion. Now only a minority were in this category; three of those voting for three motions or less were government fringe, fourteen waverers, eight opposition fringe, and twenty-five opposition, the remainder not being classified. The waverers and government fringe groups tended to vote for minor modifications to the legislation. The largest number voting on any one motion was eight, who voted to remove search by night from the seizure of arms bill. On the other hand, the opposition and opposition fringe members tended to support the earlier united attacks and then depart. Althorp's motion on the state of the country had attracted twenty, the largest number of them on any one division, while Tierney's amendment to the address attracted the next largest at thirteen. A few of these, like T. W. Coke Junior, were whigs of impeccable orthodoxy but notorious laziness, ten were known alarmists or connexions of the alarmist wing, five were county members, and the remainder fell into no recognizable category, so that no explanation can be advanced for their conduct.[2]

[1] Heron, p. 110.

[2] The ten are Lord Yarborough's two sons, Lord Carlisle's two sons, two of Lord Darlington's members, a relative of Lord Derby, Lord Carrington's brother, Pascoe Grenfell, and C. C. Western.

Whig reactions to the events of the session tended to vary with direction of gaze. To those looking for concrete results the prospect was gloomy, and Grey, congenitally inclined to low spirits, wrote: 'we are sinking fast into the torpor occasioned by despair.'[1] The bulk of the party looked elsewhere and were cheered. They looked to the county meetings, the size of the divisions, the vigour of the opposition, the number of their initiatives, and the unusual degree of whig unity. An experienced observer like Coke considered that 'they never behaved so well as in the last session of parliament since the American war'.[2] The whigs had taken a view clearly distinct from that of government, and had energetically placed that view before the public, so putting themselves in a strong position for protecting and even heading that section of public opinion most congenial to their views. This section did not include the extreme radicals: from the first the whigs had been at pains to exorcise Hunt, Cobbett, Cartwright, and all their works. Rather did it embrace the middle-class liberals and radicals, the men of property, particularly in the growing towns, such as Manchester, Leeds, Liverpool, and Birmingham. For the first time the whigs had taken a firm and clear line which could be looked up to and admired by those groups. It was this that enabled Wilson to draw, as his own moral for the session, this conclusion: 'the conduct of opposition is universally applauded and though the country has lost some of its liberties I think it has approached its redemption by the union which has been promoted between the public and the whigs.'[3]

[1] Grey to Wilson, 31 December 1819 (Grey).

[2] Coke to Roscoe, 21 February 1820 (Roscoe Papers). See also R. Russell, *Russell*, i. 209.

[3] Wilson to Grey, 24 December 1819 (Wilson Papers, Add. MSS. 30123, f. 99); Tierney to Grey, 31 December 1819 (Grey).

VII

FOR QUEEN AND COUNTRY MEMBERS 1820–1822

THE death of George III on 29 January 1820 could hardly be said to have filled whig hearts with grief. On the contrary it opened up prospects which were vaguely cheering, for not only was a general election with the possibility of further gains rendered inevitable, but the new monarch also began to quarrel with his ministers. Accession to the throne rendered imperative a decision on a question which now and for the rest of the year preoccupied George IV: divorce from his hated wife, Caroline. Encouraged by his vice-chancellor, Sir John Leach, George laid before the cabinet papers relating to the queen's behaviour. On 10 February the ministers refused to agree to a divorce.[1] George immediately announced his intention of forming a government 'upon an extended scale' and of sending for Grenville, Holland, and possibly Wellesley.[2] Rumours of resignations, reconstructions, and new administrations were soon being eagerly relayed to Grey by an excited Wilson and an anxious Holland.[3] The leader's absence in Northumberland was keenly felt, and Holland wrote to remonstrate against it and to urge Grey to make his opinions known, so that anyone sent for by the king should be able to give him

some insight of what he was to expect on seeing you upon the subjects which he has most at heart as well as upon those in which the public interests are most involved—the queen, the civil list are of the first class—catholic emancipation, late bills, augmentation of army, retrenchment, reform, treatment of Napoleon *cum multis aliis* &c &c are of the second. If for instance you did not feel yourself able to indulge him in any degree in his first object, and not disposed to

[1] A. G. Stapleton, *George Canning and his Times*, London, 1859, pp. 266–74.

[2] Essex to Grey, 7 March 1820 (Grey). Essex stated that his information came 'from the fountainhead'.

[3] *Morning Chronicle*, 11 and 17 February; Wilson to Grey, 14, 15, and 16 February 1820 (Wilson Papers, Add. MSS. 30123, ff. 127–32).

yield anything for his second, it would be loss of time and want of sincerity, as well as very bad policy to make him send for a refusal to Northumberland . . . in justice to the party and to the public ought we not to have made up our minds and to be able to state them immediately upon any application of the kind I allude to how far any and which, of the other points I have touched upon are *sine qua nons* to your acceptance of power and how far you are disposed to purchase them or any part of them by acquiescence on other matters.[1]

Ever inclined to place personal honour before party, Grey considered that to come to town would be to lay himself open to accusations of eagerness for office. He was, however, prepared to go over the questions raised, so that his views should be clear if requested. On the question of the divorce he took a flexible attitude, not being prepared to commit himself until he had seen the case against the queen, though ready, in the doubtful circumstance of the case justifying it, to bring the divorce forward. On every other subject he was less equivocal. There were to be no concessions on the civil list, on the need for economy and retrenchment, on catholic emancipation, or on the repeal of the late bills. A minister who was to undertake the divorce question, Grey pointed out, would need to seize every means of conciliating public opinion in other ways. Turning to the practical, he visualized great difficulty in forming an administration in view of the absence of any possible allies, Peel being ruled out by the catholic question, the Grenvilles by existing differences, and Wellesley being such a difficult colleague. The final conclusion was gloomy: 'a negotiation, which would not ultimately succeed, it would be better for us should be thus stopped *in limine*, than that it should afterwards be broken off on grounds which probably would be more disadvantageous, as to the effect on public opinion.'[2] Holland agreed with everything.[3]

The excitement and the definition of terms were premature, for George's initial bravado subsided, his courage, always transient, disappeared, and he gave way to his ministers.[4] Yet, though Grey had defined his position and his terms, both of which were to remain relatively unchanged for the next two

1 Holland to Grey, 16 February 1820 (Holland).

2 Grey to Holland, 18 February 1820 (Grey).

3 Holland to Grey, 22 February 1820 (Holland).

4 Essex to Grey, 7 March 1820 (Grey); Tierney to Grey, 'Monday Night' n.d. [March 1820] (Grey).

years, the process of doing so had irreparably hindered whig efforts on another front. The death of the monarch had brought the old parliament briefly together, with a whole range of important subjects likely to be touched on. Though Holland urged full consultation, Grey's refusal to come south, and the preoccupation with formulation of terms for office, meant an absence of preparation for the session in hand. On his own Tierney was unable to establish a clear policy and restrain the chafing radicals; Wynn described the result: 'the divided state of opposition . . . is far beyond anything which I have yet seen. Tierney will not vote for Hume or Creevey's motions and goes away—Grenfell votes against them, Lord Milton remains in the country and other members of the aristocratical whigs go away without attempting to pair.'[1] Disunity, lack of preparation, and low attendance all showed the opposition in a very poor light.

This lack of success cast gloom on prognostications about the forthcoming election.[2] The result was less serious than had been feared. Some of the gains of 1818 were lost, Ebrington being driven out of Devonshire, Lyttelton from Worcestershire, and Phillips from Leicestershire, while in the City opposition representation went back to one, and George Lamb lost Westminster. However, two whigs were elected in place of one in both Bedfordshire and Middlesex, Lord John Russell replaced a tory in Huntingdonshire, and R. J. Smith another in Buckinghamshire, while a series of minor changes in the boroughs also favoured the opposition. Brougham estimated a gain of fourteen, Duncannon put it at four or five in England, with even balances in Scotland and Ireland, and Tierney thought in terms of a ministerial loss of six. Claims in the *Courier* that government had gained eighteen in fact concealed some ministerial despondency.[3]

[1] C. W. Wynn to H. W. Wynn, 27 February 1820 (Wynn, 4816).

[2] Grey to Holland, 17 February 1820 (Grey); Althorp to Spencer, 13 February 1820 (Althorp).

[3] Brougham to Lady C. Lindsay, 1 April 1820 (Brougham); Duncannon to Grey, 3 and 19 April (Grey); Tierney to Grey, 5 April 1820 (Grey); the estimates of the *Courier* are mentioned in *Morning Chronicle*, 12 April 1820; H. Bankes reported ministers as calculating on a trifling loss of numbers, though Bankes's own estimates came to a difference of seven to ten; Lord Colchester, *Diary*, iii. 124; Huskisson considered that 'the dissolution has deprived us of nearly all our best and steadiest props', Huskisson to Arbuthnot, 24 March 1820 (Huskisson Papers, Add. MSS. 38742, ff. 6–7); *Morning Chronicle*, 14 April 1820, calculated that fifteen had been added to the number of 'independent members' and as many taken from government.

To consolidate the gains of 1818 in this way was a reassuring result. The state of the country promised even more advantages, for discontent remained strong in the manufacturing areas at the same time as rural distress was making a new impact. As a result even Grey observed the reform question assuming an entirely new character.[1] As a final potential advantage the king bitterly resented his treatment by ministers and began to confer evidence of favour on oppositionists. A report, which appears to have been authorized, reached Grey that royal hostility to himself and the party was at an end.[2] Nevertheless, Grey refused to come south to exploit the situation. Holland pleaded anxiously:

you must come or God knows what will happen. Parliamentary reform, Manchester enquiry, foreign politics, civil list with many other topics require serious deliberation, but might perhaps with some inconvenience be discussed in correspondence—the queen, the state of the party, the disposition of individuals, the chance if not the prospect of a change at court are not topics for a letter and yet unless there is a thorough concert about them, unless your feelings and opinions are known thereupon, and being known enforced by your presence and active co-operation, I foresee much mischief and the possibility of the party being destroyed . . . not by a revolution but by a dissolution of all its parts. . . . I do not like the prospect of seeing a party of which my uncle was and you are the head crumble to pieces for want of exertion to keep it together.[3]

Grey's only response was a letter of advice which urged a cautious policy:

In general I should recommend it to you to abstain from pressing any particular measure. The great advantage of our present situation is that it relieves from all responsibility for the measures, which the times require . . . observe the good old opposition maxim of *proposing* nothing. Wait for the measures of the ministers, confine yourselves to general principles and statements favourable to liberty and to retrenchment . . . but above all abstain from anything that borders upon a proposal of bankruptcy either virtual, or avowed . . . in our present circumstances, I am quite sure as I have already said, that if there still remains a chance of our exerting ourselves usefully hereafter it depends entirely on our discreet and cautious conduct at this moment.[4]

[1] Huskisson to Arbuthnot, op. cit.; Grey to Holland, 9 and 12 April 1820 (Grey).
[2] Lambton to Grey, 22 April 1820 (Grey); Rosslyn to Grey, 26 April 1820 (Grey).
[3] Holland to Grey, 5 April 1820 (Holland). Lady Holland added a postscript to this letter in similar terms.
[4] Grey to Holland, 23 April 1820 (Grey).

Holland, little inclined to activity with Grey absent, agreed, and Tierney was in any case constitutionally inclined to such a course.[1]

The session, therefore, opened quietly on 21 April, and the first real preparations were made on 4 May at a badly attended meeting in Burlington House. Here a plan of operations was agreed—with Brougham to lead off by a motion on the droits of the crown. Lord John Russell announced that he had a motion in reserve, while Wilson and Scarlett vainly urged an inquiry into the Peterloo massacre.[2] Brougham's motion, the next day, thus became the first party clash of the session. The whig attitude on the civil list was a clear one: the pretence of the new king's surrendering his hereditary revenues should be ended, parliamentary control recognized, and the civil list confined to a sufficient sum to maintain the dignity of the crown, everything else being paid from the consolidated fund.[3] Brougham now used the droits of the crown as a text for this sermon and rallied 155 votes against a ministerial 273. Criticism was resumed three days later, when Russell proposed a week's delay to allow inquiry, the division being much the same. The attack then diversified, the major motion now being Hamilton's on the fourth baron of exchequer in Scotland, a sinecure office to which the government had made a new appointment. Tierney had hoped that ministers would be defeated on this, but though Peel and Vesey Fitzgerald stayed away, while William Peel, Dawson, and Bagwell voted with the opposition together with several waverers, the whigs were twelve votes short of success, owing to their own lax attendance and to Castlereagh's promise of an inquiry.[4]

This failure ended the planned, organized attack. Ministers were demonstrably weak, and Wilson observed that 'The supporters of government are very angry with ministers, and indeed much more so than any of their opponents.'[5] Yet the opposition

[1] Holland to Grey, 29 April 1820 (Holland).

[2] Althorp to Spencer, 5 May 1820 (Althorp); Wilson to Grey, 5 May 1820 (Wilson Papers, Add. MSS. 30123, ff. 151–2).

[3] Holland to Grey, 19 February 1820 (Holland).

[4] Althorp to Spencer, 12 May 1820 (Althorp). Tierney to Grey, 'Thursday night' n.d. [May 1820] (Grey): 'we had in our ranks no less than 38 stragglers, 26 more of our friends were close at hand, exclusive of a great many not come to town.' See also *Morning Chronicle*, 17 May 1820.

[5] Wilson to Grey, 16 May 1820 (Wilson Papers, Add. MSS. 30123, f. 157);

could accomplish nothing against them. Attendance was very lax.[1] Tierney was still cautious: Holland reported him 'somewhat alarmed at doing anything', while others, he reported, 'are yet more alarmed at a disposition in another quarter to do all'.[2] These were the radicals who now came forward: Alderman Wood moved for a secret committee on spies, Maberly moved for accounts on exchequer bills, and Davies produced a motion on military expenditure. All were heavily defeated, but they were indicative of the lack of agreement in opposition ranks.[3] This received public demonstration when Holme Sumner moved for a committee to inquire into agricultural distress. Milton urged that it should be extended to an inquiry into all distress; Ellice, supported by Tierney and the majority of the party, moved the previous question; but Smith, Brougham, Curwen, Lambton, and others supported the motion in order to embarrass the government.[4] It did, for the motion was carried, though ministers then succeeded in effectively limiting the committee's terms of reference. After this all attempt at party warfare was abandoned.

Debates were taking place in an air of increasing unreality, since house and country were anticipating disagreements between king and ministers and speculating on the probability that the queen, then rumbling north from Italy, would precipitate political crisis by coming to England. Wilson regarded her as a firebrand certain to destroy ministers, and Lambton observed that 'everything political seems by universal consent to hinge on the queen's actions'.[5] So did something of the opposition's demeanour. Effective discussion was impossible in such an atmosphere; Grey's absence was partly due to a disinclination

Wilson to Grey, 5 May 1820 (ibid., f. 151): 'the house seems to be in a very unsettled state evidently in an attitude to extort great concessions from ministers as the price of support'; C. W. Wynn to H. Wynn, 16 May 1820 (Wynn 1793D): 'never was such a bad figure made by any set of ministers and the general opinion of their weakness is such that if there were any persons who were fit to take their places they would not remain in office twelve hours.' Also Rosslyn to Grey, 17 May 1820 (Grey).

[1] Tierney to Grey, 'Thursday night' n.d. [May 1820] (Grey).

[2] Holland to Grey, 18 May 1820 (Holland).

[3] Holland to Grey, 22 May 1820 (Holland).

[4] Brougham to Grey, 1 June 1820 (Brougham).

[5] Wilson to Grey, 5 and 13 May 1820 (Wilson Papers, Add. MSS. 30123, ff. 151 and 155); Essex to Grey, 7 March 1820 (Grey); Lambton to Grey, 13 May 1820 (Grey).

to play the vulture, and Tierney seemed reluctant to do anything which might mar the prospect of office. He was prompt to stake out the claims of the whigs by condemning any idea that there was no alternative to the existing ministry.[1]

The firebrand landed on 5 June. Ministers brought down a green bag of documents on the queen's behaviour, but when they proposed a secret committee of inquiry Wilberforce moved a week's adjournment, in order that a compromise might be reached, and ministers were compelled to accept this when tory county members rallied to it. In Tierney's view 'the king was ... disavowed by his ministers, the house being given pretty distinctly to understand that his advisers saw the propriety of bringing the question before parliament in a very different light from his majesty'.[2] At this George's anger exploded and he took steps to sound out the opposition. On 11 June the three whigs most closely in his confidence, Sir John Leach, Donoughmore, and Hutchinson were dispatched to consult Holland, Lansdowne, and Tierney, while Sir Benjamin Bloomfield consulted Buckingham and the king saw Wellesley.[3] Leach's approach to Holland was on the basis of a friendly consultation, and he went on to see Tierney on the same terms; but Donoughmore and Hutchinson made quite definite offers, for Tierney reported: 'Hutchinson assured me that the ministers would be immediately dismissed if I would say that I advised him to press the king so to do. He offered to return to Carlton House and to finish the business in half an hour.'[4] Lansdowne was given a similar understanding, and both he and Tierney were told that no hostility was now felt to Grey, and also that there was even a disposition to give way on the catholic question.[5]

All three whigs returned cautious answers. Tierney declined to advise dismissal, and pointed out that public opinion was now too roused on the divorce question for any new administration to be able to stem the pressure. Lansdowne urged the difficulty of any ministerial change while the queen's business was before parliament, and Holland went further by repeating

[1] *P.D.*, N.S. i. 978.

[2] Tierney to Grey, 8 June 1820 (Grey).

[3] Lord Holland, *Memoirs*, pp. 400–3; Tierney to Grey and Lansdowne to Grey, 12 June 1820 (Grey); *George IV*, ii. 391–2. This last memorandum has been dated by Professor Aspinall in November 1820. It should be June.

[4] Tierney to Grey, 12 June 1820 (Grey).

[5] Lansdowne to Grey, 12 June 1820 (Grey).

Grey's view that any ministry involved in difficulty with the queen would be obliged to take up popular measures, a point which did not please Leach. All three also concurred in a deference to Grey and in privately visualizing the difficulty of forming any new administration, particularly in the house of commons, where a ministry dismissed in the midst of negotiations with the queen would automatically receive the support of the country gentlemen at whose behest the discussions had begun. Influenced by these doubts Grey declined to come to London. Present, he could have given no other advice than that which the king had already received, and this in itself had precluded the possibility of change. George's conclusion from the discussion was that he would have to persevere without yielding in the smallest instance. He did persevere, and with his existing ministers, who agreed to go ahead with a bill of pains and penalties against Caroline.

This posed the problem of whig attitudes to the queen. Some sections had already made up their minds. Some older whigs, such as Erskine, remembered the doubts about the propriety of her behaviour and were inclined to think the worst of her, as were Donoughmore, Hutchinson, and Lauderdale, who were on friendly terms with George IV. A larger number were committed to the queen: Brougham and Denman as legal advisers; Western and others by the stands they had taken in her favour under Whitbread's leadership in 1813 and 1814; and Wood, Wilson, Hobhouse, Burdett, and other radicals by their enthusiasm for an undoubtedly popular cause.[1] Such prior commitments made Tierney fear that the party would be badly divided.[2] In fact, a large section, possibly even a majority, remained undecided. Grey considered that 'all that can be expected of the leader of a great party on such an occasion would be to state to his friends fairly and openly the line which a sense of duty would oblige him to take but without any wish to engage their support in it as a body'.[3] He determined to act as a judge, an intention shared by others like Mackintosh, Lord John Russell, and Derby.[4] Tierney took the same stance, though he had earlier

[1] Wilson to Grey, 6 June 1820 (Wilson Papers, Add. MSS. 30123, f. 169).

[2] Tierney to Grey, 'Sunday night' n.d. [March 1820] (Grey).

[3] Grey to Lambton, 29 May 1820 (Grey).

[4] R. Russell, *Russell*, i. 270; Derby to Grey, 5 August 1820 (Grey).

lost face within the party by arguing that no money should be granted to the queen until her character was re-established.[1] Those determined to act as judges had no liking for the 'ugly, mad woman' as a person. Tierney disapproved of those who insisted on visiting her, Fitzwilliam and Sefton refused to act as her representatives, and Lord John Russell admitted publicly to doubts about her behaviour.

This distaste was heavily outweighed by hostility to George IV, which predisposed them, if not to support the queen, at least to scrutinize carefully any action against her. Public opinion urged them in the same direction, for the popular press and the crowds had taken up the queen's cause with vigour and addresses to her began to pour in. A popular party could hardly ignore such strongly expressed feelings. Yet with the exception of those who were fervently for the queen the whig response to the situation was not a simple reflex to public pressure. They felt a quite genuine distaste for ministerial proceedings. In the whig view ministers were following a policy which was not theirs but the king's: besides being inept and ill judged it was unwilling. This was a presumption in the queen's favour and an indication of weakness. Brougham underlined the point by urging ministers to advise the restoration of the queen's name to the liturgy, claiming that if they were dismissed, no one would step forward to replace them.[2]

When ministerial proceedings against the queen resumed, the 'judging' section of the party came forward hesitantly, dwelling on procedural and tactical arguments, while the radical wing launched themselves into the campaign with chivalrous enthusiasm. Both could work together in attacking ministerial policy and urging impartial justice: 124 opposition members resisted a second motion by Wilberforce urging the queen to make concessions, their argument being that it was unfair to expect all the concessions to come from one side. Later, when ministers hesitated, 100 M.P.s voted for Western's motion to adjourn the committee indefinitely, and forty-six peers for Grey's to discharge it. When, however, ministers introduced into the lords a bill of pains and penalties against the queen, the opposition were compelled to address themselves directly to her case and

[1] *P.D.* xli. 1623–5. Tierney to Grey, 'Sunday night' n.d. [March 1820] (Grey).
[2] *P.D.*, N.S. i. 1243.

a united front had to be rebuilt from the foundations. On 17 August Leinster moved to discharge the order of the day for the bill: forty-one peers voted for this, but Grey, Lansdowne, and others opposed, on the grounds that there was no point in changing the method of procedure for which the house had already opted. On the other hand, nearly all the whigs could agree that the bill was neither necessary nor expedient. Two days later the forty were joined by twenty-four other whigs to support motions by King and Grey to this effect.

The trial completed the muster. Brougham's speech and the defence evidence brought a considerable part of the prosecution case into doubt. Grey, in a powerful concluding speech, drew attention to the danger that the bill would be rejected in the commons and to the state of public feeling; and these and other arguments helped to produce a vote of 95 to 123 against the second reading.[1] The differing motives were fully illustrated in the protests which were signed after the division.[2] Devotees and doubters all mustered together.

The second reading of the bill had been carried by a majority of twenty-eight.[3] In committee differences began to appear on the divorce clause. An attempt to delete the clause, which mustered sixty-two votes, was defeated because the majority of the whigs joined government supporters to make up a vote of 129 against it. The whigs acted from frankly tactical motives.[4] The effect of their calculation was shown on the third reading on 9 November. Three peers who had supported the second reading but opposed the divorce clause now turned round and voted

[1] Sixty-two of these had already voted for Lord King's motion on 19 August: thirty-seven were even more deeply committed, having voted for Leinster's motion two days before.

[2] The solid core of the majority was fifty-nine peers who protested against the bill on general grounds; eight whigs protested at the second reading because adultery had not been proved; ten peers, including three whigs, Somerset, Leinster, and Rosebery, argued that it has been indicated but not proved, and the accused should have the benefit of the doubt; seven peers, including Ilchester, admitted that guilt had been proved, but claimed that it was inexpedient to proceed further.

[3] *Morning Chronicle*, 8 November 1820, pointed out that if only the English titles had been considered then the majority would have been against the bill. A majority of fourteen of the Scottish peers, five of the Irish, and eleven of the bishops had voted for it.

[4] Lauderdale accused the whigs of a deliberate party manœuvre: *P.D.*, N.S. iii. 1729. Whether it was preconcerted is not known, but it was certainly avowed, as is shown by the declarations of Holland: *P.D.*, N.S. iii. 1724; Thanet: ibid.; Grey: *P.D.*, N.S. iii. 1723.

against the third reading, with one other. Eight who had opposed the divorce clause abstained on third reading, together with three others. Thus the vote against the bill rose to ninety-nine, the number for it fell to 108, and the majority to nine. This was clearly insufficient to justify proceeding with the bill, particularly in the light of the storms to come in the commons. Liverpool announced its indefinite adjournment.

This precipitated a final outburst of George's anger. He saw the withdrawal as a defeat, and the prorogation as the loss of an opportunity of settling the queen's business before delay and petitions had exacerbated the situation. On 16 November he wrote to Liverpool to announce the formation of a new administration, then decided not to send the letter.[1] In the hope that a whig administration would be able to win over the queen's major allies and deprive her of support, George decided to negotiate with Grey, only to find that he had left London.[2] Instead he sent for Donoughmore to discover whig views from him. The peer's assessment was that Grey would not take office without marking his determination to act on a new system, and that this would include repeal of the six acts and of the aliens act, reductions of expenditure in most areas of government, and concessions to the catholics. Tierney reported to Grey that

> the impression upon Donoughmore's mind was that no objection existed to the substance of what he suggested you might require as to the obnoxious bills, and retrenchments, but upon the subject of the catholic question the king declared that he would at this moment give no opinion and would only say he was not committed one way or the other. . . . With regard to the queen Donoughmore told his majesty that he could have no doubt your advice would be to drop all harsh proceedings against her and to make concessions to the feelings of the country. The king said he was ready to allow her £50,000 a year, would that be satisfactory? Donoughmore answered he thought not unless accompanied with her restoration to the liturgy. To this strong objections were at first made but it ended in acquiescence provided she would leave England. The conference concluded with renewed professions of dislike to ministers, and of a firm resolution to change them.[3]

[1] *George IV*, ii. 380.
[2] Ibid., pp. 388–90.
[3] Tierney to Grey, 21 November 1820 (Grey).

The next day, however, Donoughmore again saw the king after the latter had had a long interview with the Duke of York. He found royal attitudes materially changed and put this down to the duke's influence. This may well have been exerted but it is also clear from his own memorandum that the king was afraid of the changes in foreign and internal policy which would follow a whig administration.[1] Now the king merely requested Donoughmore to approach Tierney and discover his views on the advisability of producing letters relating to the conduct of the queen, while at the same time sounding out opposition views.[2] Tierney, however, simply emphasized his determination to be guided by Grey, and the king, when the interview was reported to him, found it 'not very encouraging'.[3] Taken with the impossibility of consulting the absent Grey this decided the issue. Rumours of change continued to the end of the month, and even prompted the *Morning Chronicle* to set out the terms on which it considered the whigs could agree to accept office, but the moment had passed, and even Canning's resignation in December left the ministry unscathed.[4] The prospect of office had never been more than the whim of a frustrated man. Holland told Grey

> that if the whole was not mere restlessness and talk the king had no other design than to ascertain if you would bid higher for him than his ministers—probably too with the further intention of raising their bidding by quoting yours. . . . It is equally clear that he is not to be gained without loss of that which both in policy and in comfort is worth much more than all he or anything of his kind.[5]

Yet the episode had had important effects. Grey and Tierney decided that any further approaches through third persons should be respectfully declined.[6] The politics of intrigue, so long important in the party's relations with the prince, were to be ended.

If this was an impetus on the road towards becoming a popular party, the whigs were pushed further in the same direction by the explosion of popular discontent at the conduct of

[1] *George IV*, ii. 390–1.

[2] Ibid. ii. 388–90. This refers to Lord D–re; Aspinall has wrongly interpreted this as Lord Dacre.

[3] Ibid. ii. 389.

[4] *Morning Chronicle*, 30 November 1820.

[5] Holland to Grey, 24 November 1820 (Grey).

[6] Tierney to Grey, 7 December 1820 (Grey).

ministers in introducing the bill against the queen and then withdrawing it. Grey angrily denounced ministers for bringing the country to the verge of revolution, and in the commons there were scenes when the house met briefly. Hobhouse and thirty-nine others came up early to try and force the speaker on to the chair at 10 a.m. Finding this impossible they came down in force in the early afternoon, with results described by Hobhouse:

> The speaker came in at quarter to two—prayers were read and two members were sworn in—two new writs were moved—at this moment Denman rose with a letter from the queen—The words Mr Speaker were not out of his mouth before the taps were heard at the door—In came black rod—We all set up a shout Mr. Denman Mr. Denman—withdraw—withdraw—withdraw—The shout lasted all the while black rod was speaking. The speaker rose from his chair —Bennet started up saying 'it is a disgrace to the nation' Tierney rose '*not one word has been heard*' said Tierney. '*What did he say?*' The speaker affected not to hear—and walked on—Castlereagh who had trembled all the while rose and followed—then we all set up a yell '*Shame Shame Shame*'!!! and fairly hooted the speaker and Castlereagh out of the house. The commotion was beyond anything you can imagine.[1]

With their own anger roused and ministers so clearly discredited the whigs could do no other than mobilize, lead, and keep up the popular indignation. A fear that further action against the queen could only be forestalled by a strong expression of public opinion prompted in the same direction.[2] Most important of all it was now clear that however severe the king's quarrels with ministers he would not replace them with whigs. Many, therefore, saw public pressure as the only hope for change. Hutchinson had already come to the conclusion that, as he says, 'If the present ministers are to be removed from office it can only be done by the combined efforts of every man in this country who wishes for domestic quiet or for liberty on the continent.'[3] In his view the opposition could expect no arrangement with the king, but could 'only by force of the

[1] J. C. Hobhouse to Burdett, 23 November 1820 (Correspondence of Sir Francis Burdett, Bodleian Library, MS. Eng. Letters, d. 96).

[2] Grey to Sir C. Monck, 23 November 1820 (Middleton–Monck Papers, Northumberland County Record Office); Grey to Sir M. W. Ridley, 29 November 1820 (Ridley Papers, Blagdon, Northumberland).

[3] Hutchinson to Brougham, 15 November 1820, copy (Brougham).

public voice most resolutely expressed dislodge these present minions'.[1] His feelings were widely shared. 'We have come to a crisis', said Bedford, 'and a blow must be struck while the country is so decidedly with us.'[2]

Though Norfolk whigs had organized a county meeting against the bill of pains and penalties in August, the first initiatives now came from the radicals; Southwark demanded the dismissal of the ministers in October, and early in December the common council of London and the electors of Westminster met for the same object.[3] The first whig efforts centred on Yorkshire; the York whig club began to circulate a requisition for a meeting at the end of October, and before the decision on the bill Fitzwilliam decided to set the county in motion, suggesting that all sections of county opinion would unite in a petition to the commons to reject the bill once it had passed the peers.[4] Soon Holland reported that many other whigs were pressing for county meetings.[5] Grey was initially more doubtful, warning of the danger of alienating those other groups who had voted against the bill, and also visualizing the possibility of producing a reaction by endeavouring to force opinion prematurely.[6] At the same time he was ready to acquiesce in anything which might be decided, and Holland's assessment of opinion in the party converted him into an enthusiastic advocate for meetings in general and a Northumberland meeting in particular.[7] Tierney and Holland took the lead in initiating meetings from London, and Lambton, seeing their enthusiasm, cancelled a trip to Paris and set off north to organize Durham.[8] Within a short time the Yorkshire preparations were being duplicated in Northumberland and Durham, in Buckinghamshire, where Folkestone took an active part, and in Sussex, where Erskine was encouraged by Grey to organize a meeting.[9]

[1] Quoted in Wilson to Grey, 14 November 1820 (Wilson Papers, Add. MSS. 30123, ff. 205–6). [2] Bedford to Grey, 6 January 1821 (Grey).

[3] *Morning Chronicle*, 25 October, 4 December, 7 December 1820.

[4] *Morning Chronicle*, 1 November 1820; Fitzwilliam to Milton, 9 November 1820 (Milton). [5] Holland to Grey, 19 November 1820 (Holland).

[6] Grey to Holland, 21 November 1820 (Grey).

[7] Grey to Holland, 9 December 1820 (Grey); Grey to Monck and Grey to Ridley, op. cit.

[8] Lambton to Grey, 24 November 1820 (Grey); *George IV*, ii. 888.

[9] Erskine to Grey, 1 December 1820 (Grey); Folkestone's efforts are mentioned in *Morning Chronicle*, 25 November 1820.

Inevitable difficulties soon cropped up: Althorp, who was hostile to the queen, declined to take any part and discouraged meetings in Northamptonshire and Berkshire; Lord George Cavendish thought meetings would alienate possible support; and Darnley refused to sign any requisition in Kent, thus imperilling the meeting.[1] Others, such as Lansdowne, hesitated, and Tierney reported that there was some unwillingness among the whigs to take any lead, a difficulty which was magnified by lack of co-ordination, for nothing had been decided before the politicians left town.[2] More serious were local reverses. In Yorkshire the reformers refused to sign the requisition unless reform were brought in, and the whigs were divided in their views on the queen. While the lower orders demanded addresses to the queen and declarations of her innocence, the higher refused to subscribe to anything of this nature.[3] The meeting was therefore given up, a fatal setback in Grey's view.[4] Brougham despaired of a Cumberland meeting because of similar disagreements between the yeomanry and the gentry.[5] In a state of despair Holland and Tierney, the London co-ordinators, both decided to give up their efforts.[6]

They did so too soon. Lambton had had difficulty in getting impressive signatures for his Durham meeting, but he eventually secured them and the meeting demonstrated that the county was more enthusiastic than its leaders.[7] Grey too secured a Northumberland meeting by giving up all thought of conciliating the tories and the cautious country gentlemen. He realized that the great mass of the middling and lower classes of freeholders would be decidedly for the petition. The meeting, called over the opposition of the sheriff, proved him right.[8] Other

[1] Althorp to Milton, 4 December 1820 (Milton); Ellice to Grey, 6 January 1821 (Grey); Brougham to Lambton, 20 December 1820 (Brougham).

[2] Lansdowne to Holland, 27 November [1820] (Holland); Tierney to Grey, 7 December and 13 December 1820 (Grey).

[3] R. Chaloner to Fitzwilliam, 6 and 8 December 1820 (Milton); Sir F. L. Wood to Fitzwilliam, 6 January 1821 (Milton); Fitzwilliam to Grey, 6 December 1820 (Grey); Grey to Fitzwilliam, 9 December 1820 (Milton).

[4] Grey to Fitzwilliam, 9 December 1820 (Milton).

[5] Brougham to Lambton, 20 December 1820 (Brougham); Bennet had no great hopes of Shropshire, see Bennet to Grey, 18 December 1820 (Grey).

[6] Holland to Grey, 4 January 1821 (Holland).

[7] Lambton to Grey, 1 December 1820 (Grey); Tierney to Grey, 13 December 1820 (Grey); *Morning Chronicle*, 18 December 1820.

[8] Grey to Fitzwilliam, 9 December 1820 (Milton); *Tyne Mercury*, 16 January 1821.

meetings began to follow rapidly, influenced both by these early successes and by a reaction against the numerous loyal addresses which tories had begun to encourage. In the next two months large and enthusiastic county meetings were held in Wiltshire, Gloucestershire, and Berkshire, all against the opposition of the sheriffs, and in Bedfordshire, Cambridgeshire, Hampshire, Middlesex, Surrey, and Kent.[1] In Derbyshire a tory attempt to claim a loyal address as that of the whole county was beaten by the intervention of the Duke of Devonshire. In Oxfordshire Holland and Jersey proposed a successful amendment to the loyal address, and an amendment was successful in Nottinghamshire.[2] Similar efforts failed in Shropshire, where H. G. Bennet's amendment had a majority apparent to the whigs but not the sheriff, and in Cheshire, where the sheriff dissolved the meeting when the Grosvenors and their supporters opposed a loyal address.[3]

Holland had hoped for uniformity in the petitions, arguing that they should request restoration of the queen's name to the liturgy and deprecate any new trials, but not demand the dismissal of ministers since this would alienate support.[4] His hopes were not fulfilled, as four of the meetings urged the dismissal of ministers and seven concentrated on the queen, either by reprobating the proceedings or by urging a settlement, while some others added other objects such as agricultural distress and, in the case of seven counties, reform. But the failures were few, and the demonstration of public feeling against the government was the most powerful since the days of Lord North, in the opinion of George Philips.[5] The whole movement had furthered the whig emergence as a popular party.

Behind the scenes the trend was further strengthened, for Grey, concerned about the terms on which the whigs could take

[1] Lansdowne to Devonshire, 17 January 1821 (Devonshire). Berkshire: *The Times*, 9 January 1821. Gloucestershire: *Gloucester Journal*, 1 January. Hampshire: *Morning Chronicle*, 15 January. Cambridgeshire: *Morning Chronicle*, 17 January 1821. Bedfordshire: *Scotsman*, 20 January 1821. Surrey: *The Times*, 3 February 1821. Kent: *The Times*, 19 January 1821. Middlesex: *Morning Chronicle*, 17 January 1821.

[2] Derbyshire: Holland to Devonshire, 10 January 1821 (Devonshire). Oxford: *The Times*, 23 January 1821. Nottinghamshire: *The Times*, 28 January 1821.

[3] Ossulston to Grey, 12 January 1821 (Grey): *The Times*, 13 January 1821.

[4] Holland to Grey, 19 November 1820 (Holland).

[5] *P.D.*, N.S. iv. 225.

office, had, at the end of 1820, begun to consult diverse sections of the party on reform and whether it should be a *sine qua non* of office. The replies were reasonably cheering. Even Fitzwilliam, who warned at length of the dangers of reform, was prepared to say that a certain type of borough was too numerous, and subsequent correspondence with his son, Milton, revealed that he was prepared to support some improvements in the representation.[1] Holland, though a 'sorry and small reformer', was now prepared to insist on reform as a condition of office, and pointed out that

> However small the quantum of reform you propose, if proposed directly and made a *sine qua non*, it gives you should it be resisted all the advantages of having proposed reform to the fullest extent with the public, and it gives the country the advantage of enlisting the popular cry under the banner of moderate practical and useful reform.[2]

The reformers too were accommodating, for Wilson suggested that they would be satisfied with giving representatives to the larger towns and taking them away from the corrupt boroughs, and Ellice, who had sounded out Hobhouse, thought that only a promise to inquire into complaints and remedy them by moderate and temperate measures would be necessary.[3]

At the same time as those difficulties in the way of taking up reform which were internal to the party were being removed, Grey saw clearly that the state of public feeling and the distress were such that only reform could satisfy the public.

> 'I am convinced', he argued, 'that this cannot be hoped for without some concession on that point. Even if there should be a change of ministry . . . calculating as the new administration must on the inveterate hostility of the court, and its determination to trip them up on the first favourable opportunity, public confidence alone could support them, which could not be had, without some concession of this nature, which I have stated and the loss of it would ensure their destruction within twelve months.[4]

[1] Fitzwilliam to Grey, 10 December 1820 (Grey); Fitzwilliam to Milton, 3 March 1821 (Milton).

[2] Holland to Grey, 24 November 1820 (Holland).

[3] Wilson to Grey, 8 December 1820 (Wilson Papers, Add. MSS. 30123, f. 220); Ellice to Grey, 7 December 1820 (Grey); Broughton, ii. 139–40.

[4] Grey to Fitzwilliam, 15 January 1821 (Milton).

At the Northumberland county meeting he therefore announced to the world:

I shall remain true to the principles with which I set out in life, and were the government offered me tomorrow—and it would be a task to which in the present circumstances of the country, and the present state of my health, I am by no means equal—I would not accept it, but upon terms satisfactory to my conscience and honour; and these terms should be nothing short of a complete and total change in the system of government.[1]

Parliamentary reform, he announced, should be a principal feature in the change of a system necessary, though whether it should be initially pressed as an indispensable and immediate object, or whether the general state of the country would be such as to demand precedence for reform, could only be determined by the circumstances of the time. By nailing his colours to the mast Grey had committed himself openly to the stands he had taken privately in the past few months.

With this commitment to popular stands and the strong general support demonstrated by the campaign of meetings, whig confidence for the coming session ran high. Lansdowne commented to Grey:

The state of the country as well as the government is really so critical that I am sure it requires all the attention that can be given to it by those who take any interest in public affairs . . . although not all [*sic*] prone to believe in changes of administration, I feel every day more convinced that the present cannot ultimately stand. I have seen a good deal of the country gentlemen in this neighbourhood since I have been here, and I find (except in those immediately connected with ministers) a great and marked change of sentiment which cannot I conclude be confined to this part of the country. . . . I am satisfied therefore that with the lukewarmness of their supporters and the strong current of popular feeling against them, nothing but some fortunate turn for them not to be counted upon, can save the present ministers and that you will probably be called upon to form a government.[2]

His optimism was widely shared, and Grey was even prepared to come up early, urging friends to be in London a day or so before the meeting.[3]

[1] *Tyne Mercury*, 16 January 1821.

[2] Lansdowne to Grey, 9 January 1821 (Grey).

[3] Grey to Lansdowne, 13 January 1821 (Lansdowne); Grey to Fitzwilliam,

Grey suggested an amendment to the address, and Tierney, though not enthusiastic, arranged to meet Brougham, Scarlett, and Denman to discuss it on 18 January.[1] Whether by their decision, or that of the full party meeting held on 22 January at Burlington House, no amendment was proposed.[2] This was perhaps unfortunate. In the lords, Grey announced that the address fell far short of what the state of the country demanded and then launched into a strong denunciation of ministers and their policy.[3] In the commons, Wetherell, a tory member, claimed the field the whigs had left vacant by moving for copies of liturgies, an obvious preface to a motion about the queen. The whigs had to support the motion, to be defeated by 169 to 260 in a premature trial of strength.

There was still every expectation that, in Althorp's words, 'the question . . . will very soon be decided, for it will depend upon the event of two or at most three debates'.[4] Tavistock now proposed to move a series of resolutions criticizing the ministerial measures against the queen as derogatory to the honour of the crown, and most of the leading figures in the party considered that this should be put forward first. Unfortunately, Lord Archibald Hamilton had given notice of a motion of his own for the restoration of the queen's name to the liturgy, and despite the persuasions of the party meeting he declined to allow Tavistock precedence, agreeing only to alter his motion from an address to the king to a series of resolutions.[5]

On 26 January he therefore moved that the exclusion of the queen's name from the liturgy was ill advised and inexpedient. He received 209 votes, better than any previous whig vote except on the property tax, but 101 behind the ministerial total. The next gun was trundled into position on 5 February when Tavistock moved his resolutions. The whigs took pains to place the issue solely on the ground of the measures taken, for Tavistock announced in the course of his speech that he would accept office under no administration, and Tierney disclaimed

15 January 1821 (Milton); Essex to Grey, 11 January 1821 (Grey); *Scotsman*, 3 February 1821. See also Aspinall, *Brougham*, p. 119.

[1] Tierney to Grey, 17 January 1821 (Grey).

[2] *Traveller*, 22 and 23 January 1821.

[3] *P.D.*, N.S. iv. 6–12.

[4] Althorp to Milton, 15 January 1821 (Milton).

[5] Mrs. Arbuthnot, *Journal*, i. 65–66; A. Aspinall, *Brougham*, pp. 119–20; Lord Colchester, *Diary*, iii. 201.

personal desire for office. Their meekness was ill rewarded. The opposition vote fell to 178, the ministerial increased to 324. A third debate, on 13 February, confirmed that the powder was damp. John Smith proposed a motion for the restoration of the queen's name to the liturgy and 178 votes were opposed by 298. The campaign was over.

The voting pattern shows clearly what had happened:[1]

	Category of member				
Vote	Govt.	Govt. Fr.	Waverers	Oppn. Fr.	Oppn.
Government vote	100% (184)	93% (74)	63% (59)	..	..
Mixed votes	..	5% (4)	14% (13)	..	..
One oppn. vote	..	2% (2)	5% (5)	14% (7)	5% (7)
Two oppn. votes	..	..	7% (6)	24% (12)	12% (18)
Three oppn. votes	..	..	11% (10)	62% (31)	83% (121)
Totals	100% (184)	100% (80)	100% (93)	100% (50)	100% (146)

The main body of the opposition had rallied with enthusiasm, voted in large numbers and frequently. Even the opposition fringe had mustered well. Yet the all-important waverers who were expected to be influenced by the pressures from the country had obstinately declined to waver in their loyalty to the government.[2] Their reasons were clear. The weakness of the government and the violence of the agitation had brought up the possibility of a change. Ministers had underlined this by making Hamilton's motion one of confidence.[3] The reasoning which dictated the votes of the waverers was made abundantly clear in speeches.[4] Stuart-Wortley explained that

gentlemen had not looked so much at the justice or injustice of the particular question then before them, as to the point to which it was directed; and it was impossible to deny, that those who had voted for it had wished to use it as a means for turning out the present ministers and putting others into their places. Now, he was sure, the country had not sufficient confidence in any other set of public men to put them in the places of the present ministers—it had no con-

[1] The government vote is known only for Tavistock's motion. The 'mixed' voters are those who voted with the government on this but with the opposition on one of the other motions. One member, not classified in any of the categories, is not counted.

[2] Whishaw thought that the minorities did not include more than 10 who were not regular opposition voters. Lady Seymour, *Pope*, p. 234.

[3] Lord Colchester, *Diary*, iii. 201.

[4] A. Aspinall, *Brougham*, pp. 119–20 for Huskisson's views.

fidence at all in gentlemen on the other side. Though the ministers had suffered much in the public estimation during the last six months, they had not yet lost the public confidence so much as to reconcile the country to having the gentlemen opposite to him as their successors.[1]

Mackintosh justly pointed out that such attitudes would supply the present ministers and all future ones with an answer to every accusation, but this was no consolation to the party whose onslaught had foundered on these opinions. The *Morning Chronicle*, like many of the whigs, drew the obvious lesson. Parliament was indifferent to public opinion and 'Till the opposition shall find out means as powerful as the repeal of a property tax for assailing these interests their speeches may convince the country in general, but they will gain them few additional votes in the honourable house.'[2]

Though serious, the reverse was not fatal. Party activity was not completely at an end. As an issue the queen was finished, but there were other issues, and attention shifted to foreign policy. The behaviour of the continental allies, who had compelled the revocation of the new constitution in Naples, brought to the fore all the old whig hostility to the holy alliance. Grey led the way with a motion for papers on 19 February and a strong criticism of the absolute monarchs who had assumed the right to dictate their views of constitutional propriety to Europe. Two days later Mackintosh proposed a similar motion in the commons: opposition support dropped to 125. Lansdowne's condemnation of the doctrines urged by the allies at Troppau fared little better, since it mustered only thirty-seven votes in the lords.

A second major seam had been quickly worked out and the only substitute was a series of minor shafts. Lennard moved for the repeal of the acts on seditious meetings and libels, Burdett for an inquiry into Peterloo, Macdonald for a cut of 10,000 men in the army. All fared badly, and, indeed, on a grant of £6,000 which the government proposed to make the Duke of Clarence the whigs split, with a large proportion of opposition voting against payment, Tierney, Wilson, Warre, and others voting

[1] *P.D.*, N.S. iv. 225–6. See also T. D. Acland, *P.D.*, N.S. iv. 661; H. Bankes, *P.D.*, N.S. iv. 392.

[2] *Morning Chronicle*, 8 February 1821.

for it. Opposition votes on three motions were as low as eighteen, thirty, and eighty-one. Only two motions on legal reform came anywhere near success: Taylor's motion on delays in the court of chancery was defeated by only four votes, Mackintosh's amendment to the forgery punishment bill by six.

The comparatively small number of opposition motions and their reduced votes both went to indicate the extent of dismay and disillusion consequent on the failure of the initial attack, followed as it was by the withdrawal of Tierney from the leadership. Such opposition initiative as remained was unofficial initiative and centred on parliamentary reform. J. G. Lambton had drawn up his own draft bill in 1819 and circulated it among the party, where it received an enthusiastic welcome from the radicals.[1] Unfortunately, the dismay of the moderates was so great that Lambton soon repented having taken the matter on, and the onset of the queen's business had provided a decent excuse for dropping it, since, as Lambton himself pointed out, the house would not then have listened even to an announcement of the coming of the Messiah.[2] Now, however, he revived the issue, and moved on 17 April for a committee of the whole house to consider the state of the representation, announcing his intention, if the motion were carried, of bringing in his bill for equal electoral districts, household suffrage, and the vote for copyholders and leaseholders. Wilson, Hobhouse, Williams, and Wyvill spoke for the motion but moderate fears were not appeased: Abercromby described it as tending to revolution, Milton thought it would turn members into mere delegates, and Honywood was reluctant to accept it.[3] The disagreements were followed by fiasco. The flow of speakers dried up on the second day of the debate; Canning, instead of giving the expected set speech against reform, claimed that members were anxious for a division. In an empty house forty-three voted for the bill, fifty-five against it. A scene was only narrowly avoided when an angry Lambton, himself an absentee, returned to the house.

The alternative approach of gradualism was tried on 9 May, when Lord John Russell proposed a series of resolutions drawing,

[1] Wilson to Grey, 17 December 1819 (Wilson Papers, Add. MSS. 30123, f. 97); W. Lamb to Fitzwilliam, 17 January 1820 (Fitzwilliam F. 49 b); Lambton to Grey, 10 January 1820 (Grey).

[2] Lambton to Grey, 29 April 1820 (Grey).

[3] *P.D.*, N.S. v. 430, 438, 439.

attention to the complaints against the system of representation and to the need to give M.P.s to places greatly increased in size. His suggestion of a select committee to consider which boroughs should be enfranchised, and the best method of doing so, was supported in a brief discussion by the whig moderates. The motion was defeated by 124 votes to 155, a majority so slight that *The Times* found it 'a cheering prospect of the final issue'.[1]

This division confirmed the whig drift to reform, but it was not in itself enough to keep the parliamentary initiative with the whigs, and in this later part of the session that initiative passed to the radicals and the country gentlemen, each of these groups following up its own interests. The number of meetings held at the beginning of the year, as well as the holding of others on reform and economy after the session had begun, had given an indication of the impact of renewed agricultural distress. Dissatisfaction among the waverers was therefore marked. However, it was mainly confined to directly practical questions and was organized by the country gentlemen themselves.[2] On 7 March Gooch urged a committee on agricultural distress, and the government, as a conciliatory measure, agreed to set this up. Then on 27 March C. C. Western, who was as much a country gentleman as he was a whig, carried the repeal of the malt tax, only to be beaten on second reading, when ministers threatened resignation, brought in new supporters, and even managed to secure the votes of a few orthodox whigs, including Alexander Baring.[3] Finally Curwen, also a country gentleman whig, moved for the repeal of the agricultural horse tax and was successful by 141 to 113. These efforts were successful, or came near to being so, because they were independent initiatives and therefore more likely to gain support from waverers, even though the main body of the whigs voted for them almost automatically.

The radicals were the other pace-makers. In 1820 they had been intermittently active. The present discomfiture of the whigs now allowed them to organize a fully fledged campaign of continuous obstruction and divisions on estimates. Their aim,

[1] *The Times*, 11 May 1821.

[2] Lady Seymour, *Pope*, p. 235; Wilson to Lambton, 8 June 1821 (Lambton); A. Aspinall, *Charles Arbuthnot*, pp. 24–25.

[3] Broughton, ii. 144.

as Creevey put it, was to bring 'into public view, and to a direct vote, every single article of the public expenditure'.[1] It was not a campaign of which the whigs approved. Tavistock pointed out to Hume that

he could not but regret the necessity the honourable member was under of bringing all these minute details of the estimates before the house. This was a new feature in the proceedings of that house. They appeared to be deviating widely from the common and ancient usage of parliament; and he was not one of those who wished to see that house assume the functions of the executive government. . . .[2]

Yet the whigs put forward no alternative, so that a large section of opposition was drawn into the new attack.

The campaign began on 2 February with the navy estimates. Creevey moved an amendment to report progress on every grant. He gave the same treatment to the war department estimates a week later. The ordnance and army estimates were actively opposed and a series of amendments forced in the committee of supply. On 1 May in the report stage of the committee of supply Bennet announced the intention of discontinuing the discussions on different items in favour of a resolution on the whole amount. But the good intentions were premature, for the attack continued with a series of motions in May and was rounded off in June with resolutions on economy and retrenchment. For all the effort the only success was the defeat of a grant of £2,000 to General Desfourneaux. Yet the radicals saw a virtue in the harassing tactics, as asserting the powers of parliament and bringing the issue before the public. Creevey's own conclusion was

that a limited minority of members of the house of commons, when they have a cause to maintain, which is as irresistible in reason as it is in justice, who avail themselves of the invaluable forms of parliament, and who are supported by the sound and intelligent public opinion of the kingdom, will eventually succeed.[3]

The session, so harassing for ministers, if not for the reasons initially anticipated, closed on 11 July with Hume characteristically in the middle of a speech. There was every indication that the next session would be very similar. Though the ministry was

[1] Creevey, *Remarks*, p. 39.

[2] *P.D.*, N.S. v. 1417–18.

[3] Creevey, *Remarks*, pp. 54–55.

joined by the Grenvilles and Wellesley in December, the new recruits hardly provided a transfusion of the magnitude required. Moreover, agricultural distress remained as strong as ever, so that the 1822 session was prefaced by another campaign of county meetings, encouraged and supported once again by leading whigs. Yet it was far wider than the dimensions of party, drawing support from tory members and peers, for there was a general feeling, as Gooch pointed out to the Suffolk meeting, that 'this was an occasion on which men of all parties and descriptions, whig and tory, churchman and dissenter, landlord and tenant must unite'.[1] Fifteen counties met, half of them in January and February, to discuss a motley array of objectives, ranging from agricultural distress to parliamentary reform, which eleven of them endorsed, a more convincing demonstration of county opinion than any since 1780.[2] Bedford, in fact, claimed of reform that 'the feeling amongst the farmers and tradesmen in the country, in favour of it, is almost universal'.[3] The campaign also promised the added bonus of a boost to the opposition, though Lansdowne predicted that Boodle's would displace Brooks's as the headquarters of faction.[4]

There was little organization to exploit the situation. At the end of January Tierney had never seen town so empty, while Grey, casually consulted by Holland a few days before the meeting, urged that the opposition should remain silent on the address, wait for the measures of ministers and the effect of public opinion on the house, and then press for economy.[5] Similar views appear to have been held in London, the only known dissident being Bedford, who wanted active guerrilla warfare.[6] No amendment was moved, Lansdowne contenting

[1] *Ipswich Journal*, 2 February 1822.

[2] Norfolk: *Norfolk Chronicle* 19 January 1822. Surrey: *Morning Chronicle*, 19 February 1822. Lincolnshire: *Morning Chronicle*, 5 April 1822. Bedfordshire: *Traveller*, 22 April 1822. Kent: *Morning Chronicle*, 12 June. Devonshire: *Gloucester Journal*, 11 February 1822. Hertfordshire: *Morning Chronicle*, 2 February. Worcestershire: *Morning Chronicle*, 11 February. Huntingdonshire: *Morning Chronicle*, 6 April. Essex: *Morning Chronicle*, 8 May. Cheshire: *Morning Chronicle*, 3 January 1822. Middlesex and Cambridgeshire: *P.D.*, N.S. vii. 53. Shropshire: *Commons Journals*, 1822, p. 204.

[3] Bedford to Grey, 19 April 1822 (Grey).

[4] Lansdowne to Holland, 21 January 1822 (Holland).

[5] Tierney to Grey, 23 January 1822 (Grey); Holland to Grey, 15 January 1822 (Holland); Grey to Holland, 18 January 1822 (Grey).

[6] Bedford to Holland, 22 January 1822 (Holland).

himself with a few innocuous remarks in the lords, while Brougham in the commons made it clear that the whigs would concentrate on a motion on distress. This allowed Hume to step forward, make one of his dull speeches, and move an amendment on economy and retrenchment which drew eighty-nine votes, nearly all of them from the opposition, but including, too, Lethbridge and a tiny number of country gentlemen.[1]

The initial impression was bad, and Lambton considered that 'at present it is impossible to conceive anything more disunited than the opposition—many anxious to be active—but not knowing what to do—and having no one to point out to them the best mode'.[2] Yet hopes were high for Brougham's motion on distress of 11 February. This was an attempt to exploit for opposition purposes the rural discontent which in the previous session had been left to the country gentlemen. In an impressive speech Brougham reviewed the extent of the distress, and moved resolutions urging a reduction of taxes suitable to the danger threatening the agricultural classes, and a vote of money to afford relief to the distressed areas. The hoped-for support materialized, Davenport, Burrell, Curtis, Fane, Lawley, Boughey, and other waverers voting for the motion. It was the performance of the whigs which was disappointing. Tierney thought the motion too strong and did not vote, twenty-one whigs were shut out, according to Creevey, and Mackintosh considered that nearly forty others were influenced by Ricardo, who, though he voted for the motion, damned it with faint praise and professions of financial orthodoxy.[3] The total of 108 votes against 212 was a severe disappointment.

Reassured, the government announced its own plans for relief: a revival of the committee on agricultural distress, and authority to issue £4million worth of exchequer bills to afford relief to the agricultural areas. To the joy of the opposition these plans were soon discovered to be insufficient to satisfy the country gentlemen.[4] Discontent remained available for exploitation: unfortunately, the problem of how this should be done remained too. Before the beginning of the session Grey had suggested that

[1] Lambton to Grey, 6 February 1822 (Grey).
[2] Lambton to Grey, 11 February 1822 (Grey).
[3] Lady Seymour, *Pope*, p. 244; Maxwell, pp. 375–6.
[4] Wilson to Grey, 16 February 1822 (Wilson Papers, Add. MSS. 30124, f. 7).

whigs should move a remission of taxation to the extent of the sums appropriated to the sinking fund. Senior figures, such as Holland, were disposed to agree, and Tierney, long a stout defender of the sinking fund, was coming round to this point of view.[1] Some were anxious to go even further, proposing to rest satisfied with nothing less than ten or twelve millions in tax reductions, though others, such as Calcraft, were opposed to any interference with the sinking fund, or were at least anxious to see a clear surplus of revenue over expenditure.[2] Possibly because of these disagreements Grey's idea was not pressed in exactly the form proposed, but on 21 February Althorp moved a resolution that the tax relief proposed by ministers was not sufficient to satisfy the expectations of the people. This allowed the opponents of the sinking fund to air their views and Tierney to avow his change of heart. The motion was, however, heavily defeated: 126 votes to 234. A week later Calcraft moved for the gradual reduction of the salt duties. The opposition vote rose to 165 as more waverers were attracted, and twenty-six members, mostly waverers, but including a few pro-sinking-fund members of opposition who had voted against Althorp's motion, now swung round to vote for what amounted to the deduction of some half million pounds from the sinking fund they had supported in the abstract.[3] Government's majority was reduced to four. To proceed from the particular to the general, from the theoretical to the practical, was to attract more votes from the waverers.

The spirit and vigour of the opposition remained high. The radicals were less effective in their diversionary efforts. No support was forthcoming from the senior figures, enthusiasm for the detailed struggles and for Hume's tedious interference was flagging, and disillusion was spreading as enormous consumption of time yielded no return.[4] In addition, the opposition had dis-

[1] Lambton to Grey, 11 February 1822 (Grey); Holland to Grey, 11 February 1822 (Holland).

[2] J. R. G. Graham to Brougham, 3 March 1822 (Brougham); Ricardo, *P.D.*, N.S. vi. 271–2; Calcraft, *P.D.*, N.S. vi. 838; Holland to Grey, 11 February 1822 (Holland).

[3] The twenty-six included five members in the government fringe, four in the opposition fringe, and seventeen waverers. Taken by type of seat, eleven were county members, two from Welsh counties, one from a large borough, seven from medium ones, and five from small.

[4] C. W. Wynn to H. W. Wynn, 30 March 1822 (Wynn, 4816); Heron, p. 133; Maxwell, p. 376; J. C. Hobhouse in *P.D.*, N.S. xv. 692.

covered the key to the exploitation of the country gentlemen's discontent: concentration on the old programme of economical reform and retrenchment. On 1 March M. W. Ridley proposed to cut the navy estimates by £2,000 so as to force a reduction in the number of junior lords of the admiralty. A mass defection of waverers enabled him to carry the motion by 182 to 128. Rosslyn observed: 'the disgrace of ministers is certainly now complete and if the experience of the last seven or eight years were not decisive against the opinion I should have believed that no men could have submitted to the degradation of retaining their places under such circumstances.'[1] More submission proved necessary, for on 13 March Normanby continued the campaign with a motion to replace the joint postmaster-generalship by a one-man administration. This was defeated by only twenty-five votes. On 2 May Normanby transformed his motion into one for an address to the king to the same end. This was carried by 216 to 201.

Ministers had unsuccessfully tried to strengthen their position in March by circular notes.[2] The cabinet now decided to threaten resignation, and a meeting of official people was told that if the government was beaten on the next two opposition motions, it would retire.[3]

> 'This', thought Wynn, 'will ensure their being rejected, particularly as I am told our country gentlemen, though much out of humour, begin to be apprehensive of the mischief they are doing, but they will not be brought to their senses till they see a change of ministers which they will not like in consequence of their vacillation and following their own wise opinions.'[4]

The last card proved a trump. On 15 May T. B. Lennard moved for a committee to inquire into the expenses of the third category of the civil list, a motion to which the whigs attached high hopes. In his reply Castlereagh stressed that it would be treated as a question of confidence. Though the whigs waxed sarcastic at the threat its effect was obvious in a vote of 147 to 274. The next day Warre's motion on the expenses of the embassy to the Swiss cantons was defeated by similar figures. This success, thought

1 Rosslyn to Grey, 5 March 1822 (Grey).
2 The note is quoted in *Morning Chronicle*, 16 March 1822.
3 Mrs. Arbuthnot, *Journal*, i. 162–3.
4 C. W. Wynn to H. W. Wynn, 10 May 1822 (Wynn, 4816).

Wynn, 'has in great measure set us up again', and the effect continued to be felt when Brougham proposed a resolution that the influence possessed by the crown was unnecessary for the maintenance of its constitutional prerogatives and destructive of the independence of parliament.[1] The scythe was even less successful than the stiletto, and opposition secured only 101 votes, ministers 216. Finally, on 28 June, Calcraft revived the popular issue of the salt tax repeal, which had seemed likely to be carried on a second attempt.[2] The government's majority increased from four to twelve.

The impact of the threat of resignation can be shown by the type of member voting. For this purpose the listed votes for the three most successful opposition motions on either side of the threat have been examined.

Motion	*Category of member* Govt. Fr.	Waverer	Oppn. Fr.	Oppn.	Total[3]
Calcraft (28 Feb.)	5% (8)	19% (33)	13% (23)	63% (107)	171 (171)
Ridley (1 March)	8% (14)	28% (51)	11% (20)	53% (97)	182 (183)
Normanby (2 May)	3% (6)	23% (51)	18% (40)	56% (126)	223 (227)
Lennard (15 May)	1% (2)	7% (10)	17% (26)	75% (111)	149 (151)
Warre (16 May)	..	7% (10)	20% (29)	73% (103)	142 (143)
Brougham (24 June)	..	1% (1)	13% (15)	86% (95)	111 (111)

The number of votes from opposition and its fringe remained consistently high. The vote from the waverers slumped heavily as alarms spread.

The lesson of a session in which the ministers had been humiliated, buffeted, and discredited, but not displaced, was reinforced by two further factors, the progress of reform, and the attitude of the king. Reform had had a most successful session. The experience of the previous year had indicated that only Lord John Russell's moderate reform stood any chance, and discussion was confined to his proposals. On 25 April he moved a general resolution that the state of the representation required the most serious consideration of the house. The number voting

[1] C. W. Wynn to H. W. Wynn, 21 May 1822 (Wynn, 4816).

[2] Rosslyn to Grey, 5 March 1822 (Grey).

[3] The second column in brackets consists of the total listed in Hansard, including those not classified in the columns.

against it was larger than in the previous year at 269, but the number in its favour, 164, was the largest ever recorded except on Pitt's motion of 1785. This reflected gains on three fronts. Sections of county opinion began to turn to reform as a device which would increase the number of county representatives and the control of agricultural opinion on parliament.[1] Whigs and mellowing Westminster radicals were drawing together, thus brightening the prospects for a moderate measure. Finally, their lack of success in parliament confirmed whig dispositions to reform. The economical reformers had always advanced patronage as the explanation of ministerial majorities; now research, both published and private, supplemented this with another. It brought out clearly ministerial dependence on Scotland and the small boroughs impervious to public opinion.[2]

For others such academic diligence was unnecessary: parliament's unresponsiveness had been graphically demonstrated. Milton, Grenfell, Alexander Baring, Lord Holland, Thanet, Lord William Bentinck, N. W. R. Colborne, Sir Thomas Baring, Charles Pelham, and the Duke of Devonshire, all now came out for reform, after having opposed it or maintained a tactful silence up to this point.[3] At the same time T. W. Coke and Tavistock, both old reformers, announced that they would not vote for a whig government which did not take up reform.[4] All this strengthened the drift to a more radical position, and created a situation in which the great bulk of the whig party was actively favourable to reform. Obstacles important earlier were either largely removed or attentuated. Grey commented:

> after the declarations of the Dukes of Bedford and Grafton, King, Albemarle &c &c on the subject of parliamentary reform and the feeling which it is producing through the country, it is in vain to think that any party looking for its strength to public opinion, either

[1] See Lethbridge in *P.D.*, N.S. viii. 1286.

[2] *An Alphabetical List of the Commons House of Parliament*, London, 1822, p. 22; *An Exposition of the British House of Commons as at present Constituted*, London, 1823, p. 38; Fitzwilliam to Grey, 24 March 1822 (Grey).

[3] Milton: *Globe and Traveller*, 24 January 1823; Grenfell: *P.D.*, N.S. iv. 223–4; A. Baring: *P.D.*, N.S. iv. 226 and *Morning Chronicle*, 15 January 1821; Holland: *Traveller*, 13 January 1821; Thanet: *Traveller*, 19 January 1821; Bentinck: *P.D.*, N.S. viii. 1148; Colborne: ibid.; Baring: *The Times*, 3 March 1822; Pelham: *Morning Chronicle*, 28 March 1823; Devonshire: Buckingham and Chandos, *Memoirs of the Court of George IV*, London, 1859, i. 116.

[4] *Norfolk Chronicle*, 27 January 1822; *Traveller*, 6 February 1821.

in or out of office can go on without taking some decisive measure upon it. What this should be still requires much consideration, but you may be assured that any nibbling at reform will not now do.[1]

The whig party was already looking for its strength to public opinion, and events after the session made it clear they could look nowhere else. In August 1822 Castlereagh committed suicide, making imperative a reconstruction of the administration, in which the only possible replacements were Canning or an unlikely choice of the whigs. There was also the possibility of a complete reconstruction, particularly if the king blocked Canning. Holland pointed out to Grey that an offer to the whigs was remotely possible and that he should be prepared with an answer.[2] He also took the precaution of writing to Lansdowne in the same terms.[3] Grey's conditions were already formulated: 'a complete change of system, both foreign and domestic'.[4] Though he thought that such a condition would end all further negotiation, he was prepared to outline his terms. These were the same as the conditions he had stipulated in 1820, with the new addition of a commitment to parliamentary reform. Reflection, consultation, and the events of the year, had convinced him that, given public temper and whig pledges, the party must demand the power of doing something. This, he thought, should not fall short of Russell's plan.[5] Holland, who was now in favour of doing as much as possible when in office, agreed with the new commitment.[6] The terms on which the whig party would take office under Grey's leadership had finally been worked out. They foreshadowed closely those on which Grey was to insist in 1830. Then they were accepted, but in August 1822 they were not even aired publicly, for Liverpool's anxiety was solely to persuade the king to accept Canning. When this was accomplished all hope of change passed.

Canning's accession to office was, although this went unobserved at the time, the end of the period of political uncertainty, which had lasted from 1820. Everything had conspired

[1] Grey to Holland, 9 February 1822 (Grey).

[2] Holland to Grey, 18 August 1822 (Holland).

[3] Holland to Lansdowne, 23 August 1822 (Lansdowne).

[4] Grey to Holland, 21 August 1822 (Grey).

[5] Ibid.

[6] Holland to Grey, 11 February and 26 August 1822 (Holland). Brougham's terms were similar: H. Brougham, *Life and Times*, ii. 447–8.

to weaken the government. The king had quarrelled violently with his ministers in 1820 and for most of 1821 was on very bad terms with Liverpool. Ministers had disagreed among themselves, and for much of the period Peel and Canning were out of office. The ministers were so weak as to be compelled to call on the Grenvilles and Wellesley in December 1821, and to be anxious, though unable, to bring in Canning. All this had availed the whigs nothing. The king had shown his determination 'to have recourse to the devil himself rather than to a whig'.[1] A weak ministry had neither broken up nor turned to them. This was not serious, for Grey had from the first disliked any prospect of power on these terms, writing in April 1820:

whatever may be the ill humour and dissatisfaction that prevail between the king and his ministers, it does not appear to me at all likely that they should proceed the length, of having a separation between them. I am sure a change of administration to be produced by such causes, is not at all to be desired by us. Indeed, though they might involve us in very embarrassing intrigues and negociations, it seems to me hardly possible they should end in bringing us into office. Nothing but a strong expression of public opinion calling for a complete change of system can have this effect.[2]

The real set-back to the whigs came with the demonstration that even a strong expression of public opinion could have little effect on their fortunes. Public opinion, though strongly voiced, had hardly influenced the house. The waverers had declined to give anything more than occasional support to the whigs and their reluctance to bring down the government had been repeatedly demonstrated.

The policy of the last seven years, direct onslaught on a despised administration, had thus reached stalemate at a time when its prospect of success had seemed brightest. The possibility of its ultimate success, which had for so long kept intermittent hopes alive, was shown to be an illusion. It was a moment for agonizing reappraisal. Grey despaired and began to withdraw from politics. Lansdowne, who had early on been convinced that no administration could be formed on what he called 'a narrow party basis', concluded that new connexions

[1] Grey to Wilson, 24 December 1820 (Grey).

[2] Grey to Holland, 12 April 1820 (Grey); Grey to Fitzwilliam, 6 December 1820 (Milton).

were necessary.[1] A large section of the party had already turned to parliamentary reform or to economical reform. Had the situation been prolonged, the more radical posture taken up from 1820 onwards would undoubtedly have hardened. It was at this point, however, that the pattern began to change, and the whigs to turn eagerly to new expedients and new policies that might replace those which had failed so badly.

[1] Lansdowne to Grey, 12 June 1820 (Grey); Lansdowne to Holland, 25 August 1822 (Holland).

VIII

DECLINE · 1823–1827

THE apparent continuity of the Liverpool administration disguises a change so extensive as to give the impression that two ministries accidentally had the same head. After 1822 relaxations of protection, the navigation laws and the corn laws, an active concern for economy, new departures from the continental alliance, and a more liberal policy in Ireland, all combined with the lifting of distress to create an increasingly liberal atmosphere. The whigs, so violently opposed to the administration since the end of the war, mellowed and even began to support government measures. At the same time, with Grey withdrawing, Lansdowne failing to take his place, and Brougham declining authority in the commons, decisive leadership was lacking and party ties tended to relax. Thus a new pattern of politics began to emerge, with the old type of party clashes disappearing. The whigs dated new beginnings in Ireland from Wellesley's appointment, but the more general changes from Castlereagh's suicide and the introduction of Canning, and though symptoms are found earlier this change of personnel does provide a convenient boundary stone.

Naturally the change was a gradual one and government–opposition hostility died away only slowly. It was, however, increasingly confined to certain specific topics rather than shown in session-long clashes. Hence it can be reviewed by issues rather than years. Only initially did conflict take the old pattern, with a clash on Spain. There King Ferdinand had been forced to grant a constitution, but the continental allies were known to be threatening invasion through the agency of France. In face of this, Grey was for an energetically independent policy on the part of the British government and urged a declaration to the holy allies:

> your principle is unjust, and subversive of the independence of nations. Your attempt, if it succeeds, must bring Spain under the

influence and power of France. We not only cannot approve but must resist measures founded on such principles and leading to such consequences. If you go to war therefore you must expect to find England not a member of the confederacy, but the ally of Spain.[1]

But though calling for energy he declined to come to London for the beginning of the session, and when Holland urged him to communicate with those peers most likely to be active in the lords, Ellenborough, Lansdowne, and Carnarvon, he did not do so.[2] To Holland he urged that the party should await ministerial explanations but make its own pro-Spanish attitude perfectly clear.[3] In the commons Brougham, whose views on Spain were almost equally strong, was determined to move an amendment. Holland, Mackintosh, and Abercromby encouraged him, but not all were agreed. Tierney was reluctant, others doubted the country's ability to make war, Althorp refused to come up for an amendment, and some, including Milton, were flatly opposed to anything which could be construed as urging the government to war.[4]

Brougham adhered to his intentions, but when the address was discovered not to mention neutrality and the mover spoke more favourably on Spain than had been expected, it was decided on the spot to withdraw the amendment. Brougham contented himself with a strong speech urging ministers to announce that they were ready to support Spain, and excused the withdrawal as producing a unanimous demonstration of opinion which would strengthen the government's hand.[5] Fortuitously, it also averted whig differences, though not for long. Grey remained warlike and found strong support; Lambton, for example, was for 'vindicating insulted honour, invaded rights, inflicted injuries and independence menaced', and regarded war as the only remedy if negotiation failed.[6] Wilson too was for a cut-price war, telling his Southwark constituents that Britain had the opportunity to enable Spain and Greece to get 'truly

[1] Grey to Holland, 5 January 1823 (Grey).

[2] Holland to Grey, 9 January 1823 (Holland).

[3] Grey to Holland, 22 January and 2 February 1823 (Grey).

[4] Brougham to Grey, 5 February 1823 (Brougham); Althorp to Milton, 3 February 1823 (Milton); Milton to Brougham, 2 February 1823 (Brougham).

[5] *P.D.*, N.S. viii. 48; *Globe and Traveller*, 3, 4, and 5 February 1823; Brougham to Grey, 5 February 1823 (Brougham); Broughton, iii. 10.

[6] Lambton to Wilson, 9 March 1823 (Wilson Papers, Add. MSS. 30110, f. 142).

representative and liberal governments, at a comparatively trifling expense to us. We have only to put to sea 30 sail of the line, manned by our brave sailors, and commanded by our gallant naval officers—to repeal the foreign enlistment bill—and to export to the continent two or three thousand stand of arms, to secure these effects.'[1] Some whigs were even anxious to propose a larger increase in the navy than the government itself desired.[2] But though this majority opinion was shared by Brougham, Denman, Macdonald, and Althorp, others, including Milton, Ricardo, Baring, and Denison, were pacific, and a few sat on the fence with Newport.[3] As a result Russell observed: 'we do nothing but abuse one another—the violent laugh at the moderate and the moderate look grave at the violent.'[4]

Confidence was still expressed in ministers. Their intentions were not, indeed, clear, but probably the main reason for this whig course was that it avoided airing party differences. On 27 March, when ministers proposed an adjournment to 10 April, they heard some warlike declamation by Hamilton and Macdonald but they were not formally opposed. When the commons reassembled Canning announced the French invasion of Spain and the English policy of neutrality. Many whigs felt betrayed, but even Grey had to admit that it was now rather late to intervene effectively. All that could be done was to raise a public subscription to buy arms for Spain and to move the repeal of legislation which prevented British subjects' enlisting.[5] The only advantage accruing to the whigs was that of being able to break their silence, by urging all help to Spain short of overt war, and retrospectively criticizing the policies which had led up to the invasion. But these criticisms could be and were met with the fatal question: would the whigs have gone to war?

Retrospective criticism was energetically pressed home after the adjournment. Grey claimed that firmness from the first would have averted war, while Brougham, shifting the emphasis, argued that to prepare for war would be to preserve peace. On

[1] *The Times*, 12 February 1823.
[2] Holland to Grey, 18 February 1823 (Holland).
[3] See *P.D.*, N.S. viii. 622.
[4] Russell to Brougham, 23 March 1823 (Brougham).
[5] *P.D.*, N.S. viii. 870; Heron, pp. 146–7.

24 April Ellenborough moved an address to the prince regent arguing that the course pursued by ministers had not been calculated to support the honour and best interests of the British people. Stressing that he was not concerned with the issue of peace or war at the present moment, he went on to claim in his resolutions that 'a more prompt, decisive, and unequivocal policy would, under all the circumstances of France and of Europe, have afforded the best hopes of preventing the commencement of a war, in which we cannot but apprehend that increasing dangers may, at no remote period, and under circumstances of accumulated difficulty, compel this country to engage'.[1] Preaching the same sermon, Grey argued: 'When the "monarchical principle" was once established—when liberty was driven from the continent—was it to be supposed that she would remain unassailed in this her last asylum? Would the despots of Europe tolerate the bitter reproaches of the free press of England, or the unshackled discussions of her independent parliament?'[2] A similar motion, with the same arguments, was introduced by Macdonald in the commons four days later. Stuart-Wortley moved an astute amendment expressing delight that England was not involved in war. Now that the fatal question had been asked, prominent waverers, such as Bankes, supported the amendment, together with many others in the opposition or its fringes, such as De Crespigny, Maberly, and Littleton. Brougham called on Macdonald to withdraw his motion, arguing that the house had unanimously condemned the French attack and the amendment contained no approval of the negotiations. But withdrawal became rout when Canning and ministerial members insisted on a division and obliged opposition members to vote in their lobby. The amendment received 372 votes with only twenty against. Militants in both houses tried to keep the discussion alive, Grey with a series of questions on Spain and a motion for papers, Palmer with a motion on the last day of the session for the instructions sent to the ambassador in Madrid. Both were obviously the nostrums of mere sections and the second was negatived without discussion or division. A gratified C. W. Wynn observed: 'our session has certainly been on the whole a triumphant one and the

[1] *P.D.*, N.S. viii. 1194.
[2] *P.D.*, N.S. viii. 1239.

opposition have lost ground by their absurd Spanish fever with which they tried to infect the country but wholly failed.'[1]

If one fault of the whig opposition was an inability to see what was well, another was to leave it alone when a matter of principle was at stake. They were reluctant to embody their criticisms of the government's Spanish policy in an amendment at the opening of the next session, for, as Holland pointed out, 'this must practically convey a censure on ministers for not making war or an exhortation now to make it, and public opinion would certainly not support, perhaps the case would hardly bear, either of these measures'.[2] Holland, therefore, contented himself with pointing out that there was no cause for congratulation on the government's Spanish policy. In the commons a more difficult situation developed when C. C. Western threatened to move his own amendment. This compelled Brougham to take a firmer stand, attacking both the continental alliance and the congratulations on non-involvement embodied in the address. Western was satisfied and did not propose his amendment. Nevertheless, on 17 February Nugent, who had been to Spain to serve in the army, moved for papers and censured the conduct of ministers. His motion, receiving little support within the party, was defeated by 171 against a meagre thirty. A further motion by Lord John Russell was negatived without division.

The successful French occupation of Spain brought to the fore another question with which the whigs had long been concerned, that of Spanish South America. Their sympathy for the cause of independence reflected both their desires for the encouragement of liberal and independent governments and the urgings of the commercial members of the party. The threat that failing Spanish resources would now be supplemented by those of the holy alliance made the question an immediate one The initiative within the party was taken by Lansdowne, who at the beginning of the 1824 session drew up a motion for the recognition of the independence of the South American republics as a guarantee against renewed Spanish efforts. The only doubts, and they were querulous ones, came from Grey, who considered that the motion was

[1] C. W. Wynn to H. W. Wynn, 8 July 1823 (Wynn, 4816).
[2] Holland to Grey, 26 January 1824 (Holland).

open to great objections. The parliamentary ground is clearly in favour of the government; and if there is any danger of its checking any disposition Canning may have to separate from the holy alliance, or of furnishing to those of his colleagues who differ from him in that matter, the means of throwing greater difficulties in his way, it is worse than useless.[1]

Grey also argued that if, as Canning had previously claimed, England had no right to stop Spain from trying to get the colonies back, she had no right to prevent Spain's allies from helping her. Still, he was in favour of recognition, and the quibbles did not deter Lansdowne, who moved an address to the king on 15 March. This was defeated by thirty-four to ninety-five. Before Mackintosh could follow it by a similar motion in the commons, ministers announced that any armament from Spanish ports during the French occupation would be regarded as not being Spanish. Mackintosh promptly withdrew his motion, to show that there was no distrust of the government's intentions.[2] Doubts revived when no action on recognition followed, and Mackintosh returned to his theme on 15 June when presenting the London petition for recognition of South America. Like Lansdowne he argued that the colonies were in fact independent already, and claimed, in words later echoed by Canning, that it was important 'to prevent the dictators of Europe from becoming the masters of the new world; to re-establish some balance of opinions and force, by placing the republics of America, with the wealth and maritime power of the world, in the scale opposite to that of the European allies'.[3] Neither this, nor Lansdowne's demands that the government should reveal its intentions, had any effect. It was not until January of the following year that Canning recognized some of the colonies, and then indirectly, by the negotiation of commercial treaties. Nevertheless, Lord King rose in the lords to claim that 'they had given an advice to ministers, which, though at first opposed and neglected, had at last prevailed. As ministers had thus come round to the opinions of opposition, he hoped it would not be the last time that he should have to congratulate them on their docility.'[4]

[1] Grey to Holland, 10 March 1824 (Grey).

[2] *P.D.*, N.S. x. 1394.

[3] *P.D.*, N.S. xi. 1392.

[4] *P.D.*, N.S. xii. 18. But others were puzzled: see Tierney to Grey, 19 January 1825 (Grey).

Foreign policy was succeeded as an issue by inevitable Ireland. Hostilities between government and opposition had been suspended on Wellesley's appointment as lord-lieutenant, and in the 1822 session the opposition to an Irish insurrection act had been minimal. But Plunket's activities as attorney-general in Ireland soon revived discontent. After a Dublin theatre riot, in which Orangemen threw wood and bottles at Wellesley's box, Plunket first indicted the rioters and then, failing to convince a grand jury, brought an *ex-officio* information against them. This tactic angered the whigs, much as they disapproved of rioting Orangemen. In 1823 Burdett and a small handful of radicals walked out when Plunket moved the catholic question. When, however, Brownlow proposed a motion charging the Irish attorney-general with harsh and oppressive measures, the whigs faced serious embarrassment. Opposed on principle to *ex-officio* informations, they were not anxious to vote with the ultra protestants. Duncannon wrote anxiously to Grey, and Lansdowne suggested moving either the previous question or a counter-motion for an inquiry into the grand jury as a means of getting round the difficulty. The problem had still not been resolved the day before the motion, and an anxious meeting that night provided no firm decision. The position was saved only on the very day of the motion.[1] Milton and Brougham then announced that the motion was too strong, and Brownlow agreed to withdraw it, on the understanding that a motion for inquiry into the conduct of the sheriff of Dublin would be substituted. This was moved by Burdett on 21 April and carried by a union of whigs and ultra protestants, 219 to 185.

The overspill of the hostility generated by this incident also promoted opposition to the renewal of the Irish insurrection act. Althorp proposed an amendment binding the house to take into consideration the whole state of Irish laws and administration with a view to their reform. This was defeated by 82 votes to 162. Then vigorous opposition was offered to the later stages of the renewal bill, particularly with Sir Henry Parnell's powerful speech for a secret committee on the Irish disturbances. On 19 June Devonshire, a rare speaker, proposed an inquiry into

[1] Duncannon to Grey, 26 February 1823 (Grey); Lansdowne to Brougham, n.d. [April 1823] and 9 April 1823 (Brougham); Bedford to Holland, n.d. [April 1823] (Holland).

the state of Ireland, while on 26 June Brougham in the commons moved to refer the Irish petition, which complained of inequalities in the administration of justice, to the grand committee for the court of justice. Though defeated, both motions served warning that the honeymoon with the Irish administration was over.

The 1824 session saw only domestic bickerings. Opposition to the insurrection act was minor and partial, though Darnley in the lords and Althorp in the commons moved for inquiries into the state of Ireland. It was not until 1825 that the activities of the new catholic association made Ireland a major subject of discussion in parliament. No amendment was moved to the address on Ireland, but Althorp pointed out to Brougham: 'we ought to abuse them through thick and thin for not saying anything about the catholic question in the king's speech, but abstain from saying anything or committing ourselves on foreign politics or on any other subject. . . . I assume that we are all agreed to make Ireland the great object of our attack.'[1] The subject was in any case to be forced on them by the government's proposal to suppress the catholic association. The threat produced a situation in which, as Lambton observed, 'there seems to be a greater chance of warmth and violence than I have seen for some time'.[2]

While some whigs, such as Hutchinson, Fitzgerald, and Brougham himself, admired the association and its achievement in uniting and pacifying Ireland, others feared this mass organization whose pressures affronted many principles dear to whigs. Spring Rice warned Lansdowne:

> The whole echaufaudage of the catholic association is complete and they may raise behind it any building their foremen masons chuse to erect. . . . It may be said for the first time that all catholic Ireland is organised from Cape Clear to the Giant's Causeway. . . . The general election will be the signal for bringing all their force into play. We shall see in every county and city candidates starting on in this new interest. . . . Tenants will be brought up against their landlords. . . . This in most places will make the separation between the upper and lower orders greater than ever.

He believed the whole association to be inconsistent with the existence of civil government.[3] Lansdowne echoed Rice's dis-

[1] Althorp to Brougham, n.d. [1824] (Althorp).
[2] Lambton to Grey, 9 February 1825 (Grey).
[3] Spring Rice to Lansdowne, 8 December 1824 (Lansdowne).

approval as well as his metaphors; Ellenborough and several fringe members, like North, Grenfell, and Sebright, supported suppression; and Tierney, though less hostile, still feared to link the whigs with the association in the public mind.[1] Yet he admitted: 'as far as I am able to collect the opinion of our friends it is in favour of the proceedings of the catholic association.'[2]

The great majority of the party still argued that to put down the association was to remove the symptoms of Ireland's malady while leaving the cause, the postponement of justice to that unfortunate country, untouched. They could also agree that the real danger was not the association but catholic unity. The association was merely an outward and visible sign, which could be suppressed but would simply reappear in one guise after another until civil liberties were removed completely. Partial measures were useless, effective ones dangerous.

On 10 February Goulburn moved for leave to bring in a bill to amend the acts dealing with unlawful societies in Ireland. After a five-day debate, in the largest vote and the clearest division of opinion for some time, 123 voted against the first reading and 278 in favour. This last figure included a few whigs such as North, Grenfell, and Sebright. The fight was sustained with a motion by Brougham to hear representatives of the association before suppression, a motion to delay the third reading, and opposition to passage of the bill. In the lords Grey, Holland, and Carnarvon also urged that the association be heard by the house, and the third reading was opposed. Defeat was inevitable, but it was the party's most effective fight for years.

There were other subjects of opposition in this period. It would have been surprising had so many sessions passed without them. Efforts to change the criminal law continued in Mackintosh's resolutions for relaxation and Williams's motion on delays in chancery; Abercromby proposed amendments to the representation of Edinburgh; Kennedy and Williams urged changes in Scottish jury legislation; and the extension of the alien act was opposed in seven divisions when Peel brought it forward in 1824. These sporadic stirrings hardly constituted opposition of

[1] Lansdowne, *P.D.*, N.S. xii. 136; Ellenborough, *P.D.*, N.S. xii. 942; North, *P.D.*, N.S. xii. 400; Grenfell, *P.D.*, N.S. xii. 433–4; Sebright, *P.D.*, N.S. xii. 577; Tierney to Grey, 17 February 1825 (Grey).

[2] Tierney to Grey, 19 February 1825 (Grey).

the old type. They were confined to a few specific issues, the divisions were small, and the opposition vote only rarely exceeded 100. All failed, though some were countered by concessions. The pressure for law reform was easing as Peel took up the work himself, and in February 1824 Williams's motion on delays in chancery was withdrawn after Peel announced that ministers would appoint a commission. On the second reading of the alien act in 1824 Canning announced that this was the last time the bill would be necessary.

As important as the absence of issues was the decline of popular pressure on the house. The beginning of 1823 saw a campaign of county meetings as large as any hitherto mounted. This had its origins in a new reform movement in Yorkshire, where, in August 1822, a meeting of leading whigs resolved that reform had become a matter of urgent necessity and decided to appoint a committee to organize a county meeting.[1] This committee met again in November, Milton, despite his father's disapproval, taking the chair. It decided to communicate with other counties on the pattern of the Yorkshire association. It is possible that the communication extended to nearly a score of counties, though only two tips of the iceberg broke surface, in Devon and Lincolnshire.[2]

The Yorkshire meeting was the largest and most impressive of the resulting series. Between 5,000 and 7,000 attended, and the petition for reform was signed by 17,083 people, including two-thirds of the freeholders.[3] In Surrey and Hertfordshire whig peers came out actively for reform, while ten other counties met for the same purpose, and two others demanded economy. Despite these successes the campaign was a serious disappointment, not because of a failure to hold meetings, though both Grey and Lambton gave up after struggles with apathy in their areas, but because some of those meetings which were held escaped from whig control.[4] In Norfolk Coke's resolutions were defeated and an amendment by Cobbett was carried, demand-

[1] *Leeds Mercury*, 24 August 1822.

[2] *Leeds Mercury*, 7 December 1822, asserted that fifteen or sixteen counties were to press for reform. Baines, the editor, was a member of the committee appointed to correspond with other counties. See *The Times*, 9 January 1823.

[3] *Globe and Traveller*, 24 January 1823.

[4] M. W. Ridley to Grey, 14 November 1822 (Grey); Lambton to Grey, 7 and 15 December 1822 (Grey).

ing, among other radical recipes, investigation into the courts of law, reduction of the size of the army, sale of the crown lands, adjustment of the national debt, and suspension of all distraints for rent.[1] In Surrey also Cobbett's resolutions, seconded by H. G. Bennet, were carried as an amendment.[2] Though Cobbett was defeated in Bedfordshire and Hampshire, similar demands were carried in Herefordshire and Cambridgeshire, while Somerset accepted Hunt's resolutions for universal suffrage. The blow to whig self-esteem was severe.[3] The growing discontent had initially seemed to offer promising campaign material and Rosslyn even thought it might shake the government: now the meetings and the diversity of petitions had ruined this prospect.[4] Lansdowne commented at the beginning of the session: 'although there is a pretty general dissatisfaction with the government pervading the country there is so much wrong-headedness and jealousy of one class against another mixed up with it, that it would require much more skill than anybody seems able or willing to exert, to direct it to any good purpose.'

The session bore out Lansdowne's predictions, for efforts on economy were brief and perfunctory: there was little left to say on the subject and experience suggested that less could be accomplished against ministerial majorities. Reform faced a similar stalemate. Russell changed his tactics by moving on 24 April a resolution that the state of the representation required the serious consideration of the house, only to have his effort followed by a discussion with no new ideas, little fire, and a vote, at 169, nearly identical with that of the previous year. On 2 June Hamilton's resolutions on the state of the Scottish county representation had a fuller house than they had achieved in 1822 but were still defeated, by 117 votes to 152. These disappointing results were the end of both campaigns. Distress, the main source of pressure for economy and reform, began to lift after the first months of 1823 and even the sharp set-back of 1825–6 hardly revived it as a political force. Apart from a few meetings on the corn laws, assessed taxes, and catholic emancipation, county meetings did not reappear until 1830.

[1] *Globe and Traveller*, 4 January 1823. [2] *The Times*, 11 February 1823.

[3] Lambton to Wilson, 9 January 1823 (Wilson Papers, Add. MSS. 30110, f. 120); Holland to Grey, 9 January 1823 (Holland).

[4] Rosslyn to Grey, 1 December 1822 (Grey).

[5] Lansdowne to Holland, 26 January 1823 (Holland).

With the fuel gone the car stalled. Lansdowne observed in 1825 that 'the prosperity of the country has driven reform almost out of the heads of the reformers'.[1] Whig interest diminished apace and the only reform motion in parliament was Russell's of April 1826, which revealed a vote fallen with public pressure: 123 to 247. In the field of economy the lack of pressure was supplemented by the replacement of Vansittart by Robinson as chancellor of the exchequer, an act which created new confidence in financial policy and dispositions to economize. Whig differences on the sinking fund also inhibited activity. Men like Calcraft, Parnell, and Lansdowne were not prepared to press tax reductions so far as to endanger the fund and there were occasional clashes in the house. On 8 March 1824, when Hume moved the reduction of the sugar duty, Bright, the opposition member for Bristol, opposed on the ground that the sinking fund had to be maintained. When Maberly moved the repeal of the assessed taxes on 3 March 1825, Calcraft opposed for the same reason. Thus opposition efforts on economy were few. In 1825 a grant of £6,000 for the Duke of Cumberland's child was energetically opposed, with some support from waverers bringing opposition votes as high as 113, 114, and 121, and ministerial majorities as low as 30, 38, and 49. In 1826, when ministers proposed to separate the offices of the president of the board of trade and the treasurer of the navy, giving both a ministerial salary, the whigs rallied against what Tierney described as 'so monstrous a job'. The battle, according to Tierney, was fought 'with perfect good humour' and 'without the least party bitterness', but the ministerial majority at eighty-seven votes to seventy-six was so low that the proposal was withdrawn.[2] Finally, in 1827, when the ministers proposed an extra grant to the Duke of Clarence, it was attacked by the bulk of the opposition, though Fitzgerald and Calcraft came out in favour of it. Together with a couple of motions by Calcraft this was the sum total of opposition attempts to secure economy. Hume was still active, instigating about half the total number of divisions on economy and tax reduction, while Maberly made repeated efforts to cut the assessed taxes. Neither could command much support from the main body of opposition, and

[1] Lansdowne to Holland, 17 January 1825 (Holland).
[2] Tierney to Holland, 10 April 1826 (Holland).

even their efforts were dilatory compared with those of 1821 and 1822.

Lack of issues and absence of public pressure meant dull politics. Complaints of this became frequent from 1823 onwards; Grey, for instance, saw the state of the country in 1824 as being 'as dull and monotonous as anything can well be conceived to be. There is no public question which excites, no public feeling which produces any sympathy, no public prospects which can engage one in future speculations.'[1] The number of divisions declined with the level of interest. From eighty-eight divisions in which government and opposition had clashed in 1822 the number dwindled to fifty-nine in 1823, fifty-six in 1824, twenty-nine in 1825, and twenty in 1826. The wide-reaching and deep political disagreements which had lasted since 1815 were gradually coming to an end.

In this climate opposition was bound to change its nature and lose its bitterness. The change was greatly accelerated because Canning and his liberal tory followers were putting themselves forward as mediators between government and public opinion and were attempting to respond to the new and more liberal public mood. The result was a new feature on the political scene: approbation and support for government policies from an opposition which felt that the principles it had long advocated were at last being put into effect. When Canning had been appointed to office in 1822 whig reactions had been mixed. Some considered that he would step into Castlereagh's shoes, by taking over his policies, and Allen, after long conversations with Canning, formed the opinion that he considered himself as directly opposed to the whigs.[2] These were not, however, majority opinions. Holland expected that Canning would try to conciliate both public opinion and opposition, while Brougham immediately speculated:

> Given Canning's hostility to reform, improvement, liberty generally and whigs personally—supposed his agreement with us on Irish and on foreign policy and the enmity of almost all his colleagues towards him—to find the course we should steer in order to aid him on the points of agreement, to increase his differences with his

[1] Grey to Wilson, 19 August 1824 (Grey). See also: Bedford to Grey, 15 February 1824 (Grey); *The Times*, 3 July 1823, 7 July 1825.

[2] Allen to Brougham, 3 September 1822 (Brougham).

colleagues, and not to commit ourselves on points of difference with him? My solution is 'abstinence' from needless attack for a while.[1]

The clash on Spain the following session appeared to belie these expectations, but the contradiction was superficial. A large section of opposition considered that Canning was in favour of a strong policy in respect of Spain but was being held back by the more reactionary elements in the cabinet.[2] It became an aim of policy, therefore, to help him and to try and distinguish between him and the rest of the government. Even in the later stages of the affair Brougham still declared

that when the minister for foreign affairs, rose and uttered sentiments which, as an Englishman, a statesman, and an orator, did him the highest honour . . . he observed, while those expressions were heard with delight by all who sat on the opposition side of the house—while the loudest expressions of gratification were heard . . . a 'death-like silence' was preserved by the gentlemen opposite—that the faculties of those who administered the government, and their various adherents and supporters appeared to sink into a 'dread repose' astounded, he supposed, at the liberality of the principles which they had so unexpectedly heard. . . .[3]

Opprobrium was reserved for the rest of the cabinet. Partial satisfaction in foreign policy was supplemented in this session by growing delight at economic and financial policy, and the budget particularly came in for high praise from men who were normally vigorous critics.[4] The result was a steady change in the tone of the house of commons. Milton, paying a rare visit, commented that

it was so long since he had attended the house, that he hardly knew by whom he was supported, or to whom he was opposed. . . . He contrasted with much gratification the policy by which ministers were now governed, with that on which they had formerly acted. He could not help feeling that the country had a new government—a government new in all its feelings, and in all its views on great public questions.[5]

[1] Holland to Grey, 23 December 1822 (Holland); Brougham to Lansdowne, 18 December 1822 (Lansdowne).

[2] See, for example, Wilson's view: 'Canning now stands high and backed by parliament and country united. . . . I have some good reason to believe that he has been sincere throughout': Wilson to Grey, 7 February 1823 (Wilson Papers, Add. MSS. 30124, f. 66).

[3] *P.D.*, N.S. viii. 899

[4] See, for example, *P.D.*, N.S. ix. 1420–1.

[5] *P.D.*, N.S. viii. 231.

Wynn too observed that he and the other ministers 'have only to sit quiet and blush with maidenly modesty at our own praises'.[1] The only sour note was a personal attack on Canning delivered by Brougham in a moment of anger.[2]

Since the following session was unblemished by major differences on foreign policy, except for South America, the flirtation continued more openly, with lavish praise of economic and financial policy, and Sir Robert Heron began to visualize opposition dwindling to nothing.[3] By 1825 the opposition was even beginning to claim the credit for having first proposed the measures now initiated by government, and though there were disagreements on the catholic association the growing importance of the catholic question itself helped to strengthen prevailing trends. It was clearly the major issue in politics, and it was also a subject on which the opposition and the more liberal section of the administration agreed most strongly. It is hardly surprising that opposition figures now began to urge publicly and privately an administration favourable to the catholics.[4] As a result of the importance of the catholic question even the 1826 election failed to drive the liberal ministers and their opposition suitors further apart. Instead, for the first time, the results of the election were very rarely recorded in terms of party gains or losses for government and opposition: observers concentrated on calculating the numbers of 'catholics' and 'anti-catholics'. In Peel's view there had never been an election less characterized by serious political differences bearing on the general policy of government.[5] If there was an issue in the election, it was the catholic question, and though its importance lost seats for the pro-catholics in England, it brought the supporters of emancipation, whether whig or ministerial, closer

[1] C. W. Wynn to H. W. Wynn, 11 March 1823 (Wynn, 4816). See also Heron, p. 148.

[2] *P.D.*, N.S. viii. 1091.

[3] Lansdowne in *P.D.*, N.S. x. 15–16; Baring in *P.D.*, N.S. x. 337; Parnell, *P.D.*, N.S. xi. 595–6; Hume, *P.D.*, N.S. xi. 597–8; Heron, p. 151.

[4] Lambton to Grey, 12 February 1825 (Grey), reports Burdett as saying 'he thought the main object ought to be to form an administration on the express basis of conceding the catholic claims. I said what without any stipulation on reform? He answered, "Certainly that is a secondary consideration." ' For more public declarations, see *P.D.*, N.S. xi. 720–1 and xii. 341.

[5] Peel to Wellesley, 1 July 1826 (Wellesley Papers, Add. MSS. 37304, f. 152). The result of the election was a loss of seats for pro-catholics in England and a gain in Ireland, making over-all a net loss: Heron, p. 161.

together. The same trend was strengthened by increasing whig support, in parliament and out of it, for Peel's legal reforms, and, at the end of 1826, by the whig approbation of the dispatch of troops to help the constitutional government in Portugal.

While this flirtation between the opposition and the liberal tories was developing, it was also clear that there was an increasing disenchantment between these same liberal ministerialists and the more conservative section of the government. Policy towards Spain and the continental alliance, South America, the catholic question, distress, and the corn laws, all provoked disagreements, some of them violent, within the administration. Since some of these divisions were known outside government circles, they encouraged the whigs to regard themselves as the supporters of Canning and his group against their obscurantist enemies. Public witness could soon be given to this situation: internal differences within the cabinet were supplemented by differences between it and some of its supporters in parliament. Open discontent centred on three particular issues, brought to the fore by a sudden new recession provoked by the collapse of the speculation of 1825. Currency, corn laws, and protection suddenly became important, and techniques for relieving the distress could probably be added as a fourth issue. The government's remedy for the speculation was to prohibit the country banks issuing notes under £5, a measure which affronted country bankers, their clients among the country gentlemen, and those currency reformers who saw inflation as a solution to distress. The government's solutions to the threatened food shortages were to take power to open the ports to corn at a fixed duty and to amend the corn laws. Finally, protection became an issue when Ellice, the member for Coventry, demanded a committee on the silk trade, since this had been injured by the government's switch from prohibition to protection. The pattern of voting against the government on these questions is shown in the table:[1]

	Govt.	Govt. Fr.	Waverer	Oppn. Fr.	Oppn.	Totals
Currency, 1826	13% (5)	8% (3)	23% (9)	10% (4)	46% (18)	39 (41)
Ellice's motion	3% (1)	7% (3)	34% (14)	12% (5)	44% (18)	41 (42)
Corn imports	10% (6)	10% (6)	35% (22)	8% (5)	37% (23)	62 (65)
Corn law, 1827	24% (13)	11% (6)	44% (24)	5% (3)	16% (9)	55 (78)
Edinburgh representation			5% (5)	9% (9)	86% (83)	97 (100)

[1] Since some members are not classified, they are left out of these calculations

Though the numbers involved are small, the distribution of support for the first four motions was very different from that of a more usual opposition vote, as represented by the division on Abercromby's motion on Edinburgh. Discontent was also wider than the figures suggest, for to vote against ministers was to take an unusually bold step. Moreover, the desertions of the country bankers and their clients on the small-notes bill, and of embattled country gentlemen on the corn measures, represent a reaction against the government's whole policy.[1] While the country had been prosperous this discontent had been silent. When distress returned in 1826 government supporters and waverers tended to blame it on the new policies. The Earl of Malmesbury, for example, declared 'old fashioned people like himself would say, that it proceeded from those principles of free trade lately introduced by his majesty's ministers'.[2] Tampering with the corn laws stirred all these prejudices, producing frequent denunciation of 'political economists'. T. S. Gooch said 'he was heartily sick of political economists altogether, and he wished them no further harm than that a clause should be inserted in the present bill, enacting that every vessel laden with foreign corn destined for this country should take back, instead of ballast, a cargo of political economists'.[3] It was attitudes such as these, the direct opposite in nearly every respect to his own views, which caused an angry Canning to declare in the commons:

I have not to learn that there is a faction in the country. . . . I should, perhaps, rather have said a sect, small in numbers and powerless in might, who think that all advances towards improvement are retrogradations towards jacobinism. These persons seem to imagine that, under no possible circumstances, can an honest man

and listed only in the final total in brackets. Their numbers are small, except on the 1827 corn law, which was debated in a new parliament, many of whose members were newly elected and hence outside the 1820–6 categories. The division classified in the table as 'currency' is on Baring's amendment to the promissory notes bill.

[1] The government minimized discontent on its corn importation measure by modifying it after introduction. Sir J. Brydges commented that at first he had felt 'with many other honourable members, that he would be called upon to give a vote, either against the intended proposition of his majesty's ministers (to support whom it was ever his desire), or against his own conviction'. Modification had ended his difficulty, *P.D.*, N.S. xv. 974. See also Broughton, iii. 133–4.

[2] *P.D.*, N.S. xv. 1057. See also Robertson in *P.D.*, N.S. xiv. 43.

[3] Curteis, *P.D.*, N.S. xvii. 178; Gooch, *P.D.*, N.S. xvii. 198.

endeavour to keep his country upon a line with the progress of political knowledge, and to adapt its course to the varying circumstances of the world.[1]

The discontent compelled the government to rely for support on a large section of opposition which now declined to exploit the situation to attack the government in the way it would have done in the past. When ministers proposed their currency measures Althorp reported: 'I hope the ministers will be able to carry their two measures but I do not think it at all sure, they appeared very weak in the house last night: I do not know how people will vote but the only people who like what they proposed, were about half the opposition.'[2] Had it been backed by the opposition the discontent of the country bankers could have endangered the government's measures. Though a section of opposition did disapprove of these measures, the main body supported them and Canning frankly acknowledged that opposition support had secured their passage.[3] Once again the opposition neither encouraged nor combined with the discontented, and Ellice congratulated himself that 'ministers were again last night in our hands and we carried them against the attacks of their friends'.[4] In the lords too the measures passed for the same reason, even though Grey and Bedford took a different view from that of the main body of their party. Lord Limerick warned:

> He would call upon his majesty's ministers to look upon those by whom they were supported, and those by whom they were opposed. Their household troops, as he might call them, in which number he included himself, were voting against them, and his majesty's ministers were found leaguing themselves with his majesty's opposition.[5]

Despite their experience in 1826, the government still pressed ahead in 1827 with a proposal to alter the corn laws. Embattled

[1] *P.D.*, N.S. xiv. 854.

[2] Althorp to Milton, 11 February 1826 (Milton).

[3] A. G. Stapleton, *Canning*, p. 232; Duke of Wellington, *Despatches, Correspondence and Memoranda of Field Marshall Arthur, Duke of Wellington*, London, 1877, iii. 116–17; see also Huskisson to Grenville, 9 March 1826 (Huskisson Papers, Add. MSS. 38747, f. 208).

[4] Ellice to Lambton, 3 May [1826] (Lambton).

[5] *P.D.*, N.S. xv. 1068. See also the very similar declaration of Alderman Heygate in *P.D.*, N.S. xiv. 393.

country gentlemen again opposed any change and ministers again had to rely on the votes of that majority of opposition which was in favour of liberalization. Opposition members gloated and government supporters complained that the measures passed only because the votes of opposition were cast for the government, particularly in the most severe test, Lord Clive's resolutions, which ministers survived by 229 to 160.[1]

Similar events followed over other questions.[2] Both country gentlemen and mercantile members among the government's supporters were urging it to issue exchequer bills to relieve distress. On 23 February Alderman Wilson presented a petition from London merchants praying for relief, and Bright, John Smith, Baring, Sumner, and Manning, representing a wide range of opinions, urged issue. Canning, influenced by Liverpool's flat refusal to consider the expedient, rose to announce that if parliament wanted an issue of bills it would have to put power in other hands.[3] This made it probable that Wilson's motion of 28 February for the issue of bills would become a crucial test for the government, particularly if, as seemed likely, many of the opposition would support the motion.[4] It survived the test by authorizing the bank to issue credit on receipt of goods. Wilson withdrew his motion and the opposition declined to drive the issue to a vote, a complaisance which Croker felt had saved the government from defeat.[5]

The government's proposal to take power to allow temporary imports of grain caused an angry discontent later in the session. Tierney reports that 'all the landed interest are in a terrible commotion and they speak very confidently of beating ministers in the lords if they should fail, as I think they certainly will, in the house of commons'.[6] These years, then, brought out a new concept of opposition, that of 'his majesty's opposition', one which had taken it upon itself to support a section of the

[1] Knatchbull, *P.D.*, N.S. xv. ii. 197: 'those who composed the majority by whose vote the resolutions were carried on a former evening, were members in the interest of government, aided by members who composed what should be the opposition.' See also Hobhouse in *P.D.*, N.S. xvi. 1158–9 and Rosslyn to Grey, 10 March 1827 (Grey).

[2] See, for example, Broughton, iii. 127.

[3] *P.D.*, N.S. xiv. 727.

[4] Tierney to Holland, 23 February 1826 (Holland).

[5] Tierney to Holland, 13 March 1826 (Holland); L. J. Jennings, *Croker*, i. 315–16.

[6] Tierney to Holland, 4 May 1826 (Holland).

administration. Baring told the chancellor of the exchequer at the beginning of the 1826 session that 'Opposition as a party was at present that which the right honourable gentleman had no cause to apprehend . . . at no period of modern times was there less of party feeling evinced in the discussion of matters proposed by ministers.'[1] Tierney, too, claimed:

> we are certainly to all intents and purposes, a branch of his majesty's government. Its proceedings for some time past have proved, that though the gentlemen opposite are in office, we are in power, the measures are ours, but all the emolument are theirs. . . . I think that government do want support. I never saw a session when they wanted it more . . . he would, without our support, have been long ago driven from his present honours. If we take away our support out he must go tomorrow.[2]

Privately the former whig leader now confessed that his only object was to support that branch of the administration whose principles he most approved.[3]

While this was the view of a clear majority, it was not unanimous. Althorp and Tavistock were suspicious of Canning.[4] A handful of old guard whigs, such as Bedford, Rosslyn, and Jersey, distrusted him personally and were horrified at the tendency to support him.[5] Grey never varied in his hostility. As late as 1825, when the songs of praise for Canning were ringing out, Grey wrote: 'If in some way or other his meanness is not exposed and punished it will be a bad example for all politicians. The only difference between him and Castlereagh seems to me to be that he can make brilliant speeches, and disguise with a hypocritical profession of better views, the same base policy.'[6] His own protectionist views on the corn laws and his scepticism about the prospect for carrying the catholic question by a combination of opposition members and liberal government supporters supplemented this dislike. Grey, therefore, asked the basic question preoccupying the party at this

[1] *P.D.*, N.S. xiv. 194.

[2] *P.D.*, N.S. xv. 145–6.

[3] Tierney to Holland, 13 March 1826 (Holland).

[4] D. Le Marchant, *A Memoir of John Charles, Viscount Althorp*, pp. 209–10; Camden, pp. 36 and 38.

[5] Bedford to Holland, 9 May 1826 (Holland).

[6] Grey to Holland, 3 February 1825 (Grey).

time, and answered it in a manner very different from that of the majority of his fellow whigs:[1]

What interest we can have in supporting him against his colleagues I really cannot conceive; doubting very much whether an administration purely of ultra tories, would be so mischievous, as the present motley government, by which an effectual opposition is prevented by the hope (as it appears to me the absurd hope) that liberal principles will ultimately prevail, while in the meantime the exclusion of the catholics is maintained, and even the adoption of right principles in some cases rendered useless by the weakness and inconsistency which this state of things inevitably produces in the measures that are taken for giving them effect.[2]

Yet Grey took no active part in politics from 1823 to 1825, spending the winters in Portsmouth for his wife's health, and existing 'Without a single occurrence to interest, or any society to engage or amuse me, vegetating from day to day without utility to myself or others, my blood stagnant, my mind torpid, and all the listlessness of advancing years increasing upon me from day to day.'[3] When he did resume a partial activity in 1826 his views were treated with some impatience by former friends.[4] He was clearly out of touch with the whole trend of the times.

This lesson was underlined by Holland, who pointed out to Grey the increasing convergence of opposition and the liberal section of the ministry, and warned him that only Lansdowne of the old leadership group was in accord with the new mood:

On trade and South America and I suppose corn bills he is in opinion if not nearer at least warmer with Huskisson &c &c than you or I who do not care about or perhaps understand such matters so much or so well. As Irishman as well as politician he considers catholic question yet more paramount to other considerations than most of our friends—such are in truth the only questions now at issue—and the great parties in parliament must ultimately be distinguished by their respective and opposite opinions on one or most of

[1] Grey to Wilson, 30 November 1823 (Grey); Grey to Holland, 28 August and 4 September 1825 (Grey).

[2] Grey to Ellice, 7 February 1827 (Ellice Papers, packet 11, National Library of Scotland).

[3] Grey to Wilson, 19 August 1824 (Grey).

[4] Tierney to Holland, 4 May 1826 (Holland): 'I am vexed to see our friend after professing to withdraw from all political activity availing himself of the very first opportunity to attack ministers by cooperating with Lord Malmesbury and the most violent of the tories for that purpose.'

these topics. In that case a jumble of *men* must ensure a liberal ministry with an intolerant court opposition, or an intolerant court ministry with a liberal opposition. . . . Now the question as personally affecting any of us old ones, and you in particular is this. Will you endeavour to accelerate or to retard, or will you leave entirely to chance and keep neutral and aloof from such a revolution of parties.[1]

Yet Holland's warning did prompt a definite transfer of the leadership to Lansdowne, a transfer effected with the full knowledge on both sides that it might be the prelude to new arrangements with the government. Grey commented: 'I think it nearly impossible that under these circumstances they should not seek for some additional strength, before long, and . . . I have told Lansdowne that I wish him decidedly to understand that I stand out of the way.'[2] Lansdowne himself informed Grey 'from the moment you had told me of your own intention not again to take any office under any circumstances, I felt that sooner or later it must lead to my forming with that view some political connection to which I might not otherwise have looked'.[3]

The new arrangement, then, was not a simple transfer of authority but a recognition that party in the old style was at an end. Not only was the role of supporter to the government a new one, but Lansdowne, while perfectly satisfied with it for himself, was prepared to allow individuals in the party to make their own connexions with the administration.[4]

Even ahead of this relaxation of internal cohesion, observers and participants were already beginning to point out that party was at an end. As one voice among the many, Brougham tersely commented: 'We have ceased to act as a party and the country has naturally given over talking about what has no existence owing to ourselves.'[5] In such a situation it was hardly surprising that rumours, however unjustified, began to spread of negotiations between Canning and Lansdowne.[6] Ellice put into words

[1] Holland to Grey, 2 September 1825 (Grey).

[2] Grey to Holland, 16 February 1826 (Grey).

[3] Lansdowne to Grey, 29 April 1827 (Grey).

[4] Lansdowne to Brougham, 4 January 1827 (Brougham).

[5] Brougham to Lansdowne, 1 April 1827 (Lansdowne). See also *The Times*, 17 April 1826 (Lord Howick), 19 June 1826 (Lord Stanley); Grey to Ellice, 24 March 1827 (Ellice Papers, packet 11); Holland to Grey, 21 December 1826 (Holland); Lansdowne to Brougham, 4 January 1827 (Brougham).

[6] Lambton to Grey, 13 February 1823 and 26 August 1825 (Grey); W. J. Fitzpatrick, *Correspondence of Daniel O'Connell*, London, 1888, i. 137.

a prevailing expectation of imminent change, when he commented at the beginning of 1827 that 'great changes, not only affecting the situation of parties but the vital interests of the country, are not far distant, and that the death of one or two individuals, or any other accidents within the compass of a reasonable probability, may accelerate them beyond the expectation of any party'.[1]

Though the expectation that liberals, whig, and tory, would draw together against illiberals was understandable, real obstacles stood in the way. Canning consistently mistrusted whigs as doctrinaires, and claimed that though they might appear as his suitors, in fact another mistress, parliamentary reform, was more dear to them.[2] Nor could he agree with their views on the repeal of the test and corporation acts and the six acts, or on the catholic association. Even on catholic emancipation he felt the house was so far ahead of public opinion that a divided administration was the only possible one. Though Canning's banner and those of the whigs might be mingled for a time, in his view this could be no more than accidentally. Even had he mistrusted the whigs less, there was little reason for him to break with existing colleagues. In disagreements on policy Canning, with the backing of Liverpool, nearly always had his way. From the end of 1824 he began to draw closer to the king. Thus uncertain seas had no attraction, and the most that he was prepared to do was to make a vague approach to Lansdowne in November 1826 to assure himself of whig support for liberal measures.[3] This entailed no attempt to undermine the administration.

Yet Canning was a master politician who could adjust to events as they developed. More important as a barrier on the path designated by the pundits was Lord Liverpool. Mediating constantly between the two sections of the administration, defending Canning's views to the illiberal group, Liverpool became a major bond of unity. Even had he not been this, so long as he remained prime minister there was no need for a basic reshuffle or a redistribution of power such as might have provoked the two sections of his administration to disagree and fall apart. One man blocked the emergence of the new pattern.

[1] Ellice to Grey, 29 January 1827 (Grey). [2] *P.D.*, N.S. xi. 716–17.

[3] See A. Aspinall, 'Canning's Return to Office in September 1822', *E.H.R.* lxxviii, 1963, p. 544 n. 1.

IX

FALL · 1827–1828

On 17 February 1827 Liverpool suffered a seizure which left him, in the words of *The Times*, 'if not actually, at least politically dead'.[1] The administration appeared to founder and the country and the political world awaited the decision of the king. Speculation became the only reality with Grey anticipating a new tory administration, tories fearing a government break-up, and optimistic whigs awaiting a call to Lansdowne.[2]

The only way whigs could bring any influence to bear was through the catholic question, already the decisive issue of the session. A meeting of the leading whigs on 8 February had decided to proceed by means of a general resolution, but Grey now urged delay lest a defeat for the catholics should influence Canning or the king in the negotiations about the new administration.[3] Though Norfolk, Rosslyn, Bedford, Macdonald, and Lansdowne agreed, discussions at Lansdowne House saw Spring Rice and others urging immediate action.[4] But Canning returned to the parliamentary scene advocating early action and tipped the balance against delay. On 8 March the motion was defeated by four votes.

Despite their tactical differences the whigs agreed in opposing another divided administration. Grey was flatly against

> a continuation of the same system, by which the question, of all others the most immediately affecting the peace and safety of the country, is excluded from the deliberations of the cabinet, and left to be perpetually agitated and perpetually debated between the

[1] *The Times*, 19 February 1827.

[2] Grey to Holland, 21 February 1827 (Grey); Howick to Grey, 22 February 1827 (Grey); H. Twiss, *Eldon*, ii. 583–4.

[3] Burdett to Huskisson, 8 February 1827 (Huskisson Papers, Add. MSS. 38748, f. 245); L. Melville, *The Huskisson Papers*, London, 1931, pp. 214–16; Grey to Howick, 28 February 1827 (Grey).

[4] Camden, pp. 24–25; Rosslyn to Grey, 1 March 1827 (Grey); Broughton, iii. 169. Hobhouse states that Lansdowne was against delay (Broughton, iii. 170).

members of the same government, professing different opinions. I declare most seriously and conscientiously my firm conviction that an administration decidedly anti-catholic would be infinitely less mischievous than such a state of things.[1]

His views were echoed by Duncannon, and Althorp, as well as by many others who were more inclined towards Canning.[2] Even Brougham urged a united and vigorous opposition to any divided administration.[3] Althorp asked Brougham to move an address to the crown for a united administration, and a small meeting at Althorp's rooms, attended by Milton, Tavistock, Brougham, and others, appears to have agreed that this should be done, a decision confirmed next week by a larger meeting at Burlington House. When Brougham went north on legal business, the initiative was taken by Tierney, who suggested on 30 March that supply be withheld until a decision had been taken on the ministry and demanded 'a strong, an efficient and a united administration'.[4] He lost by 153 votes, several members having left thinking the motion would be withdrawn. Tierney renewed his opposition when ministers adjourned the house on 12 April without reporting the progress made in arranging an administration; he did not force a division since he did not want a majority of tories.[5]

While the stick was being brandished others were preoccupied with the carrot. Immediately after Liverpool's seizure the Duke of Devonshire offered (without response) to go down to Brighton to see both Canning and the king and open up communications with Lord Lansdowne.[6] About the same time a small meeting of the moderate opposition, including Fazakerly, Abercromby, and Lord John Russell, offered to support a Canning ministry even without a settlement of the catholic question. Their views were communicated by Fazakerly to E. J. Littleton for transmission to the foreign secretary.[7] Though both moves were

[1] Grey to Holland, 7 March 1827 (Grey).

[2] Althorp to Brougham, 26 March 1827 (Althorp); Lambton to Wilson, 25 March 1827 (Wilson Papers, Add. MSS. 30111, f. 335).

[3] H. Brougham to J. Brougham, 1 April 1827 (Brougham); Brougham to Lansdowne, 1 April (Lansdowne).

[4] *P.D.*, N.S. xvii. 157–64; *George IV*, iii. 212.

[5] Tierney to Holland, 12 April 1827 (Holland).

[6] Duke of Devonshire's Diary, 19 February 1827 (Devonshire).

[7] A. Aspinall, 'The Coalition Ministries of 1827: I Canning's Ministry', *E.H.R.*, 1927, pp. 202–3, and Camden, p. 23.

premature they were soon followed by an intervention from Brougham. Away in York, and anxious lest Canning should overrate his difficulties and the hostility of the whigs, Brougham asked Sir Robert Wilson to urge Canning to reject any limitation of his power and to promise whig support and Brougham's own disinterested services. With Lansdowne's and Duncannon's agreement Wilson gave the substance of the communication to Lord Erskine, who was seeing Canning on other business.[1] Back through the same channel came a request for Lansdowne's own views. He observed to Brougham:

a great anxiety was expressed yesterday, to ascertain my sentiments and probable line of conduct under certain contingencies. I have pledged myself to nothing, nor did the sort of communication require it; but took the opportunity of insisting as strongly as I feel it, on the unequivocal recognition of power, and the subsequent use of it, with a direct view to the prosecution of those objects on which we are agreed, as that upon which everything must ultimately hinge, and as affording the only chance of *advancing* under present circumstances.[2]

Thus Canning now knew that he could expect whig support for himself but opposition to a divided administration. His hand was strengthened, though not his inclination, which was for a reconstruction of the existing ministry with himself at its head.

Canning was forced, rather than led, to other expedients. The king saw him and Wellington on 28 March and discovered that Canning would serve under no one else. For George this was decisive, and on 10 April he asked Canning to reconstruct the administration on the old basis. Peel, Wellington, Westmorland, Bathurst, Melville, and Eldon vetoed the scheme by resigning, and they alone made Canning turn to the whigs. Even then he first sought tory support, appointing Anglesey master general of the ordnance, making Copley chancellor, and persuading Bexley not to resign as chancellor of the duchy.

Canning's reluctant approach to the whigs was on his own terms, affecting individuals and not the party. On 12 April Canning offered his old friend, Carlisle, the privy seal, and Devonshire the office of lord chamberlain. Like good whigs both

[1] Sir R. Wilson, *Narrative*, pp. 4–8.
[2] Lansdowne to Brougham, 26 March 1827 (Brougham).

deferred to Lansdowne, whom they found to be willing to support a government acting upon liberal principles, but reluctant to go any further.[1] At Canning's suggestion a discussion between him and Lansdowne was arranged at Carlisle's house on 19 April. It was unsuccessful. Canning stressed that ministers could act freely on the catholic question despite the king's refusal to let it be made a cabinet question, and offered Lansdowne the home office, but the whig leader apparently stipulated that the Irish administration must be pro-catholic. When Canning renewed his overtures to Devonshire and Carlisle and made an offer to Spring Rice, he found them unwilling to accept, and Scarlett, to whom Canning had offered the post of attorney-general, was advised by his patron, Lord Fitzwilliam, to decline.[2] A meeting of leading whigs at Lansdowne House confirmed the decision not to accept office and the insistence on the Irish administration, and Lansdowne prepared to set off home to Bowood.[3] Negotiations were apparently over.

All now depended on two things: concessions by Canning and whig reactions to their leader's stipulations. Whig divisions over the previous five years were approaching a climax. Already on 30 March several whigs, including Wilson and Calcraft, had voted against Tierney's amendment or stayed away.[4] When Sir Thomas Lethbridge announced that he would move for a united administration the party found itself split. A meeting was held at Lansdowne House, but, as Holland reported,

> the result was not satisfactory, for though there was no difference of opinion nor any ill humour in discussing the matter, there was little or no agreement in the practical result—some being bent on voting for Lethbridge (especially Althorp and Duncannon) some disposed to vote against it (Burdett and Sir Robert Wilson) and some for moving amendment, previous question or going away. I understand there is to be a larger meeting of opposition at Althorp's and I fear many of the best men of the party will be for supporting a proposition which certainly contains their opinion and that of many (myself

[1] Devonshire's Diary, 12, 14, and 16 April 1827 (Devonshire); Lansdowne to Grey, 15 April 1827 (Grey and Lansdowne).

[2] Devonshire's Diary, 20 April 1827 (Devonshire); Fitzwilliam to Grey, 22 April 1827 (Grey).

[3] Wilson, *Narrative*, p. 22; Camden, pp. 172 and 147; Tierney to Holland, n.d. [April 1827] (Holland); Bedford to Grey, 23 April 1827 (Grey).

[4] *George IV*, iii. 213.

among them) who would vote against it. I could not vote for it when moved by such a person and with such a design for I could not sleep in my bed if I thought I had directly or indirectly helped to form an Orange government.[1]

The gulf could not be bridged, for the subsequent meeting at Althorp's allowed each individual to express his own opinions, though in the end the motion did not go to a division.[2]

The differences widened gradually. Most strongly against union with Canning was Grey, influenced partly by what he called his 'rooted distrust' of the man, but also by his concern with the dignity of the whig party as a major power in the state, entitled to an equal share of places and patronage.[3] Grey would agree to a juncture only if the catholic question was made a government issue, and grew increasingly sure that Canning had agreed to exclude this possibility.[4] Grey also resented the failure of his own colleagues to consult him regularly or inform him in advance of the decisions taken, and personal pique clearly influenced his attitude.[5]

Though Grey's attitude had been made clear to Lansdowne it was seconded in that quarter only by Ellenborough. Holland was less firm, for though he was critical of union, inclined to argue that Canning had made too many concessions on the catholic question, and certain that if he did go in Lansdowne should insist on leading the lords, Holland was still very reluctant to do anything that might help the ultras.[6] Althorp and Duncannon were also doubtful about joining an administration not committed to the catholic claims, though their doubts were made known only to Brougham and Wilson, who were unlikely to publicize them.[7]

All the other pressures on Lansdowne were for union, and

[1] Holland to Carlisle, n.d. [1827] (Carlisle).

[2] *The Times*, 7 April 1827.

[3] Grey to Holland, 13 March and 14 April 1827 (Grey); Grey to Fitzwilliam, 18 April 1827 (Milton); Camden, pp. 96 and 98; Grey to Holland, 14 April 1827 (Grey).

[4] Grey to Howick, 19 February 1827 (Grey); Grey to Holland, 14 April 1827 (Grey).

[5] Camden, p. 95. Lambton later claimed that attempts had been made to reach Grey but they had been unsuccessful: Lambton to Grey, 9 January 1828 (Grey).

[6] Holland to Lansdowne, 18 April 1827 (Lansdowne); Holland to Grey, 13 April 1827 (Holland); Camden, pp. 81–82.

[7] A. Aspinall, *E.H.R.*, 1927, pp. 217–18 and 220; Camden, p. 69.

Tierney observed that people were 'quite mad' about a junction.[1] The liberal press was similarly unbalanced. Darlington, Mackintosh, Baring, and his own members Abercromby and Macdonald, all urged Lansdowne on, while Lord Auckland and Lord John Russell, though realizing the difficulties, were on balance inclined to accept.[2] Brougham, back in London, was using all his influence for union with Canning. He asked Wilson to summon M.P.s to meet at Brooks's on Friday, 21 April, when thirty to forty whigs, including the most Canningite—Brougham, Wilson, Burdett, Calcraft, Spring Rice, and the Knight of Kerry—met in a critical mood. After Brougham had reported on the Lansdowne House meeting and condemned its decisions, the meeting sent Lord Auckland and the younger Calcraft to Lansdowne to urge him to change his mind. He declined to postpone his departure from London. Lord Dudley was also approached to resume negotiations with Canning.[3]

The role of this meeting has probably been exaggerated. The opinions of many of those present were already known. Other pressures on Lansdowne may well have been more influential, for he admitted he was overwhelmed with letters favourable to union. Finally, his mind was clearly not made up after the meeting, which was only one of several efforts to reopen negotiations, precipitated by the whigs most likely to come into office. Scarlett wrote to Canning to urge renewal, and Devonshire, who had noted in his diary: 'it makes me sick to think of the absurd way in which our wretched whigs always cut their own throats', saw Canning again on 21 April.[4] Canning gave him until the Monday to decide whether to take office. After meeting Lansdowne's members, Macdonald and Abercromby, Devonshire went with Carlisle to see Canning, who assured them that the offer of the home office to Lansdowne was still open.[5] Devonshire then saw Macdonald, Abercromby, Granville, Seaford, and Morpeth, and found them favourable, though he discovered that Holland

[1] Tierney to Holland, [April 1827] (Holland).

[2] Camden, pp. 94–95, 131, 78–80, 157–8; Mackintosh to Lansdowne, 22 April 1827 (Lansdowne); Lord John Russell to Lansdowne, n.d. [April 1827] (Lansdowne).

[3] Tierney to Holland, n.d. [April 1827] (Holland); Camden, pp. 133–4, 142, 152; Maxwell, p. 456.

[4] Camden, p. 141; Devonshire's Diary, 19 April 1827 (Devonshire).

[5] Devonshire's Diary, 21 April 1827 (Devonshire).

still insisted that Lansdowne should be leader in the lords.[1] The duke travelled down to Bowood and persuaded Lansdowne to name his conditions for taking office.[2] Lansdowne specified that if the lord-lieutenant was not to be a pro-catholic, the secretary for Ireland should be. He professed indifference to the leadership in the lords, but as his friends were anxious he should have it, suggested he should be employed on foreign-policy addresses. Finally, he insisted on freedom to resign at any time without specifying reasons.[3] Devonshire took the document outlining these stipulations back to London, but Canning declined the stipulations. Once more it appeared that negotiations were broken off.

However, Lansdowne himself now came to London and saw Canning on 27 April. The meeting succeeded where correspondence had failed. Canning appointed William Lamb as Irish secretary and Lansdowne therefore agreed both to advise his friends to take office and to come in himself later.[4] No stipulations were made on reform, for though the administration was to oppose the measure, Lansdowne and Tierney both declined to bind themselves against it. The procession to power now began. Devonshire, William Lamb, and Scarlett accepted office immediately: in May Carlisle took over woods and forests, Abercromby became judge advocate, while Lansdowne joined the cabinet as minister without portfolio and Tierney as master of the mint; and Macdonald entered the board of control in June. Not until July did Lansdowne come into the home office, with Spring Rice as his under-secretary, and Carlisle become privy seal. Of fifteen ministers three were whigs, while of thirty-seven other places they got a mere half dozen.

Despite their meagre share of power the juncture satisfied most of the party, who saw it as the logical culmination of the developments of the last four years.[5] To some it closed the door on the intolerant tories, to others it guaranteed that the liberal economic and foreign policies of the old cabinet would be maintained, and to still more it gave a prospect of doing good for Ireland, even, in time, of carrying catholic emancipation.

[1] Devonshire's Diary, 21 April 1827 (Devonshire).
[2] Ibid., 22 April 1827.
[3] Memorandum in Devonshire's Diary (Devonshire).
[4] Lansdowne to Holland, 26 and 27 April 1827 (Holland).
[5] Lansdowne in *P.D.*, N.S. xvii. 490.

A large section of the opposition transferred in early May to the government benches.

Two small groups in the old party did not share in the rejoicing. Grey, though at pains to proclaim his independence, was followed in his disapproval by a few peers, Bedford, Rosslyn, Jersey, Albemarle, Ellenborough, and even fewer in the commons, including Creevey, Lord George Cavendish, and Grey's son, Howick. Besides partisan dislike of Canning their reasons were two: Canning had not stood up firmly to the king on the catholic question; and the whigs had sacrificed a strong position (since Canning had little support) to become impotent junior partners in a divided administration, thereby breaking up the whig party and humbling it in the public eye—a crime the old stalwarts found in hard to forgive.[1] Thus they prepared to take up an aloof attitude, neither supporting the government, nor aiding the tories. Only Ellenborough verged on outright opposition.

The second block was largely in the commons. A small group of members led by Althorp, but including Milton, Lord John Russell, Tavistock, Hobhouse, the Ponsonbys, Ebrington, and Sir Robert Heron, were reluctant to leave their old opposition places. Approving neither of Grey's attitude nor of the government's, they proposed to support those ministerial measures which they approved and oppose those they did not. But before long the embittered ultra tories under Sir Thomas Lethbridge began to come out in hostility to the new administration, and Althorp pointed out that, as he says, 'it is impossible for us not to see, that the time is now arrived, in which we must choose between a government actuated by liberal and enlightened principles, and one of toryism in its most odious forms'.[2] Carnarvon and Holland in the lords were similarly disposed.[3]

Despite these discontented whigs and the more numerous disgruntled tories, the government was in a strong position. Its opponents were divided, and with the support of whigs, liberal tories, and regular government supporters prepared to carry on in their old allegiance, it probably had a majority in the

[1] See, for example, Lord G. Cavendish to Grey, 27 September 1827 (Grey); Jersey to Grey, 29 April 1827 (Grey).

[2] *P.D.*, N.S. xvii. 583. See also Nugent in *The Times*, 26 June 1827.

[3] Carnarvon to Lansdowne, 18 July 1827 (Lansdowne); Holland to Grey, 18 May (Holland).

commons, though in the lords it was shortly defeated by ten on an amendment by Wellington to its corn-bill proposals.

Even so, its main difficulties were internal. Embarrassments were not lacking. Some were precipitated from outside, as when Hume moved the repeal of the stamp duty on small publications, part of the six acts opposed by the whigs in 1819. This attempt to embarrass the whig ministers was supported by Howick and Milton, but opposed by Newport, Wilson, Lord George W. Russell, and Lennard, and defeated on the previous question.[1] Such embarrassments would be renewed with a new session, but arrangements to deal with them proved difficult. After the long opposition years the whigs inevitably made heavy demands on patronage, and Lambton, Baring, and others were shortly being put forward for titles, Holland acting almost as a self-appointed broker. Patronage became a symbol of the balance of power within the administration. Facing disgruntled whigs outside it who claimed that too much had been surrendered, the whigs inside had to press both for patronage and for more cabinet posts, particularly one for Holland. These squabbles kept alive dangerous divisions between the two wings of the administration.

Reform promised even more serious difficulties, for the whigs had by no means abandoned their concern. With no general pressure, general reform was no longer an issue, but there was developing a pressure for partial reform, to which whigs were responding. In counties with a large manufacturing interest this body was already beginning to play its part in the choice of M.P.s, and commercial men had been elected in Middlesex in 1820 and in Yorkshire in 1826. In addition, the increasing complexity and volume of commercial business made it difficult for county M.P.s from the landed classes to represent the manufacturing towns adequately.[2] Conflicts between interests, as on the corn laws, also enhanced the value of representation. The result was a growing demand for individual representation from manufacturing towns, a demand with appeal even to those in them who saw general change as leading to revolution. The Grampound disfranchisement bill in the previous parliament had shown the way, for though the lords had insisted on a transfer

[1] *George IV*, iii. 244.

[2] See, for example, J. W. Ward, in *P.D.*, N.S. iv. 591–2.

to Yorkshire, not to Leeds, a darn at least had been made in the sacred fabric of the constitution.

Now, in the 1826 election, both Penryn and East Retford had laid themselves open to disfranchisement. Lord John Russell gave notice that if Penryn were disfranchised he would move a transfer of the seats to Manchester, a move which Lord Stanley seconded by writing to the borough-reeve of that town, suggesting that the wishes of the inhabitants should be made known.[1] A large meeting was held in Manchester, which unanimously agreed to petition for representation, and set up a committee representing all shades of political opinion.[2] On 28 May Russell moved to disfranchise Penryn and transfer the seats as requested. Canning opposed, but many tories stayed away on the vote, others were away by accident at the Pitt dinner, and the whig supporters of the government voted for disfranchisement, a demonstration of Canning's weakness where the whigs were pledged.[3] The embarrassment was prolonged when Tennyson proposed to transfer the seats from East Retford to Birmingham and a great public meeting was held in that town.[4] On 22 June a motion to disfranchise Retford and transfer the seats to Birmingham was carried in the commons. Since committees in both Manchester and Birmingham now began to draw up draft bills and the problem of the lords would have to be faced, the reform embarrassment promised to be a serious one for the government.

On 8 August Canning died. Once again there was a brief burst of speculation, some ruminating on Wellington's chances of the premiership, others on Lansdowne's, and Wellesley on his own.[5] But George promptly sent for Lord Goderich, who under-

[1] Minute Book of the Manchester Representation Committee, 4 April 1827, ff. 3–6.

[2] *The Times*, 25 May 1827; A. Prentice, *Sketches*, pp. 306–7. An indication of the complexion of the committee is given by the inclusion of H. H. Birley, who had commanded the cavalry at Peterloo. The radicals had to move an amendment even to secure representation.

[3] Grey to Ellice, 31 May 1827 (Ellice Papers, packet 11, National Library of Scotland).

[4] J. K. Buckley, *Joseph Parkes of Birmingham*, London, 1926, pp. 37–39; J. A. Langford, *A Century of Birmingham Life*, Birmingham, 1868, ii. 530–1.

[5] L. J. Jennings, *Croker*, i. 382; Burdett to Ellice, 8 August 1827 (Ellice Papers, packet 44, National Library of Scotland); Hardinge to Londonderry, 8 August (Londonderry Papers); Ellenborough to Londonderry, 8 August (ibid.); Memorandum (Wellesley Papers, Add. MSS. 37297, f. 371).

took to reconstruct the government with as few changes as possible and no further whig appointments. When Lansdowne again urged the admission of Holland, the king refused on these grounds.[1] He promised only to consider the demands of Holland's friends in the future.[2] More trouble arose over the exchequer. The king's first choice, Sturges-Bourne, was a Canningite acceptable to the whigs. When he declined, Goderich turned instead to J. C. Herries, a tory and anti-catholic, who was persuaded by the king to accept. The whigs learned of the appointment in council on 17 August, and refused to agree.

At once Lansdowne was exposed to a series of pressures almost comparable with those of April. Holland wrote to Lansdowne, Carlisle, and Tierney to urge that Herries's views were incompatible with those of other ministers and to point out the threat to the confidence of government supporters.[3] Carlisle agreed, and Abercromby also came out for resignation.[4] But Baring, Spring Rice, Macdonald, and Brougham, all urged submission, Brougham arguing:

> I should not make this the ground of a change and of letting in the enemy. It may—probably will—come to this ultimately and on some other ground. But for God's sake reflect on the force we go out in after a year's cooperation compared with our present force. If we break up now Goderich and company take back Bathurst and co. and Wellington is P.M. and commander in chief. Surely in a year after much fighting together we shall have a far better prospect of our own allies going right and leaving office with us?[5]

Lansdowne, already reluctant to carry on, felt Herries's appointment would give a tone to the administration which the whigs could not accept, and began to consult Abercromby on his own resignation, though he was willing for others to stay.[6]

[1] Goderich to Lansdowne, 11 August 1827 (Lansdowne).

[2] L. Melville, *Huskisson*, p. 228. Holland himself was opposed to any pressure for his own admission: Holland to Althorp, 28 August 1827 (Althorp); Holland to Lansdowne, 22 August 1827 (Lansdowne).

[3] Holland to Lansdowne, 22 August 1827 (Lansdowne); Holland to Carlisle, 22 August (Carlisle); H. K. Olphin, *Tierney*, pp. 236–7.

[4] Carlisle to Huskisson, 25 August 1827 (Huskisson Papers, Add. MSS. 38750, ff. 88–90); Abercromby to Devonshire, 29 August 1827 (Devonshire).

[5] Brougham to Abercromby, n.d. [August 1827]. Sent by Abercromby to Lansdowne (Lansdowne).

[6] Abercromby to Lansdowne, n.d. [August 1827] (Lansdowne); Lansdowne to Carlisle, n.d. [1827] (Carlisle).

To avert disaster Goderich offered to promote Darlington and Camden in the peerage, make Stanley under-secretary to the colonial office, and appoint Mackintosh to the India board at the next vacancy.[1] When the whigs met the night before Lansdowne's visit to the king, it was decided to do nothing precipitately, and some had clearly softened.[2] Yet Lansdowne set out for his interview determined on offering his resignation, and only George's direct request to carry on as a personal favour finally changed his mind.

The immediate crisis had been averted, but the lesson Lansdowne drew was to be 'resolute for the future, another such concession would ruin us completely'.[3] Whig resistance was also stiffened because of a growing conviction that both the cabinet and its head were dangerously feeble.[4] A prime minister of a stature so much below that of Canning seriously reduced both the whig security for the maintenance of liberal opinions and the government's strength against the king. Goodwill had disappeared, and so, when the king in December revived a plan for Wellesley to enter the cabinet, the whigs insisted that Holland should come in too, and Goderich's feeble equilibrium disintegrated. Persuaded to send an ultimatum to the king to bring in both men, he ended up by practically offering his own resignation. Only the king's agreement that Holland should come in at Easter averted a split.

Not surprisingly, therefore, the outsiders who had looked with reserve at Canning, who commanded respect, looked askance at Goderich, who drew only derision. Ellenborough burst out laughing when he heard who had been sent for as prime minister, Grey nicknamed him 'Lady Goderich', Milton thought the new arrangement would give power to the king.[5] The admission of Herries also stiffened hostility. The result was a growing feeling for independence among those who had tended to support Canning. As the government became weaker

[1] Lansdowne to Carlisle, 2 September 1827 (Carlisle).

[2] J. E. Denison to Huskisson, 1 September 1827 (Huskisson Papers, Add. MSS. 38750, f. 170); Tierney to Holland, 1 September 1827 (Holland).

[3] Lansdowne to Carlisle, 2 September 1827 (Carlisle).

[4] Holland to Lansdowne, 3 September 1827 (Lansdowne).

[5] Ellenborough to Hardinge, 12 August 1827 (Hardinge Papers); G. Le Strange, *Correspondence of Princess Lieven and Earl Grey*, London, 1890, i. 95; Grey to Ellenborough, 24 August 1827 (Ellenborough Papers, P.R.O. 30/12/24); Milton to S. Rice, 9 September 1827 (Monteagle).

even the argument that the tories were the only alternative carried less and less weight. Some began to think a tory ministry dependent on the house better than a liberal one dependent on the king.[1] There was still no attempt to organize whigs uncommitted to the government, but the inclination was stirring. Lord George Cavendish commented:

I consider the whig party as completely annihilated and every one at liberty to act as he thinks best. If Lord Tavistock, Lord Althorp and Lord Milton were to erect an independent party I should be inclined to give it my support, but I doubt for different reasons the probability or practicability of it. Many however would flock to their standard, for with the exception of such, as have made their bargains, there must be those who cannot be satisfied with the present state of things. For my own part I have so long acted in party, and so constantly, with one short exception, with my family that I feel myself, as you may imagine, in an awkward situation, and my inclination is rather to give up politics altogether.[2]

Althorp was coming round to the view that a group of men pledged not to take office without carrying the catholic question could prod changes out of the administration.[3] He considered a meeting to sound opinion, but abandoned it—from natural diffidence, puzzlement about what line to take, and perhaps even a disinclination to party.[4] Tavistock certainly felt so:

I am sick of party, and when I reflect upon who and what our leaders were, and how they have treated us, I am not disposed to make any efforts to bring them back to us. The king and Canning (the natural and avowed enemies of the whigs) have divided us, and defeated us. If we go to the wars again it must be in guerrilla parties.[5]

The only agreement, and that tacit, was to consult together, but take no more positive steps to union.[6]

[1] Spencer to Holland, 23 December 1827 (Holland); Bedford to Holland, 9 September 1827 (Holland).

[2] Lord George Cavendish to Grey, 27 September 1827 (Grey).

[3] Althorp to Lord John Russell, 2 October 1827 (Russell Papers, P.R.O. 30/22/1 Althorp to E. D. Davenport, 11 November 1827 (Bromley–Davenport Papers).

[4] R. Russell, *Russell*, i. 271–2; Althorp to Davenport, op. cit.; Tavistock to Hobhouse, 5 January 1828 (Broughton Papers, Add. MSS. 36464, f. 166); Broughton iii. 233.

[5] Tavistock to Hobhouse, op. cit. (ff. 169–70); see also Jersey to Grey, 9 January 1828 (Grey), quoting from a letter of Tavistock's.

[6] Jersey to Grey, op. cit., and Althorp to Russell, 2 October 1827 (Russell

More alarming to ministers was a rumoured alliance between Lord Grey and the high tories.[1] Grey's first reaction to the new government had been to scrutinize measures but not change his own policy.[2] Gradually he became more hostile, as most government patronage went to tories and anti-catholics, but he stayed independent of all connexions except personal friendships, such as those with Rosslyn and Bedford.[3] He believed the rumours were started to frighten the king, but in fact they probably grew from the efforts of Ellenborough and Lauderdale. Ellenborough was on friendly terms with both Grey and some old tories, and was urging an active course probably intended to bring the two groups together.[4] He received some response on the tory side, but none from Grey.[5] Lauderdale was clearly hopeful of an informal grouping under Grey, for he told Brougham 'when a man unites character and talent to the extent he does, it requires no letter of service to place him in a situation to which in the estimation of all, except those who have kicked him over, he has an undisputed right'.[6] Yet a man as devoted to consistency as Grey would hardly have risked anything beyond occasional and accidental concurrence with those he had so long opposed.

A third danger was that Brougham would go into opposition, or at least prove hard to handle.[7] The course of the meteor was as erratic as ever, for Brougham was flaunting his influence by writing to friends 'I pray you for a moment to consider what kind of reforms you will have carried next session', suggesting, apparently without any authorization, that Rosslyn might take office in the ordnance, and even urging that Grey should form an active opposition to diminish the power of the court.[8]

Papers, P.R.O. 30/22/1); *The Times*, 10 January 1828, stated that a party of 'watchers' forming round Althorp was at least forty strong.

[1] S. Rice to Newport, 20 December 1827 (Monteagle); Aspinall, *E.H.R.* 1927, p. 550.

[2] Grey to Ellenborough, 24 August 1827 (Ellenborough Papers, P.R.O. 30/12/24).

[3] Rosslyn to Brougham, 20 October 1827 (Brougham); Grey to Howick, 8 December 1827 (Grey); Grey to Fitzwilliam, 15 December 1827 (Milton).

[4] Mentioned in Grey to Ellenborough, 24 August 1827 (Ellenborough Papers, P.R.O. 30/12/24).

[5] Hardinge to Londonderry, 11 December 1827 (Londonderry Papers).

[6] Lauderdale to Brougham, 26 December 1827 (Brougham).

[7] Duncannon to Abercromby, 19 August 1827 (Lansdowne).

[8] Brougham to the Revd. W. Shepherd of Liverpool, 4 September 1827 (Brougham); Rosslyn to Brougham, 31 October and 7 November 1827 (Brougham); Rosslyn to Grey, 4 December 1827 (Grey); Maxwell, p. 482.

Yet these activities indicate no hostility to the government on Brougham's own part. He was too much involved in the government to oppose it, and overt tory opposition was bound to bring him to its defence.

Though hostility to the government grew, the opposition was embryonic and divided, and the ministry's chief difficulties still came from its own supporters and its internal differences. Burdett was ready to go into opposition, Sefton was reported to have withdrawn his support after Navarino, and the Irish catholics were preparing simultaneous meetings in 1828 to bring pressure for action.[1] More serious, any desire to carry on seems to have disappeared. The final blow came over Althorp's chairmanship of the parliamentary finance committee. After this had been agreed by Huskisson and Tierney, Herries announced that if the appointment were made he would resign. Goderich went to the king, for his last visit. George dismissed his incompetent premier and the administration ended, not with a bang, but a whimper, at the whim of a banker.

On 9 January the king asked Wellington to form a government. It was bound to draw heavily on those who had left office the previous year, but Wellington and the king also wanted to retain the most efficient members of the old administration from the Huskisson group, who promptly accepted, and some of the whigs, who declined. No offer was made to Lansdowne, partly because he would have wanted to retain all his friends in office, which would have offended the tories, and partly because he might have taken the chance to refuse. Without him neither Carlisle, Devonshire, nor Scarlett would stay in, while Rosslyn for different motives also declined, and only Ellenborough accepted.

The acceptance of office by Huskisson and company shattered the hopes of pundits and papers for a new pattern of politics, liberal opposed to illiberal. Hopes remained of reviving the old pattern of whig against tory, for Lambton saw the opportunity for whig unity, and Lord John Russell and his father hoped to put the clock back to the time before Canning's ministry.[2]

[1] Broughton, iii. 232; Maxwell, p. 143; O'Connell to S. Rice, 29 November 1827 (Monteagle); W. Lamb to S. Rice, 13 December and 4 January 1828 (Monteagle); S. Rice to Brougham, 1 October 1827 (Brougham).

[2] Lambton to Grey, 21 January 1828 (Grey); Althorp to Lord J. Russell,

But these hopes too were unrealistic. Grey, condemning 'the fatal error of last year', was extremely angry at Brougham, the 'devil incarnate', and bitter at the attacks which had been made on himself.[1] On the other hand, many who had supported Canning felt with Fazakerly: 'I shall ever attribute a great part of the mischief to such men as Lord Grey and Althorp who instead of supporting their friends and giving him the means of increasing his strength and acting with vigour, distracted him.'[2] Agreement was rendered harder because no leader was now acceptable to both wings.[3] It was finally ruled out by wide differences of attitude to the new administration, its personnel, and its still emerging policies. The next few weeks revealed three main groups. Althorp, Fitzwilliam, Milton, and Normanby openly opposed the administration, distrusting its members, its principles, and its origins.[4] More were inclined to approve of it, for the exclusion of Eldon helped create hopes of a liberal policy. Bedford thought it impossible to find an alternative, and Rosslyn, although he declined office, was favourably disposed. So too were supporters of the previous government, such as Wilson, Calcraft, and even Lansdowne.[5] Perhaps larger still, at this uncertain stage, was a group inclined to watch and wait and prepared to support those measures of which they approved. In it, besides Brougham, Spring Rice, and Stanley, who had supported the late administration, were Russell and Hobhouse.[6] Grey, unwilling to commit himself, held aloof from all groups.

13 January 1828 (Althorp); Bedford to Holland, 21 December 1827 and 15 January 1828 (Holland); R. Russell, *Russell*, i. 272.

[1] Grey to Fitzwilliam, 20 October 1827 and 21 January 1828 (Milton). Account by Grey, February 1828 (Grey), and Maxwell, pp. 491–2.

[2] Fazakerly to Spring Rice, 16 January 1828 (Monteagle).

[3] Ellice to Hobhouse, 15 January 1828 (Broughton Papers, Add. MSS. 36464, f. 182): 'how are we to act with the lawyer? . . . Do what we will in the way of party he will be the stumbling block. I am more for acting alone at least till we can find a leader in whom we can place confidence.'

[4] Fitzwilliam to Grey, 21 January 1828 (Grey); Milton to Scarlett, 24 January 1828, copy (Milton); *P.D.*, N.S. xviii. 68; Althorp to Milton, 20 January 1828 (Milton), and *P.D.*, N.S. xviii. 61.

[5] Bedford to Holland, n.d. [1828] (Holland); Calcraft, *P.D.*, N.S. xviii. 68; Lansdowne, *P.D.*, N.S. xviii. 300–2; Wilson, Rosslyn to Grey, 18 January 1828 (Grey).

[6] Hobhouse to Place, 12 January 1828 (Place Papers, Add. MSS. 35148, f. 10); Brougham, *P.D.*, N.S. xviii. 55; Rice, *P.D.*, N.S. xviii. 76; Russell, *P.D.*, N.S. xviii. 66–67; Stanley, *P.D.*, N.S. xviii. 51; Ridley, *P.D.*, N.S. xviii. 79.

With no semblance of party and a large part of the old opposition inclined to await its measures, the government was strengthened by the divisions among opponents and the absence of any alternative. Yet Wynn observed: 'the government is weak on account of the non-existence of any regular or organised opposition. They do not know who are their friends or upon what questions they may be left in the lurch.'[1] The difficulties were soon shown when Lord John Russell moved for the repeal of the test and corporation acts. Here was an issue which all members of the old opposition supported, but which was also taken up by liberal supporters of the administration and only half-heartedly opposed by the liberal tories in office. The motion passed by a majority of forty-four, and the government decided to give way gracefully and see the measure through the lords.[2] When a motion for a committee on the catholic question was also carried, even those originally inclined to hostility, like Fitzwilliam, began to congratulate themselves that the country was in fact being governed by the opposition.[3]

At first confidence in the government largely reflected the presence of the liberal tories. In May they resigned over a dispute on the Penryn and East Retford disfranchisement bills. The government had decided that it could agree to the transfer of only one of the boroughs, the other to be thrown open to the hundred. Even this was too much for the lords, who struck out Manchester from the Penryn bill and enfranchised the neighbouring hundred. Through the resignations the government lost its only real debating talent in the commons. Yet if the departure added to the party confusion it did not subtract from the confidence even of reformers, for this was increasingly based on the hope that the government's intentions remained liberal, and the knowledge that if they were not Wellington could hardly implement them, while he was weak enough to be prodded in a liberal direction. As Abercromby pointed out, 'The duke has the real support of no party. . . . In this state he must be weak and may be forced to yield what would not be conceded by a more liberal government.'[4] There were even growing hopes that

[1] C. W. Wynn to H. Wynn, 8 April 1828 (Wynn 4817); Maxwell, p. 489.

[2] Brougham estimated that of 240 on the majority side 190 to 200 were known party men; *The History of the Times*, London, 1935, i. 259.

[3] Fitzwilliam to Milton, 21 March 1828 (Milton).

[4] Abercromby to Brougham, 13 July 1828 (Brougham).

some whigs might be taken into the administration, as Ellenborough was urging.[1] The only immediate change, however, was the admission of Calcraft as paymaster of the forces.

The unstable political situation placed a premium on organization to exploit it, yet there was still no one to take the lead. Grey, committed to independence, was becoming more favourably inclined towards the government. Lansdowne's position had been seriously undermined by the events of 1827, when his dilatoriness and lack of either application or firmness had stood revealed to all: Bedford, for instance, comments that 'he is sadly lost in public estimation, we can never replace him where he was'.[2] Lansdowne had, in any case, determined not to repeat the experiment of becoming a party leader and had deliberately lapsed into inactivity.[3] Brougham was seriously ill, and even after recovery had to keep up with the accumulating demands of his legal practice. Althorp, whose stock was on a bull market, was still bearish: when he was suggested as a leader he replied to Graham: 'I believe with you that a great many of our party fancy that I should be a good leader (so they did about Lord Lansdowne) but I know I should not. I should not have been leader two months before I had fallen into the greatest possible contempt, at present I am overrated, then I should be underrated.'[4] In addition, he was deeply involved with the work of the finance committee, and inclined to wait until next session before acting against the government, in the hope that in the meantime it would act on the catholic question.[5] The semi-retirement of the veteran generals left the field to the subalterns; the absence of general plans opened the way to partial ones. Edward Stanley, only twenty-nine but already a rising star, began to gather a small moderate following and made an overture to C. W. Wynn, now out of office and independent, which was favourably received. The object, according to Wynn, was 'not to form an opposition but a party to support the liberal

[1] Ellenborough's memorandum of May 1828 (Ellenborough Papers, P.R.O. 30/12/24).

[2] Bedford to Holland, 15 January 1828 (Holland). See also: Broughton, iii. 232; Ellice to Lambton, 6 December 1827 (Lambton); E. J. Littleton's Diary, 10 February 1828 (Hatherton Papers, Staffordshire Record Office); Abercromby to Brougham, 28 December 1829 (Brougham).

[3] Lansdowne to Holland, 19 January 1829 (Holland).

[4] Althorp to Graham, 17 December 1828 (Graham).

[5] Althorp to Graham, 2 July 1828 (Graham).

division of the government whenever we have an opportunity'.[1] The resignation of this liberal section changed the position, and Graham was shortly urging a broader union and a more active role, writing to Stanley:

> I hope you will take the field in force: and I think you will find a strong and respectable body willing to act under you. Much of course must depend upon the events which may occur before parliament reassembles: but the prospect of affairs is so clouded by difficulties, that the chances are some capital blunder may be committed, and then will arrive the golden opportunity of forming a party in the house of commons on some broad and intelligible principle, without any reference to leaders in the house of lords and without any direct compact with Brougham.[2]

These were plans for the future, and in that long perspective, or in any general union, Stanley's prospects were not bright. Abercromby pointed out: 'Stanley has been moving as if he wished to be leader in the house of commons. I should hardly think that will do. Brougham is not yet absolutely a cypher and such nomination would greatly rouse him. Stanley may be and probably is a proper person to be looked to but is he ripe for so difficult a charge?'[3]

Though the session ended with no general opposition or concert it was clear this could not last. Everything depended on the catholic question, which was rapidly eclipsing every other issue. The growing agitation reported in dramatic terms by Irish whigs, the strength of the catholic association, and O'Connell's election in Clare, impelled the issue to the forefront. In the general perplexity over the duke's intentions two things alone were clear. If the duke did propose a government measure he would have firm, vigorous, and united support from the old opposition.[4] If he did not, there was an increasing likelihood that he would be opposed: the whigs could hardly stand unshaken while Ireland was a bursting world. Not only was catholic emancipation one of the few things on which all the old opposi-

[1] C. W. Wynn to H. W. Wynn, 29 April 1828 (Wynn, 4817). See also Ellenborough's Memorandum, op. cit.

[2] Graham to Stanley, 15 July 1828 (Graham).

[3] Abercromby to Carlisle, 10 November 1828 (Carlisle).

[4] Althorp early on told Arbuthnot that he and, he thought, many others would support Wellington generally if he settled the Irish question. Brougham to Lambton, n.d. [1829] (Brougham).

tion agreed but it was also becoming a question of national interest.[1]

A wide range of voices was beginning to urge unity to further catholic claims. Holland was an active proponent. As early as October E. D. Davenport was drawing up schemes for a new party unity, and E. G. Stanley, the budding leader of the previous session, was prepared for a regular and broader opposition based on the catholic question.[2] It was left to Lord Lansdowne to channel this groundswell of support. In December, he began to urge:

> I think it would be disgraceful to us all as individuals and a complete derelection of public duty, if we did not buckle on our armour at the very outset of the approaching session and fight the catholic question resolutely as a party—not overlooking other points but giving it the precedence which its urgency as well as its importance claims. When I say *as a party* I do not mean it would be practicable, nor do I think for our purpose it would be necessary, to effect a strict party alliance between all the scattered fragments who are friendly to our principle—but I am much mistaken if there is neither a satisfactory measure announced, nor a negotiation opened with the king at the time of the meeting neither of which I expect, and we do not find nearly all, ready to act together upon the basis of supporting no government that will not undertake to settle it. I think whether openly declared or only privately understood no assistance would be worth having without such a resolution,—but it might be also understood that this point once carried all were individually at liberty.[3]

Lansdowne wrote to Spring Rice, Lord John Russell, and Stanley about his plan and also saw Althorp and Brougham in London and J. E. Denison in Paris.[4] Everywhere the reaction was favourable.[5]

The general principle was readily and quickly accepted: the

[1] Abercromby to Brougham, 6 December 1828 (Brougham).

[2] Holland to Brougham, 28 October 1828 (Brougham); Holland to E. D. Davenport, 9 November 1828 (Bromley–Davenport Papers). Stanley's views are in R. Russell, *Russell*, i. 282.

[3] Lansdowne to Spring Rice, 26 December 1828 (Lansdowne).

[4] Lord J. Russell to Lansdowne, 4 January 1829 (Lansdowne); E. G. Stanley to Lansdowne, 31 December 1828 (Lansdowne); Lansdowne to Brougham, 26 December 1828 (Brougham).

[5] Milton to Spring Rice, 25 January 1829 (Monteagle); Tavistock's views are mentioned in Countess of Carlisle to Earl, 18 December 1828 (Carlisle); Holland Brougham, 20 December 1828 (Brougham).

details and the tactics provoked disagreements. Holland thought the only hope of real unity was a commitment to secure power and then share it evenly.[1] This was further than Lansdowne wanted to go. Spring Rice, believing that the government could not survive if the whigs and the Huskisson groups combined, wanted to bring the Huskisson group into the union, and so opposed Lansdowne's suggested repudiation of any government which did not carry emancipation.[2] There was no agreed leader: many now looked to Althorp, whose diffidence still held him back, but Lord John Russell continued to favour Brougham, whom he considered *facile princeps*, and others may still have preferred Stanley.[3] Holland, devoted to old-style party and slightly cynical about the new, observes that 'All our best men in both houses speak of an array of strength, concert, cooperation and what not. But I do not hear of a leader, nor exactly know whether the efforts are to be directed to a change of ministry or exclusively to one measure.'[4]

Grey was determined not to join in the preparations, believing that the duke intended to act on the catholic question and that an organized opposition might discourage him.[5] Like Bedford, Albemarle, and Jersey, he favoured neutrality. Rosslyn argued that the main concern should be to assure the duke of support extending even beyond emancipation, while Cleveland even urged a written declaration to the same effect and asked his members to abstain from attacking the government.[6] These minority views were justified when the session began. In the last few days before the meeting the rumours that the duke was to act appeared definitive.[7] The king's speech confirmed them and all pretext for opposition was removed. A great change took place in the feelings of the critics. Even Tavistock was inclined to throw over his long-formed habits and become a

[1] Holland to Lansdowne, 17 January 1829 (Lansdowne).

[2] Mentioned in E. G. Stanley to Lansdowne, 31 December 1828 (Lansdowne).

[3] Althorp to Graham, n.d. [December 1828] (Graham); Lord J. Russell to Brougham, 26 November 1828 (Brougham).

[4] Holland to E. D. Davenport, 5 January 1829 (Bromley–Davenport Papers).

[5] Grey to Holland, 10 January 1829 (Grey); Grey to Howick, 1 February 1829 (Grey); H. Brougham, *Life and Times*, ii. 500–2.

[6] Rosslyn to Brougham, 1 January 1829 (Brougham); Cleveland to Grey, 6 and 27 January 1829 (Grey).

[7] E. G. Stanley to Spring Rice, 29 January 1829 (Monteagle); Tankerville to Grey, 2 February 1829 (Grey).

ministerialist, and Brougham told the government it had nothing to fear.[1]

The rest of the session was an anti-climax. Whig support for the government measure was automatic, and the only point of difficulty, the measure disfranchising the 40-shilling freeholders, was speedily settled. On 6 March a meeting was held at Burdett's, which revealed strong and general hostility to this measure. But as it was realized that opposition might endanger emancipation, Althorp and Spring Rice went as delegates to represent the views of the meeting to Peel, and when they were told that without the measure the bill could not be carried, the meeting agreed to support it, and only a handful of opposition members voted against.[2] The session, dominated by emancipation, yielded little legislation and less difficulty. Wellington had anticipated trouble, but *The Times* thought him safe and was proved correct.[3] Since many unforgiving ultra tories began to criticize and attack a government which they felt had betrayed them, whigs could hardly encourage opposition, even had they been organized or inclined to do so. Catholic emancipation and disunity outside the government ranks had enabled the duke to avoid organized opposition. In the opinion of *The Times* he could go on doing so: 'let him rule well and show a cool determination and hardy bearing and he will not be without sufficient support, both in and out of parliament.'[4]

[1] Rosslyn to Grey, 9 February 1829 (Grey); Jersey to Grey, 9 February 1829 (Grey); C. S. Parker, *Peel*, ii. 103–4.

[2] Mrs. Arbuthnot, *Journal*, ii. 250; Howick, Journal, 6 March 1829 (Grey); Abercromby to Brougham, n.d. [March 1829] (Brougham).

[3] Russell to Brougham, n.d. [1829] (Brougham); *The Times*, 21 April 1829.

[4] *The Times*, 4 August 1829.

X

TOWARDS OFFICE · 1829–1830

CATHOLIC emancipation left a legacy of political confusion. Canning's administration had split the whigs, 1828 had split the liberal tories away from the main body, and 1829 had sundered the solid trunk of the tory party. 'The pack of cards', as Wynn put it, 'has been . . . completely shuffled.'[1] The old party system appeared to have gone for ever. Yet in the event all the auguries of 1829 were to be belied. The situation which had developed by the end of that year proved to be a purely temporary one. It vanished within a year, for by then the whig party had drawn together, and once again the old personnel were urging the old principles under the old leaders. Only the context was new, and there all the changes favoured the whigs. By the end of 1830 their long-standing difficulties and problems had been removed or solved. Difficulties over the leadership, the hostility of the crown, the unity and strength of tory party and government, the disagreements over reform, all those things which had stood between the party and office had ceased to hamstring and hinder them. The year 1830 thus became a conclusion, pulling together all the threads of the previous fifteen years and ending a political deadlock maintained since the Napoleonic wars.

This could hardly be foreseen in 1829, or even early in 1830 because all observers were then agreed that party and organized opposition were at an end. There remained only political groups which could be differentiated by the new litmus test of political allegiance: reaction to Wellington's administration. Outside the government's own supporters, observers defined three main groups, disagreeing only over exact boundaries and subdivisions. The first was the group defined by Ellice as 'the discontented and still more bitter old tories, who will make no peace with Peel, and are generally the most formidable'.[2] Bitterness was the

[1] C. W. Wynn to Lord W. Bentinck, 16 June 1829, copy (Wynn, 10804).
[2] Ellice to Grey, 18 January 1830 (Grey).

characteristic of this party. It had no other *raison d'être*, for, as Spring Rice pointed out,

the talisman of the party is broken. No popery was the only cry that could raise adherents even among the parsons. That cry no longer finds an echo. The loose fish are quitting the shoal. The Duke of Chandos and others have given in their adhesions. The tories gravitate naturally towards power and the ultras are left contemptible in character and acquirement, worthy of the leaders by whom they are disgraced.[1]

Whigs found the idea of tories in opposition inconceivable and continually expected the ultras to rejoin the government.[2]

The same expectations did not attach to the second group; Huskisson and his followers, who included Palmerston, Melbourne, the Grants, Sturges-Bourne, and Wortley. Their break with the government had been too bitter, their present antagonism was too strong. This was a group of generals without soldiers, weak in numbers, strong in ability, and regarded with suspicion by the other groups in opposition, mainly because of Huskisson's reputation for self-interested unreliability. However, at the beginning of 1830 there was a small spate of rumours that Huskisson was to give up the leadership so that the group could conciliate wider support.[3]

Finally came the whigs, and a series of divergent opinions on the number of groups into which they could be divided. Londonderry saw three, a nucleus of the old party which could be secured by the government, the Lansdowne group, and the 'ultra whigs' under Grey.[4] Spring Rice saw only one, Wellington two—the Lansdowne and the Grey groups—, and Ellice two—those backing the liberal tory attacks on the ministry, and the 'watchers' under Althorp.[5] All these views were over-simplified, for the whigs had spread over a whole spectrum of opinion.

One extreme hue approximated to the colour of the government. Rosslyn joined Wellington as privy seal, with Grey's

[1] Spring Rice to Abercromby, 9 January 1830 (Monteagle).

[2] Grey to Holland, 29 December 1829 (Grey).

[3] C. Wood to Sir F. L. Wood, 7 February 1830 (Hickleton Papers); Ellice to Grey, 18 January 1830 (Grey); Spring Rice to Lansdowne, 24 January 1830 (Monteagle).

[4] Londonderry to Hardinge, 6 July 1829 (Hardinge Papers).

[5] Spring Rice to Abercromby, 9 January 1830 (Monteagle); Ellice to Grey, op. cit.; Duke of Wellington, *Despatches*, vi. 532–3.

half-hearted consent, in May 1829; Scarlett, with the cautious blessing of the Fitzwilliams, joined the government in June. They were followed by the Knight of Kerry, who became vice-treasurer of Ireland in March 1830, and Jersey, who accepted office as lord chamberlain in July, after declaring his confidence at the beginning of the year.[1] The recruits were a symptom of a wider-reaching friendship to the government. Cleveland announced his adherence in January 1830, Durham commenting that he had stuck to the government like plaster ever since it was formed.[2] His son, Darlington, moved the address at the February meeting of parliament, but his members were allowed freedom of action and only Brougham found another seat. Bedford declared his support for Wellington in June 1829 and gave his proxy to Rosslyn at the end of the year.[3] Darnley, too, was known to be favourable, as were Grosvenor, Norfolk, Albemarle, and individual M.P.s, such as M. W. Ridley, M. A. Taylor, Alexander Baring, J. C. Hobhouse, and Sir Ronald Ferguson. Most of these were prepared to give the duke general support, while reserving to themselves the right of opposing anything contrary to their principles. It nevertheless appeared that they might be drawn in more closely and become the bridgehead for a larger whig recruitment.

At the other extreme were those men, mostly from the left of the old party, who would have no contact with the administration. Burdett, Waithman, Protheroe, and Davenport felt that government inactivity was dangerous at a time when the country could not afford to stand still.[4] A rather different hostility was that of the moderate section of the whigs, small in number but including such important figures as Sir James Graham and Morpeth, who were close to the Huskisson group and sympathetic towards it.[5] They now shared something of its hostility. Between the extremes of active support and hostility came the great mass of the former opposition, finely differentiated by the

[1] Jersey to Grey, 15 February 1830 (Grey).

[2] Durham to Grey, 20 January 1830 (Grey); Cleveland to Grey, 12 January 1830 (Grey).

[3] Bedford to Grey, 2 and 6 June and 20 December 1829 (Grey).

[4] See Burdett in *P.D.*, N.S. xxii. 174–5.

[5] Graham was later reported as saying 'that he was a whig, and that he certainly should not leave his party; but that he had been in communication with Huskisson on matters of business, and that this he intended to continue'. Arbuthnot to Peel, 8 July 1830 (Peel Papers, Add. MSS. 40340, f. 226).

gradations of their reactions to Wellington. Perhaps the most sympathetic was Lansdowne and his small group of personal friends such as Spring Rice and Stanley, who were ready to give support if the government continued economy and retrenchment.[1] Like them, Milton and Fitzwilliam felt that the debt of gratitude owed to Wellington precluded opposition, while Tavistock even saw in ministerial weakness a virtue which made the administration 'too weak for evil and yet strong enough to carry through any measures that may be fixed upon'.[2] More central was Lord Holland, who was hostile to the government's foreign policy yet prepared to praise ministers for their internal policies because 'they swallow their physic like good boys'.[3] Others were equally torn between support for internal and hostility to foreign policy.[4]

Althorp's more hostile attitudes probably represent the bulk of whig opinion. In the summer of 1829 he had urged, through Arbuthnot, that Wellington should take in further whig recruits. In October he was given to understand that the duke had done all he could.[5] Compelled to decide for himself, he was pressed by conflicting sentiments; gratitude was countered by concern at ministerial weakness, and anxiety to bring pressure for further reforms by a desire not to serve the ends of Huskissonians and ultras.[6] As a result he hesitated and puzzled, awaiting events and hoping that the duke would rescue him from his 'great embarrassment' by bringing Grey into the government.[7] Brougham, with whom Althorp conferred fully before the 1830 session, shared very similar views, and Howick, originally more sympathetic, quickly came round to them when no offer was made to his father.[8] These views also appealed widely because they promised independent activity without binding commitment. Some were more extreme: Lord John and Lord William Russell were urging organization and union:

[1] *P.D.*, N.S. xxii. 54–55.

[2] Milton describes the evolution of his views in a letter to Scarlett, 28 July 1830, copy (Milton); Tavistock to Milton, 8 July 1830 (Milton).

[3] *P.D.*, N.S. xxii. 398; R. Russell, *Russell*, i. 295.

[4] Abercromby to Brougham, 26 December 1829 (Brougham).

[5] Wellington, *Despatches*, vi. 198–200.

[6] *P.D.*, N.S. xxii. 112–13; Althorp to Grey, 19 February 1830 (Grey).

[7] Mentioned in Lord John Russell to Devonshire, 18 December 1829 (Devonshire).

[8] Howick to Grey, 11 March 1830 (Grey); Broughton, iv. 7–8.

the machine is ricketty and unsafe, and it becomes us to take a decided line. I therefore propose—1st—That we should support our own measures, commercial freedom, an honest currency, parliamentary reform &c. without any reference to ministers, or whether we may hurt them or help them.—2d. That we should look at no long time hence to a co-operation with Huskisson, Grant &c. . . . 3d. . . . that none of us should take office without Lord Grey's being considered . . . 4th. that we should declare ourselves early on foreign politics.[1]

To reinforce this decided line Lord John Russell looked to a restoration of union and regular leadership, visualizing Holland in the lords and Althorp and Brougham jointly in the commons.[2] Outside, perhaps above, the general spectrum mused Grey, his attitudes changing with the fortunes of the ministry and the fluctuating hopes of his own accession. Initially he had been well disposed towards the government, although stressing that he was unconnected with it or, indeed, with anyone else.[3] Sympathy lingered, although increasingly combined with an awareness of ministerial weakness.[4] Yet he still declined to go into opposition, for he was weighing up the situation, emphasizing in his letters sometimes the weakness of the government and sometimes the magnitude of its difficulties and the impossibility of securing any replacement. Until his mind was made up he resolved to stay away from parliament.

Disunity and lack of decision gave the initiative to the government. Throughout 1829 and into 1830 observers expected it to seize this by recruiting additional strength from one or more of the groups outside, for most considered it weak, and a few doubted that it would continue to stand.[5] Whigs in particular hoped that the choice would fall on Grey and possibly some other whigs with him. This was being urged on the duke by whigs already in office, and Lord Ponsonby informed Grey early in December 1829 that although the king's hostility was a barrier he thought it 'highly probable' that Wellington would be able

[1] Lord John Russell to Brougham, 30 January 1830 (Brougham); Lord G. W. Russell to Lord J. Russell, 9 February 1830 (Woburn Abbey MSS.); R. Russell, *Russell*, i. 301–2.

[2] Ibid. and Russell to Devonshire, 18 December 1829 (Devonshire).

[3] Grey to Fitzwilliam, 30 June 1829 (Milton).

[4] Grey to Adair, 19 February 1830 (Grey).

[5] Grey to Howick, 9 May 1829 (Grey); Grey to Holland, 9 February 1830 (Grey); C. W. Wynn to Southey, 8 February 1830 (Wynn, 4814).

to overcome it sufficiently to offer Ireland to Grey.[1] The hopes received a set-back later in December, when Rosslyn visited Grey and made it clear that there was no thought of gaining extra support, and that the continued hostility of the king ruled out any offer of place to Grey himself.[2] Definitive to Grey, this was far from being so to others, partly because it was not generally known, partly because it was assumed that Wellington could overrule the king's reluctance if necessary, and that necessity must soon be driving him. 'I never recollect a moment in which the intentions of government seemed to be involved in so much mystery, or the course of the independent party so doubtful and uncertain', commented Spring Rice at the beginning of 1830.[3] These two features were closely interconnected, for until it was clear whether and how the government would strengthen itself, the whigs were unlikely to take a decided course. They might have been more active had the duke's real intentions been known. Whig fears that he would treat with the ultra tories were unrealistic, but so were whig hopes that he would turn to Grey or to whig groups.[4] The reasons were numerous, and included disbelief that Grey would bring much gain in strength, reluctance to share power with another strong personality, and unwillingness to change the character of the administration.[5] To choose Grey, or indeed any major group, would be to imply the rejection of the other groups outside the government, to give the administration a decided hue, to recreate party, and to unite an opposition.[6] The best safety was in keeping all expectations alive, all avenues open. It is hardly surprising that Wellington confined his efforts to 'the picking-off system' by recruitment of individuals, not groups. This brought neither votes nor numbers, but the duke saw little reason for either, considering that the hostility of the independent groups to each other was greater than to the government, and that the government party was stronger than all the others combined.[7]

[1] Noted in Howick, Journal, 2 December 1829 (Grey)

[2] Grey to Ellice, 17 December 1829 (Ellice Papers, packet 11); Grey to Howick, 8 January, 18 February 1830 (Grey).

[3] Spring Rice to Newport, 18 January 1830 (Monteagle).

[4] Wellington, *Despatches*, vi. 70–71.

[5] Londonderry to Hardinge, 6 July 1829 (Hardinge Papers); Wellington, *Despatches*, vii. 106–8; Mrs. Arbuthnot, *Journal*, ii. 293 and 316.

[6] Spring Rice to Lansdowne, 25 August 1829 (Lansdowne).

[7] Wellington, *Despatches*, vi. 70–71 and 532–3.

The opening of the session confirmed Wellington's first calculation and dispelled his second. No amendment was moved by the whigs, but Knatchbull, a disgruntled ultra, came forward with one which portrayed the distress as more general than the government had allowed, and requested a full consideration of remedies. This received the support of ultras, Huskissonians, and over sixty whigs, including Althorp, Brougham, Morpeth, and Lord John Russell. Several whigs presumably abstained, but twenty-six or twenty-eight others, who included Howick, Hobhouse, William Smith, George Philips, and William Marshall, voted for the original address, and allowed ministers to survive by fifty-three votes.[1] The next few debates saw variations on the same theme of party confusion. Blandford's motion for reform received support from radicals and a few fellow ultras. Hume's efforts for retrenchment received practically no support from ultras or from the Huskissonian group.[2] The government's prospects appeared to revive after its initial setback.

Yet if Wellington was counting on the continuation of disunity, he was ignoring the state of the country. This was shortly to transform the political situation as it made its influence felt on parliament. Industry and trade were beginning to recover from the depression of 1829, but recovery was patchy. Depression was still severe in some centres, such as Birmingham, and the urban working class in most areas was still suffering from marked unemployment and a slight decline in wages. Agriculture was in more serious difficulties, for the harvest of 1829 had been a bad one, that of 1830 was to prove but little better, and the general depression affecting all sections of the agricultural community produced a deep gloom early in 1830. Though neither as severe or as general as that of 1816 the distress of 1830 was marked enough to produce considerable political repercussions. Grey spoke of 'A state of general distress, such as never before pressed on any country, so intense and so extensive, that the minister can find nothing to say upon it . . . and for which he does not hold out even the hope of a remedy.'[3] Some envisaged revolutionary results, and the counties and grand juries

[1] *The Globe*, 5 February 1830, gives the number as 28 and lists 26; Howick to Grey, 5 February 1830 (Grey), gives the number as 26; Broughton, iv. 8, says 28.

[2] Howick to Grey, 16 February 1830 (Grey).

[3] Grey to Adair, 19 February 1830 (Grey); Spring Rice to Newport, 18 January 1830 (Monteagle); L. Melville, *Huskisson*, 310–12.

brought the distress to the attention of parliament by petitions and addresses: twenty-two county meetings were held on distress or taxation in the first three months of 1830, the first campaign of this kind since 1823.[1]

As before, distress brought forward a series of new issues, as community and parliament cast about for solutions. Some solutions, changes in the corn laws and currency, or a property tax, were widely discussed but threatened to disrupt different sections of whigs. They were less important than the others, economy and reform, on which whigs could achieve a broad measure of agreement. The new importance of these two questions hastened unity. This was particularly true of economy, which had always been the highest political wisdom for the whigs and their inevitable cure-all for distress. It was difficult to see how economy could be implemented, but means were the concern of government. Whigs could rest content with pointing to the end, and giving ministers a series of pushes on the way.

The first move was made by Graham on 12 February, with a motion to reduce official salaries to the level of 1797. Dawson moved a series of counter-resolutions pledging economy and Graham withdrew his motion. Everything now depended on the government's reductions of expenditure, announced on 19 February, and on the budget, introduced on 15 March. Some welcomed both, but Althorp was far more cautious, commenting that the reductions were good 'as far as they went' and expressing the wish that ministers had run risks by reducing more taxes.[2] Public pressure brought the after-thoughts round to this point of view; Howick thought the remissions less than the country required, and his father, Grey, argued that they would offer little relief.[3] In earlier years such extensive concessions

[1] Norfolk: *The Times*, 19 January. Kent: *The Times*, 22 January and *Morning Chronicle*, 15 March. Cambridgeshire: *The Times*, 23 January. Cumberland: *Leeds Mercury*, 30 January. Essex: *The Times*, 12 February. Worcestershire: *The Times*, 4 March. Herefordshire: *The Times*, 15 March. Cheshire: *Morning Chronicle*, 20 January. Lincolnshire: *Morning Chronicle*, 9 January. Devonshire: *Morning Chronicle*, 20 January. Buckinghamshire: *Morning Chronicle*, 1 March. Northamptonshire: *Morning Chronicle*, 15 March. Hertfordshire: *Morning Chronicle*, 11 March. Huntingdonshire: *Morning Chronicle*, 9 April. Lancashire: *Leeds Mercury*, 30 January. Wiltshire: *Spectator*, 30 January. Somerset: *Spectator*, 30 January. Gloucestershire: *Spectator*, 30 January. Rutland, Surrey, Northumberland, and Hampshire: *Commons Journals*, 1830, pp. 172, 182, 219. [2] *P.D.*, N.S. xxiii. 34304, 347–8, 336.

[3] Howick to Grey, 23 March 1830 (Grey); Grey to Howick, 19 March 1830 (Grey).

would have been welcomed with incredulity. Now they were received with ingratitude. A campaign for further economy soon gathered pace and motions became more frequent. Hume ferreted; Poulett-Thomson moved for a committee to review taxation; on 26 March a motion was carried by eighteen votes to abolish pensions awarded to the Hon. R. Dundas and the Hon. W. L. Bathurst; and three days later Graham attempted to secure the abolition of the office of lieutenant-general of the ordnance. Some weeks after this the government gave in to demands for a return listing the offices and emoluments of privy council members, and for changes in the crown's right of importation. Thus, continued pressure placed the government on the defensive where it had tried to take the initiative. The impression, a welcome one to whigs, was created that ministers were prevaricating. Coke spoke for many, when he claimed that no reductions would have taken place at all, had it not been for pressure from the opposition side of the house.[1]

Reform, too, was becoming an issue again. The long discussion before 1830 had laid an effective groundwork and removed the stigma of novelty. The arguments in its favour and against the defects of the existing system had been endlessly rehearsed, and the liberal climate of the 1820's had allowed them to be digested by the community. Different sections of the community had grown familiar with the idea of reform, albeit for different reasons; the agricultural interest thinking in terms of strengthening the county representation, the commercial interests viewing it as redressing the balance in their favour, the urban working class thinking in terms of a relief from distress. Also the whig party had associated itself so closely with reform that, whatever the quibbles about its being or not being a party doctrine, in the public mind it was part of the whig image. Moreover, previous experience indicated that it was something that the whigs were bound to take up if it again became as important as it had been in 1822. Now the signs indicated that it was, in fact, assuming just this importance. The political union formed in Birmingham took up reform, and was imitated in other towns as distress revived interest among the working and middle classes.[2] Agriculturalists also turned to reform as a solution to their difficulties

[1] *P.D.*, N.S. xxv. 281.

[2] Attwood to Davenport, 25 February 1830 (Bromley–Davenport Papers).

and petitions came in from Kent, Worcestershire, and Hertfordshire. Grey even claimed that there appeared to be 'a stronger feeling in favour of that measure than has for some time, or perhaps ever, existed'.[1]

Even in this early stage of the movement the whigs resumed their fickle courtship of reform. On 11 February, when Calvert moved to enlarge the East Retford franchise into the neighbouring hundred, Tennyson proposed a transfer to Birmingham; and Howick, despite the efforts of his father to dissuade him from any public commitment, moved a series of resolutions on the need for a general reform as an alternative to the piecemeal treatment of boroughs. Transfer and resolutions were defeated, and the growing strength of reform sentiment emerged only with Lord John Russell's motion to enfranchise Manchester, Leeds, and Birmingham. The dangers of revolution had always been an argument of the anti-reformers. Now Russell stole these clothes and appeared in them to argue that 'it is more than ever expedient to unite, as much as possible, persons representing every kind of property, and connected with every kind of interest, in order to remedy the evils that now oppress us, and to avert the dangers that may hereafter threaten the country'.[2] The regular reformers were now joined by new recruits, such as Lord William Powlett, Henry Bright, and Huskisson, who would agree to a partial remedy for pressing grievances, and by a handful of tories, including Blandford and Gascoyne. The motion secured 140 votes, but because several tories abstained, it was defeated by a majority of only forty-eight. Further discussion was delayed until 28 May, when O'Connell conjured up the bogey of radical reform, which the whigs exorcised in mechanical fashion. A series of counter-resolutions for moderate reform, proposed by Russell, were defeated by a majority of nearly a hundred. Reform was a long way from success, but it had been seriously discussed for the first time since 1826. The majority of the whigs had supported it, and thus Milton could argue that nearly all of them were prepared to support the general proposition, and some measure of detail.[3] New recruits had been secured, and the

[1] Grey to Howick, 10 February 1830 (Grey).

[2] *P.D.*, N.S. xxii. 860.

[3] P. C. Scarlett, *A Memoir of the Rt. Hon. James, First Lord Abinger*, London, 1877, p. 145.

discussion itself helped to keep the issue before the country and encourage new support.

The renewed interest in such old staples as economy and reform was a clear indication of the new pressures working on the political scene. On economy the government had made concessions viewed by the whigs as insufficient. On reform it stood firm. As a result, opinion began to move against the ministers, a development encouraged by Wellington's failure to recruit additional strength. The lack of speakers was so glaring that Brougham predicted the alteration of the rules of the house to allow Peel to speak up to thirty times on all questions, and Charles Wood considered that the debate on both sides of every question was carried on from the opposition benches.[1] Ministerial want of numbers was so marked that Lord Wallace predicted defeats on any issue on which even two of the groups outside it united; and Grey points out that 'the amount of the majorities on questions directly attacking the government is very small; and the numbers in the house show so little power in the ministers to procure an attendance, that they can only be considered as dragging on a precarious existence from day to day'.[2] Clearly the government did not have the strength necessary to deal with the deteriorating situation. The hostility and the self-confidence of the groups outside the government increased apace.

The first effect was to strengthen the internal cohesion of the independent groups, and in March separate meetings of the Huskisson group, the ultras, and the whigs were reported.[3] The most important of these was the meeting of the old whig opposition. A movement to bring a section of it together was initiated by three county members, Francis Lawley, E. B. Portman, and Edward Pendarves, who approached Althorp with a request that he should accept the leadership of a small group. Although doubtful, he recognized that Brougham was too unpopular with many to be an alternative, and after consulting Brougham, Graham, and Lord John Russell, he determined to accept.[4] A meeting was called for 3 March at Althorp's rooms in the Albany

[1] C. Wood to Sir F. L. Wood, 7 February 1830 (Hickleton Papers).

[2] Lord Wallace to Sir Charles Monck, 22 February 1830 (Wallace Papers, Northumberland County Record Office); Grey to Ellice, 16 March 1830 (Ellice Papers, packet 11).

[3] Adair to Grey, 11 March 1830 (Grey).

[4] D. Le Marchant, *Althorp*, pp. 245–6.

and attended by twenty-seven members, nearly all from the old opposition.[1] After initial agreement to co-operate to enforce reduction of expenditure and taxation, disagreements began to emerge. The question of the currency had to be left open and Althorp and Howick had to give up their urging of a property tax in deference to the meeting.[2] Further decisions were postponed to a second meeting three days later, when forty M.P.s found themselves able to agree to support every measure of economy no matter who proposed it, and to make a public announcement of their union.[3] It may be that it was only at this second meeting that Althorp agreed to act as leader, though the first one had unanimously chosen him. Immediately after it he wrote to Grey and Brougham to tell them of the party and of his own position as spokesman.[4]

What had been formed was a reconnaissance group rather than a party; the objects were limited to economy, there was no intention to act in hostility to ministers or bring them down, and concert with other groups was to be eschewed. Since the members differed on many questions and even on what economies could be made, it is hardly surprising to find that Grey was very dubious about the group and its degree of unity.[5] Even the first public appearances were inauspicious. On a resolution by Gordon, Burdett, who was a member of the group, advocated increased expenditure. On Graham's motion on the treasurer of the navy some supported, others, including Althorp, did not. A third meeting held on 16 March produced a larger attendance and a larger measure of agreement, but even then a tiny handful declined to give up their support of E. D. Davenport's effort to expand the currency.[6] Although the meeting agreed to support Poulett Thomson's motion for a committee on taxation, and

[1] Known names are the three movers, Guise, Wrottesley, Lord John Russell, Howick, Fazakerly, Warburton, and Heron. Lord Stanley and E. G. Stanley excused themselves, Burdett went out riding instead.

[2] Graham to Morpeth, n.d. [March 1830] (Carlisle); Howick to Grey, 3 March 1830 (Grey); Howick, Journal, 3 March 1830 (Grey).

[3] Howick to Grey, 6 March 1830 (Grey); C. Wood to Sir F. L. Wood, 8 or 9 March 1830 (Hickleton Papers); Le Marchant, *Althorp*, p. 245; Howick, Journal, 6 March 1830 (Grey).

[4] Le Marchant, *Althorp*, p. 267; *Morning Chronicle*, 9 March 1830; Althorp to Brougham, 6 March 1830 (Althorp).

[5] Grey to Howick, 9, 14, 16, and 28 March 1830 (Grey).

[6] Howick to Grey, 17 March 1830 (Grey); Howick, Journal, 16 March 1830 (Grey).

even though this decision was confirmed by a small meeting on the 25th, Althorp, to the dismay of his colleagues, went on to advocate a property tax. Howick blamed this obstinate honesty for the poor division: 78 votes against 179.[1]

It was from this low point that the group began to grow into the broad nucleus of a reviving whig party, and one which, retaining Althorp as its leader, solved that problem of leadership in the commons which had for so long weakened the old party. The group made up the hard core of the 124 votes cast against government on the ordnance estimates, and a large section of the 104 whigs who were joined by twenty-three ultras and four Huskissonians to defeat government on the Dundas–Bathurst pensions. When meetings resumed after Easter, they were both more numerous and more united, and a small vigilance committee was set up to scrutinize government legislation and report back to the general meetings in order to facilitate a united policy.[2] Unfortunately the only reports of meetings which survive are those of a meeting on 1 May, held to whip up attendance for Huskisson's motion on banking, and of a meeting early in July when over fifty members turned up, with several others out of town or unable to attend. Although this meeting was unable to agree on how to deal with a forthcoming motion by Grant, disagreement on this unusually thorny problem did not conceal either the steady growth in size or the new degree of unity attained by the group. In June a dinner had been organized at Brooks's which, according to Normanby, consisted of 'all that is most venerable and revered in whiggism . . . and looked more like a revival of party than anything that has happened for some time'.[3] In July new recruits began to attend the meetings: on the 4th Morpeth and Graham came, and said that they had not attended earlier because they had not considered the group sufficiently hostile to ministers.[4] Finally, the ground of attack was widening as hostility to the government grew. The July meeting decided that if the government had not strengthened itself by the meeting of the new parliament the party would go into regular opposition to turn them out.[5]

[1] Howick to Grey, 26 March and 1 April 1830 (Grey); Howick, Journal, 28 March 1830 (Grey)

[2] Le Marchant, *Althorp*, p. 246.

[3] Normanby to Devonshire, 23 June 1830 (Devonshire).

[4] Broughton, iv. 36.

[5] Althorp to Spencer, 5 July 1830 (Althorp); *Morning Chronicle*, 5 July 1830.

While this development was in progress Grey was beginning to move into opposition. In his earlier state of doubt he had been inclined to his normal melancholy. In March, the day after his sixty-sixth birthday, he wrote to his son:

> I am altogether unequal to the discharge of the duties of any laborious office. It has been therefore for some time my determination not to take any, . . . though I might assist by occasional exertions in parliament, in the formation of a new government, I could not take upon myself the weight of active parliamentary and official duties. I have no longer the powers of either body or mind that are required for such a task.[1]

Nevertheless, by May Grey was ready to emerge from harbour, his sails bellied out by the rising winds of public and personal discontents.[2] Concern at government weakness was probably supplemented by indignation at the slight implied by the failure to offer him any position. In April Grey had thought it possible that some office would be offered to him on the accession of the new king, although not one he could accept.[3] Thus Grey came into the open, and was even prepared to face the consequences of defeating the government. Howick recorded in May: 'my father said that if his being at the head of the government should be considered absolutely necessary (which it would), he would not refuse.'[4] His inclinations were confirmed after George IV's death on 26 June. No office at all was forthcoming, even though the new monarch had no personal hostility.

The process of whig reunion, already under way, required nothing more than that Grey should take an active role. He alone could be looked up to as the leader of any group that emerged; Althorp, indeed, had already thought it proper to notify him of its formation. Informal communication appears to have begun in May, when Grey and Althorp were reviewing possible members of a whig government, and by the end of June it was followed by full consultation.[5] On 29 June Peel announced a message from the king recommending a temporary provision for the public service. Howick, Stanley, Wood, and Althorp

[1] Grey to Howick, 14 March 1830 (Grey).

[2] Howick, Journal, 5 May 1830 (Grey).

[3] Howick, Journal, 29 April and 13 May 1830 (Grey).

[4] Ibid., 13 May 1830.

[5] Howick, Journal, 13 May 1830. There is a minor illustration in Broughton, iv. 28.

discussed the question at Brooks's and decided to move an adjournment of twenty-four hours. Stanley then talked with Grey and found him fully in agreement, so the next morning Stanley, Althorp, Holland, and Lansdowne met Grey at his house and agreed together to move an adjournment in both houses; failing that, an amended address was to be proposed, but not divided on. This was specially written by Grey and Holland.[1] The same day, Grey and Althorp declared against the government. Grey also pointed out that his motion 'had originated from a consultation with one or two friends with whom he had always been in the habit of acting'.[2] Thus almost immediately Grey was, as he himself put it, 'though without any formal union, supported by the favourable disposition of all the parties not connected with government'.[3] This, in turn, boosted the Albany meetings. Durham told Grey: 'it was stated by Sir J. Graham and others that they only consented to belong to the party, when re-formed last year, [i.e. session] on the express understanding that you were to be the leader over all, and the house of commons leader acting in every respect under you. Stanley repeated the same thing the other day at Heaton.'[4] Small wonder that observers began to talk of the reunification of the whig party.[5]

The trends drawing the whigs together also pulled them towards Huskisson's group. Russell had argued in January that the whigs should look to a co-operation with them, since they had men of official experience while the whigs had numbers; and in March Grey had warned his son that Althorp's group should do nothing to alienate the small party round Huskisson, since no administration could be formed without them.[6] For their part, Canning's old followers were also beginning to feel both their own isolation and the impossibility of rejoining Wellington's cabinet on their own. They began to envisage a return accompanied by Grey, as a safeguard which would prevent their being dominated by Wellington.

Early in May Littleton told Howick that the Huskissonians

[1] Howick, Journal, 11 July 1830 (Grey).

[2] *P.D.*, N.S. xxv. 764.

[3] G. Le Strange, *Lieven*, ii. 20.

[4] Durham to Grey, 4 October 1830 (Grey).

[5] Wallace to Monck, 1 July and 21 July 1830 (Wallace Papers).

[6] Russell to Brougham, 30 January 1830 (Brougham); Grey to Howick, 9 March 1830 (Grey).

hoped to see Grey in charge of foreign affairs, and that if this appointment were made, they would no longer consider themselves as hostile to the administration.[1] In June Grey was approached by Wellesley, who claimed to have heard from Huskisson that he favoured systematic opposition and was prepared to serve under Grey in a government. Grey declared himself disinclined to any junction, but in favour of thorough scrutiny of the government's measures, and prepared for closer co-operation if the measures made this necessary. Huskisson appears to have been satisfied with this answer.[2] Similar approaches were made by Tennyson to Durham, who replied that Huskisson would be one of the first people to whom Grey would make proposals if he were in a position to do so.[3] Thus, although there was no actual junction between parties, each group had some knowledge of the other's mind, through informal communication. This knowledge may have constituted one among the many factors which inclined the Huskisson group to decline offers of place. In July an attempt was made to secure Melbourne, together with Grant and Palmerston. He replied that he could not accept without Huskisson and Grey, a stipulation which prevented prompt renewal of overtures.[4]

The last days of the session heavily underlined both the drawing together of parties and their growing hostility to the government. In moving their twenty-four-hour adjournment on 30 June, Grey and Althorp insisted that the regency question should be discussed, and decided, before the house was dissolved. This was supported by Huskisson and his group, by C. W. Wynn, alone and out of office since 1828, by Melbourne and Goderich in the lords, and by Grosvenor and Norfolk, who had hitherto been sympathetic towards the government. It was followed by a fiasco on 6 July, when Grant moved an unpopular address to the king on provision for a regency, and secured a very low vote. Yet it was still a vote in which whig and Huskissonian were both represented.

[1] Howick, Journal, 5 May 1830 (Grey).

[2] Howick, Journal, 27 June 1830 (Grey).

[3] K. G. Feiling, *The Second Tory Party, 1714–1832*, London, 1951, p. 380; Tennyson to Huskisson, 6 July 1830 (Huskisson Papers, Add. MSS. 38758, ff. 194–5): 'I ventured to state *my conviction* from what I had heard you express.'

[4] E. Ashley, *The Life and Correspondence of H. J. Temple, Third Viscount Palmerston*, London, 1879, i. 211.

The debates of these few days provided the opportunity for a series of attacks. Grey declared his hostility to the government, announcing that it was incapable of forwarding the honour of the country.[1] Brougham, intemperate, irritated, and possibly intoxicated, described ministers as 'the mean fawning parasites' of the duke, and Graham announced that the administration had been weighed in the balance and found wanting.[2] Wynn's comment on the whole demonstration was that 'the opposition to the duke of Wellington seem to be *banding* themselves more than one has yet seen'.[3] The *Manchester Guardian* noted that a regular opposition had at last emerged.[4]

Wellington saw the danger symptoms, but he appears to have underestimated their importance, being confident both of the government's ability to face a united opposition, and of the support of crown and country. Opinion in the house was moving ahead of opinion in the country, as measured even by the liberal press, and Wellington counted on new reinforcements and support from the general election made necessary by the death of the king.[5] This was to be an appeal to the country to endorse his government.

After the polling in July and early August contemporaries attempted to assess the success or failure of this appeal in numerical terms. Their views conflicted. On the government side Hardinge was very much on his own in visualizing a loss of two or three, for Lowther reported Holmes as thinking that government had gained twenty-one, and he himself put the figure at twenty-five, while Planta, who did a detailed analysis, estimated the gain at twenty-two.[6] The opposition were equally confident, for Durham thought that ministers had lost fifty, the *Spectator* forty or fifty, Brougham, after originally bidding higher, decided on a loss of thirty-four and an opposition gain of twenty-

[1] *P.D.*, N.S. xxv. 765.

[2] *P.D.*, N.S. xxv. 825, 894–5; Milton to Scarlett, 28 July 1830, copy (Milton); Duncannon to Milton, 27 June 1830 (Milton).

[3] C. W. Wynn to H. W. Wynn, 11 July 1830 (Wynn, 4817).

[4] *Manchester Guardian*, 3 July 1830.

[5] Wellington, *Despatches*, vii. 107; Wynn commented: 'I hear the grand duke talks of obtaining an accession of 25 votes', C. W. Wynn to H. W. Wynn, 23 July 1830 (Wynn, 4817).

[6] Hardinge to Ellenborough, 5 September 1830 (Ellenborough Papers, P.R.O. 30/12/7); Lowther to Lonsdale, 20 and 30 August 1830 (Lowther Papers); Planta to Wellington, 30 August 1830 (Apsley House Papers).

five, while Duncannon estimated that government had lost nearly thirty.[1] All these estimates were based on the same lack of evidence about the opinions of the new members, and even on dubious estimates of the opinions of the old.[2]

'It is folly to talk of the influence of numbers', Abercromby pointed out, 'when you see that the character and spirit of the elections is so decidedly popular.'[3] There were many appearances which went against the government. In several prestige contests, particularly in counties such as Yorkshire, Suffolk, Surrey, Essex, Cambridgeshire, and Devon, government candidates had fared badly, opposition ones well, while in some of the counties independent movements among freeholders had broken or weakened long-established preponderances.[4] Peel's relatives had suffered defeat, and the attempts to eject Huskisson's supporters had proved fruitless. It was also clear that the government was weak in the more popular constituencies: Brougham, ever inclined to put the obscure precisely, calculated that, of 236 members returned by popular election, seventy-nine were ministerialist, 141 opposition.[5] In addition, the mood of the country, and particularly the pressing concern for economy, and even for reform, had been clearly brought out, and several candidates had been obliged to pledge themselves to economy and retrenchment in deference to the insistence of their electors.[6]

[1] Durham to Grey, 17 August 1830 (Grey); *Spectator*, 14 August 1830; Brougham to Denman, n.d. [1830] (Brougham); Brougham to Devonshire, 20 August and 8 or 12 September 1830 (Devonshire); H. Brougham, *Life and Times*, iii. 55; Duncannon to Brougham, 27 August 1830 (Brougham).

[2] The pamphlet *Observations on Two Pamphlets lately publicly attributed to Mr. Brougham*, London, 1830, claimed that, of fifty-two opposition members listed by Brougham in his pamphlet, a third had no community of sentiment with him, while, of fifty-two government members whom Brougham had counted as displaced, 12 to 14 had not voted once with ministers the previous session (p. 70).

[3] Abercromby to Lansdowne, 17 August 1830 (Lansdowne). See also Huskisson to Littleton, 8 August 1830 (Hatherton Papers, Staffordshire Record Office).

[4] Coke commented that in Norfolk tory strength had been broken by such an independent movement and that 'the like spirit has manifested itself in most counties which leads me to hope we shall live to see the parliament independent', T. W. Coke to Roscoe, 25 August 1830 (Roscoe Papers). In most counties these movements worked against tory influences. Occasionally whig influences were attacked, as in Bedfordshire.

[5] *Edinburgh Review*, no.ciii, October 1830, p. 268; *Morning Chronicle*, 14 August 1830.

[6] *Spectator*, 23 August 1830; Buckingham and Chandos, *Courts and Cabinets of William IV and Victoria*, London, 1861, i. 45; Devonshire's diary, 7 August: 'the Derbyshire election well over and the old tories gave Mundy a lecture instead of

Hardinge was sceptical about the effect of the pledges, thinking they could count only on 'finicking questions', yet they did cut down the government's freedom of manœuvre at a time when it already had dangerously little, and the same pressures which imposed pledges inevitably encouraged whig members to greater efforts against the government.[1] The pressures were particularly strong in Ireland, owing to the imposition of new taxation earlier in the year. Duncannon commented: 'there has been a spirit shown in almost every county in Ireland, that must alarm the members, and I am much mistaken if you will not see a very obstreperous set from this country'.[2] He gave opposition a net gain of six, while O'Connell put it at eight and added several cases of pledges or of alarm at the state of public opinion.[3] Because of this situation, Ireland saw a greater increase in the number of contests and a greater turnover of members than did the rest of the kingdom.[4]

In view of the pressures to which members had been exposed, the *Leeds Mercury* considered that the new house would be the most independent ever elected; Abercromby, too, thought it would be the least controllable.[5] The elections were comparable in the scale of activity only with those of 1818, which had also placed the then administration in a very difficult position. Just

Lord George—reform retrenchment . . . etc.—its like a whig county now' (Devonshire). Examination of newspapers indicates that twenty-nine elected members, eighteen of them new ones, took pledges. The list is far from comprehensive, since many pressures, those on Mundy, for example, went unrecorded and old opposition members hardly needed to pledge. In assessing the allegiances of members Planta classified nine of these members as 'friend', two as 'bad doubtfuls', four as 'moderate ultra', and ten as 'enemy': Peel Papers, Add. MSS. 40401, ff. 182–95. The effect of the pledges can be illustrated by the vote on the motion of 15 November on which ministers fell. Taking all except those counted as enemies, eleven voted against government, one for it, and the rest absented themselves. Nearly half of the pledged members were Irish, an illustration of the greater pressures there.

[1] Hardinge to Ellenborough, 5 September 1830 (Ellenborough Papers, P.R.O. 30/12/7).

[2] Duncannon commented: 'these taxes of Goulburn's have nearly driven the people crazy', Duncannon to Milton, 27 June 1830 (Milton); Wellington, *Despatches*, vii. 80–81; Duncannon to Brougham, 27 August 1830 (Brougham). See also *Dublin Evening Post*, 10 July and 26 August 1830.

[3] Duncannon's estimates are quoted in Brougham to Devonshire, 8 or 12 September 1830 (Devonshire); O'Connell to Hume, n.d. [1830] (Hume Papers).

[4] Ireland returned 22 per cent. of the members who had not sat in the last parliament, but only 13 per cent. of those who had.

[5] *Leeds Mercury*, 4 September 1830; Abercromby to Lansdowne, 17 August 1830 (Lansdowne).

as had been the case then, the large numbers of new members were uncommitted by any loyalties the government had been able to build up for itself, and probably more responsive to the mood of the country. Apparently they were more inclined to hostility toward the government than the old members, and in the division of 15 November, when the government fell, their votes were to be the decisive ones.[1] In August and September, however, their views were largely unknown and the experts were trading hypotheses in a vacuum. Until the vote only two things were clear. The mood of the country was more hostile than ministers had expected, and the fact that opposition and government estimates could cancel each other out so neatly indicated that the expected government gains had not materialized. Ministerial hopes were vitiated and the government was weaker than it had been in early July. Wellington refused to despair. Influenced possibly by Planta's analysis of party strength in the new house, he was confident of both government numbers and speaking talent. At a time when the possibility of gaining new recruits was slim, he was still reluctant to take in any but isolated individuals.[2]

If Wellington failed to learn the lesson of the election, the whigs knew it by heart. Stuart-Wortley comments that they have 'acquired double confidence from the elections *in the present state of* affairs and I cannot help saying, as it appears to me, not without some reason'.[3] Hostility to ministers rose with expectations. Sefton voiced a widespread mood when he wrote anxiously to Brougham:

If we are not organised, his miserable weakness will still prevail. For God's sake, concert with Grey a regular plan for an union of parties and don't put it off till it is too late. . . . An avowed party in opposition is indispensible. . . . There never was such a moment. You supported ministers as long as you could, but their imbecility

[1] If the votes of 15 November from the slightly inaccurate Hansard list are analysed, the following trend appears:

	For Govt.	Against	No vote	Totals
Not in previous parliament	25% (42)	44% (76)	31% (54)	172
In previous parliament	33% (162)	34% (163)	33% (161)	486

[2] Wellington, *Despatches*, vii. 240–1.

[3] J. Stuart-Wortley to Arbuthnot, 7 September 1830 (Peel Papers, Add. MSS. 40340, f. 234).

and utter incapacity for conducting the government has become so obvious that it is impossible to support them or even tolerate them any longer.[1]

The leading figures in the party agreed. Grey, Graham, Durham, Russell, and Brougham shared a conviction that only whig bungling and mistakes could save the government.[2] The opposition now envisaged was one to turn the ministers out, for, as Lord John Russell pointed out, 'the duke has now lost three quarters of his merit as a minister, namely the authority of his name and I can see no use in looking to any combination with him. He must be left to pursue his tottering course as he can.'[3] Some even began to envisage victory and to review policies in the light of office.[4] Even the attitude of those whigs who had hitherto been attracted to the administration stiffened, for Calcraft, Ebrington, and Lord Stanley were all reported as more hostile.[5]

Hostility stimulated preparation. Lansdowne called on Grey on 20 October at Howick and reviewed the political situation; Grey came up early, arriving in London on 29 October; the meetings at Althorp's were resumed before the session began.[6] Although badly attended, the first meeting showed more unanimity than the earlier ones, and agreement was reached on strategy. Howick reported:

Althorp began by saying that at ye beginning of ye last session he had been unwilling to do anything which might have ye effect of driving out ye government but that in consequence of its inefficiency and ye apparent determination of ye duke not to strengthen it he had no longer any such feeling, after a good deal of talking which came to very little Maberly said that a party could only act upon some principle and it was agreed that retrenchment and parliamentary reform were to be our great objects.[7]

[1] Sefton to Brougham, 27 August 1830 (Brougham).

[2] H. Brougham, *Life and Times*, iii. 44–46; Graham to Brougham, n.d. [October 1830] (Brougham); Russell to Brougham, n.d. [1830] (Brougham).

[3] Russell to Grey, n.d. [October 1830] (Grey).

[4] Graham to Brougham, 25 September 1830 (Brougham); Grey to Holland, 19 October 1830 (Grey); Brougham to Durham, n.d. [August 1830] (Brougham).

[5] *Morning Chronicle*, 11 October 1830; R. W. Horton to Littleton, 17 August 1830 (Hatherton Papers, Staffordshire Record Office); *Manchester Guardian*, 7 August 1830.

[6] Grey to Holland, 19 October 1830 (Grey).

[7] Howick, Journal, 31 October 1830 (Grey); Althorp to Milton, 2 November 1830 (Milton).

Although the meeting decided against any amendment it was still clear that an organized onslaught on the government was building up.

This was a simple acceleration of earlier developments, but a new dynamic was now accelerating the processes. Brougham had kept himself in the background of affairs ever since 1827, but the parliamentary clash at the end of June, followed by his own election for the largest constituency in the country, now revitalized him. At the beginning of July he had published, anonymously, a pamphlet, *The Country Without a Government*, launching a bitter attack on both Wellington and his government, and urging the whigs to co-operate with Huskissonians and ultra tories. He argued the same case with greater succinctness in the July issue of the *Edinburgh Review*, followed it up with a further pamphlet on the result of the general election, and rounded off by reviewing his own efforts for the *Edinburgh Review*. In addition, he bombarded fellow whigs with letters urging activity, telling Lord Durham, for example, to excite Grey to action, and stressing the need for a regular and organized party to turn out the government.[1]

All this proved worrying to some, and especially so to Grey and Howick, both of whom feared that Brougham's head had been turned by the Yorkshire election. In particular they feared that he would challenge for the leadership. Howick noted:

> he must know that there are not half a dozen people who would follow him. I fear we shall find him very troublesome next session, his return for Yorkshire seems to have increased his before intolerable vanity to the highest pitch and I should not be the least surprised if he should insist on managing everything in spite of his total want of discretion (and I cannot but think of honesty).[2]

Ellice added: '*I see on all sides* great jealousy of Brougham's assumption of the office of leader, great distrust of his prudence or intentions, and much apprehension of his committing some fault which will strengthen ministers.'[3]

Yet Durham defended Brougham stoutly, arguing that Brougham fully realized that the elected leader in opposition

[1] Brougham to Durham, 5 August and n.d. [August] 1830 (Brougham).
[2] Howick, Journal, 27 August 1830 (Grey). See also Ellice to Grey, 30 September 1830 (Grey).
[3] Ellice to Grey, 28 October 1830 (Grey).

would become leader of the commons in office, and that since he would not sacrifice his legal profession to be the one, he could not expect to be the other. His present activity, Durham explained, originated not in an anxiety to be leader, but in a passionate desire to turn out the Wellington administration.[1] This interpretation appears to contain a large element of truth. Certainly, if Brougham had challenged the leadership which Althorp was in the process of establishing, the consequences could have been disruptive for the party. Considered with his long reluctance to take the lead in the 1820's, and his consent to Althorp's experiment earlier in the year, this failure to challenge may indicate that Brougham realized his unpopularity and was not, in fact, anxious for the position. He may, of course, have been delaying until his immediate enthusiasm, the overthrow of the government, was achieved, but a creature of sudden passionate enthusiasms may well not have calculated the situation as fully as this. Whatever the reason, Brougham's failure to challenge at this point settled the question of the leadership in the commons, just as Grey's re-emergence had settled the problem in the lords.

Brougham combined his efforts for whig unity with a strenuous advocacy of some measure of understanding with the Huskisson group, now only just under a dozen in number, but still strong in experience and ability. Like Durham, he wanted to co-operate, but stop short of an open coalition, which might alienate the ultras, since their support, too, was necessary to defeat the government.[2] Many other whigs, including Grey, agreed with this assessment, and with the view that a government could not be formed without the group.[3] The only doubts concerned the attitude of the Huskisson group themselves, for July and August saw a spate of rumours that the government was making approaches to them.[4] The doubts were not dispelled until Huskisson was sounded out by the leading whig contact,

[1] Durham to Grey, 4 October 1830 (Grey).

[2] Brougham to Durham, 5 August and n.d. [August] 1830 (Brougham); Durham to Grey, 29 August 1830 (Grey).

[3] Durham to Brougham, 7 September 1830 (Brougham), quoting Lord Grey; H. Brougham, *Life and Times*, iii. 44–46; Howick Journal, 27 August 1830 (Grey).

[4] Grey to Milton, 25 July 1830 (Milton); Lady Holland to Brougham, 6 August 1830 (Brougham); C. W. Wynn to H. W. Wynn, 25 August 1830 (Wynn, 4817); *Morning Chronicle*, 21 September 1830.

Graham. He elicited a comprehensive declaration from Huskisson:

> I agree with you that the present ministry ought not to stand the shock of the next session and that it is the interest of all public men . . . that they should come to an understanding not to listen to any separate overtures for reinforcing it, unless upon the preliminary admission of an entire *reconstruction*, so as to exclude no one, and to admit to a fair participation of influence and power in the deliberations and management of the state persons more competent than those who have now the charge of some of the most important departments. I do not expect, I own, that the Duke of Wellington will consent to negotiate upon such a principle, but I am sanguine, from all that has come to my knowledge, since the close of the session, that he will not find in the country any man of *real weight* inclined to treat with him upon any other.[1]

The next step was clearly up to the whigs. Both Graham and Brougham planned to meet Huskisson on 15 September, at the opening of the Liverpool–Manchester railway, and discuss the situation in the opposition coach.

Death met Huskisson first. For the whigs this removed a major obstacle to an agreement with his followers. Many whigs had strong doubts about Huskisson's character, but no one had any reservation about his supporters.[2] The death also eliminated the danger of alienating ultra tories, for their objections too had been to Huskisson.[3]

In this situation Brougham once again began vehemently to urge junction; but a definitive understanding was due to the actions of Lord Grey.[4] Grey now asked Holland to see Melbourne and Palmerston, and discover whether the loss of Huskisson would make them any more inclined to join Wellington. In his interview Holland was delighted to find that the opposite was in fact the case. He also came to this conclusion: 'As to other junctions they evidently imply and almost say that there is no public principle or personal feeling which stands in the way of

[1] Huskisson to Graham, 26 August 1830 (Graham).

[2] Duncannon to Brougham, 22 September 1830 (Brougham); Althorp to Spencer, 24 September 1830 (Althorp).

[3] C. Arbuthnot to Peel, 17 September 1830 (Peel Papers, Add. MSS. 40340, ff. 236–7).

[4] Brougham to Devonshire, 18 September 1830 (Devonshire); Brougham to Graham, 17 September 1830 (Graham); Brougham to Carlisle, 17 September 1830 (Carlisle).

a union between them and the whigs and in hinting at such matters they point more directly to you, as the leader under whom they would willingly range them.' Their only doubts, in fact, were about Althorp's judgement and Brougham's lack of it.[1] This appears to have been the only direct negotiation between the two parties, although Melbourne had informed Brougham of his views, but Grey considered it adequate:

> I think matters now stand in the best way, that is with a disposition to co-operation on both sides, and without any positive engagement, till we see what the measures of the government are to be. Agreement on these will naturally lead to a more intimate union, and it is in this way only that such junctions can ever be hoped to succeed with the public. To such a result I shall be most ready to lend myself.[2]

It was also the arrangement which best suited the Huskisson group, for they may have been reluctant to merge with the whigs at this stage.[3] Independence did not, however, mean any willingness to join the government, for without the protection afforded by Huskisson's reputation and stature, the danger that they would be swallowed up in a tory government was enormously increased. An invitation to join the administration was to Palmerston 'like asking me whether I was disposed to jump off Westminster Bridge'.[4] In any case, there was little incentive to join a declining administration. An overture from Wellington through Lord Clive was therefore turned down by Palmerston, and he promptly disappeared to Paris to avoid further embarrassment.[5] On his return he refused a renewed offer in a six-minute interview with Wellington.[6]

Matters were bound to rest here until the session made possible further co-operation between whigs and Huskisson's friends. Yet before this could be achieved some understanding had to be reached on parliamentary reform, always a whig favourite and a Canningite phobia. The problem was a real one, because for

[1] Holland to Grey, 25 September 1830 (Holland).

[2] Grey to Holland, 8 October 1830 (Grey).

[3] Palmerston to Littleton, 25 September 1830 (Hatherton Papers).

[4] A. Aspinall, *Brougham*, pp. 182–3; Palmerston to Littleton, op. cit.; Melbourne to Brougham, 19 September 1830 (Brougham).

[5] E. Ashley, *Palmerston*, i. 211–12; Wellington, *Despatches*, vii. 281; Broughton, iv. 60; A. Aspinall, 'The Last of the Canningites', *E.H.R.*, 1935, p. 662.

[6] E. Ashley, *Palmerston*, i. 212–13; Mrs. Arbuthnot, *Journal*, ii. 395.

the first time the three branches of the reform movement in the country at large were now beginning to move in unison. In the immediate post-war years the reform movement had been largely an affair of mass working-class discontents and of small nuclei of urban radicals. In the early 1820's it had been a concern of sections of county opinion activated by distress. In the late 1820's it had been the preserve of urban middle-class interests anxious for representation. Now the slowness with which industrial distress was lifting and the prolonged depression in agriculture caused all three movements to revive at the same time, a situation partially demonstrated in the election by demands for pledges on reform and movements against established political influences in several counties. The excitement produced by the revolution in France provided a further boost, and the new strength of the demand for reform was such that Peel visualized it as 'the all important question' of the session: rumours soon began to circulate that Wellington was to satisfy the country by introducing a government measure.[1]

If Wellington could be thought to be considering reform, the whigs could be expected to be obsessed with it. Grey took little active part in the discussions on the issue, but there was no need for him to do so. His opinions on reform were known; as he himself pointed out, 'I of course must support my old opinions. . . . I must be found in the ranks of its supporters.'[2] Silence was in any case the best policy; as a symbol, Grey could conciliate moderate and violent reformers, but, as a partisan committed to some definite scheme, he would risk alienating one or the other group. When Sir James Graham asked him to make a declaration against the nomination boroughs, he declined, and kept public expression of his views to very general terms.[3]

It was Brougham who took the initiative. In the enthusiasm of the Yorkshire election he had come out as a strong protagonist, declaring, 'I will leave in no man's hand, now that I am member for Yorkshire, the great cause of parliamentary

[1] C. S. Parker, *Peel*, ii. 161; C. W. Wynn to H. W. Wynn, 28 October 1830 (Wynn, 4817); Graham to Brougham, 1 September 1830 (Brougham); Holland to Brougham, 13 September 1830 (Brougham); Grey to Holland, 19 September and 19 October 1830 (Grey); *Morning Chronicle*, 12 October 1830.

[2] Grey to Holland, 19 October 1830 (Grey).

[3] Mentioned in Lord John Russell to Grey, October 1830 (Grey).

reform.'[1] At a great Yorkshire dinner at the end of September he unveiled his own plan of reform, which envisaged giving the representation to the large towns, carrying on the poll at several places in each county, enfranchising copy-holders, disfranchising non-resident electors, and reforming the representation of Scotland.[2] Brougham then returned south to begin the preparations for a reform motion and whip up support—to the horror of some of the older whigs, who would have preferred the subject in the safer hands of Lord John Russell.[3] His first step was taken at the party meeting before the session, and the events are again described by Howick:

> Althorp . . . gave notice that J. Russell meant in the present month to give notice of ye renewal of his motion for giving representatives to the three great towns but the feeling of all present was so strongly expressed that such a motion as not going far enough ought not be made that he engaged to write to J. R. to induce him to give it up. Brougham complained that his plan of reform had been much misrepresented and said that he was determined to move certain resolutions preparatory to bringing in a bill or rather four or five distinct bills for the purpose of enabling different persons to support those parts of his plan of which they might separately approve and he repeated what he had said at Sheffield of being resolved not to give up this subject to anybody that he followed others long enough and he now expected them to follow him.[4]

After staking his claim, Brougham dined with Althorp, Stanley, and Denman, and agreed to return with Graham and Macdonald to talk over the plan, before it was put to another meeting. As now elaborated, this envisaged, in addition to the earlier components, the subtraction of one member each from all the rotten boroughs, and some of the smaller towns, and the concession of the vote to inhabitant householders.[5] Brougham now commissioned Sir James Graham to help him in the task of sounding out opinion on the scheme. Graham himself was

[1] *Leeds Mercury*, 2 October 1830 and 27 July 1830.

[2] *Leeds Mercury*, 2 October 1830.

[3] Brougham to Ellice, 25 October 1830 (Ellice Papers, packet 36); Grey to Holland, 8 October 1830 (Grey); Holland to Grey, 10 October 1830 (Holland).

[4] Howick, Journal, 31 October 1830 (Grey). See also Tavistock to Lord G. W. Russell, 5 November 1830 (Woburn Abbey MSS.). Tavistock claims that Brougham was heard 'in cold silence'.

[5] Brougham to Graham, n.d. [October 1830] (Graham); C. W. New, *Brougham*, p. 413.

enthusiastic about the plan because it was moderate, and sought 'a practical remedy for an admitted evil at a moment of great excitement'. He was also delighted that the question had been taken up by Brougham, 'because', as he says, 'the public will be satisfied with *less* from you than from any other member of the house of commons, when you declare that you bring forward *all*, which you can hope to carry with a due regard to the circumstances of the present time'.[1] Nevertheless, he allowed himself to be convinced by Grey that the plan of taking only one seat each from the rotten boroughs was no longer sufficient.[2]

As the main contact with the Palmerston group he then had to discover their views. These were much more cautious, but the group was prepared to vote for a general resolution such as Brougham was considering 'if vaguely worded'. Howick, who received his account of the discussions directly from Graham, recorded the latter's impression that, if it became necessary to form a government, the Palmerston group would consent to a great deal more than they were now prepared to accept.[3] As a result, Graham went away satisfied.

Brougham, meanwhile, was taking his own soundings. His first intention was to give notice of his motion on the first day of the session, but both Graham and Durham feared that this might alarm people, unless it were understood that the motion came from Brougham and not the whigs as a body. They preferred a motion in general terms, and wanted Brougham to confine his efforts on the first day to a simple announcement of his intention. The difficulty was to get him to agree to this without making him think that the whigs wished to disclaim him or his motion, and this was accomplished only after lengthy persuasion by Durham, and a letter from Graham.[4] Whig fears relaxed and Althorp noted the next day that 'Brougham is in a much more controllable state'.[5] The opening of the parliamentary session set the seal on the emerging agreement when the duke of Wellington alienated all moderate opinion by declaring against reform. The final steps were then decided with unani-

[1] Graham to Brougham, 1 November 1830 (Brougham).

[2] Howick, Journal, 6 November 1830 (Grey).

[3] Ibid., 7 November 1830.

[4] Graham to Brougham, 1 November 1830 (Brougham); Durham to his wife, 2 November 1830 (Lambton).

[5] Althorp to Milton, 2 November 1830 (Milton).

mity at a dinner at Brougham's, attended by Morpeth, Stanley, Denman, Althorp, Hobhouse, Graham, Howick, and Macdonald. It was decided to make reform the first division against the government, and Hobhouse gave up a motion of his own on Belgium to make way for it. It was also decided that Brougham would move, on 16 November, for a committee to inquire whether the state of the representation required attention.[1] These decisions and the general commitment to reform were confirmed by a further meeting at Althorp's on 13 November. With 104 present this was the largest of the series, as well as the largest recorded attendance of M.P.s at any whig meeting since the war.[2]

Whig reunion, the *rapprochement* with Palmerston and Melbourne, and the concerted pressure for reform, all meant danger for the government. It was in a weak position to face this, and Wellington was therefore pressed by supporters, particularly after the opening of parliament, to conciliate the opposition, and remain master of the situation, by making concessions on reform. Fitzgerald, Lord Talbot, and Lord Stafford all argued or pressed, and E. J. Littleton took it upon himself to make an unauthorized approach, holding out the prospect of support from Palmerston's group, if the government gave satisfactory explanations on five points, one of which was moderate reform.[3] Wellington remained obdurate, refusing to violate his principles, calculating that the government could survive, and hoping, perhaps, that fear of revolution would bring in additional support.[4] The ministry was to meet the situation unchanged and unchanging.

When the session opened on 2 November, reform immediately became the major preoccupation. In the lords Grey stressed the

[1] Howick, Journal, 7 November 1830 (Grey); Countess of Carlisle to Devonshire, 8 November 1830 (Devonshire); Brougham to Devonshire, 8 November 1830 (Devonshire); Broughton, iv. 60.

[2] Brougham to Creevey, 16 November 1830 (Creevey transcripts); Le Marchant, *Althorp*, p. 256, gives the attendance as more than 200.

[3] M. Fitzgerald to Wellington, 5 November 1830 (Apsley House Papers); Lady Granville to Devonshire, 4 November 1830 (Devonshire); C. S. Parker, *Peel*, ii. 163–6.

[4] Lowther to Lonsdale, 27 October 1830 (Lowther MSS.), 'It is said he is heartily tired of concession and conciliation'; C. W. Wynn to H. W. Wynn, 28 October 1830 (Wynn, 4817), 'The great object of government will, I imagine, be to raise alarm.'

danger of revolution and the need to avoid it by redressing grievances, and reforming parliament, before public pressure became overwhelming.[1] In the commons Brougham gave notice of his motion for a fortnight's time, and Althorp, taking that leading position in the debate on the address which was now rightfully his, announced the hostility of his party to the government and their readiness to displace it, following up with a declaration of his own conviction of the need for parliamentary reform.[2] Wellington countered the public urgings of the whigs, and the private urgings of his supporters, with his famous declaration against all reform. Hopes of ministerial action were dashed and the government seemed to many to be certain to founder on its sudden access of toryism.[3] Wharncliffe, Lord Talbot, the Earl of Harewood, and other tories were reported to be angry, Richmond, the leading ultra, declared for moderate reform, Lord Bath withheld his proxy from the government, while Tavistock and Darnley, belated whig supporters, dropped away.[4]

While the political world anxiously awaited the discussion of Brougham's motion, which was generally assumed to be the government's major test, the situation outside parliament deteriorated rapidly. Towards the end of October Howick notes in his diary that 'ye most violent democratical principles are daily spreading and are avowed and proclaimed by bodies of respectable people in a manner not a little alarming'.[5] Devonshire noted in his a fortnight later: 'If Wellington does not resign and a popular government form itself there must be a crash soon.'[6] This deterioration was accelerated by financial crisis. On 10 November the Bank of Scotland requested a credit which the Bank of England felt obliged to refuse.[7] Five days later the Bank

[1] *P.D.*, 3rd ser. i. 37.

[2] *P.D.*, 3rd ser. i. 63–64.

[3] Countess of Carlisle to Devonshire, 8 November 1830 (Devonshire); Mrs. Hardcastle, *Lord Campbell*, i. 484; John Wood, M.P., stated that he had changed his intention to support government after the declaration, *Morning Chronicle*, 6 November 1830. It is possible that other individuals classified by Planta as government supporters or friendly were lost in this way. The *Manchester Guardian* also renounced its support, 6 November 1830, as did the *Globe*, 3 November 1830.

[4] Countess of Carlisle to Devonshire, op. cit.; Tavistock to Lord W. Russell, 5 November 1830 (Woburn Abbey MSS.); Durham to his wife, 10 November 1830 (Lambton); C. C. F. Greville, *Journal*, ii. 58–60.

[5] Howick, Journal, 22 October 1830 (Grey).

[6] Devonshire, Diary, 9 November 1830 (Devonshire).

[7] Bank of England Minutes of the Court 1830/1, p. 234.

of England was warning its own Birmingham branch that continuation of the drain for another two or three weeks would necessitate an increase in interest rates.[1] Distress and financial crisis were becoming cumulative processes. With them came disturbance and rural violence; and, several paces ahead, and magnifying all that occurred, alarm verging on panic. The government cancelled the king's visit to the city of London, for fear of disturbance.

Some observers expected alarm to have its usual effect, and to produce a rally of support to government and *status quo*, the same kind of reaction which had destroyed high whig hopes in 1792, 1817, and 1819.[2] The expected event failed to materialize. Long discussion had deprived the demand for reform of its revolutionary associations, and it now had respectable sponsors in county and urban opinion. More important, Wellington's government was too weak to serve as a rallying point. The decline in ministerial fortunes from the beginning of the session was unchecked. The government's own supporters were reported to be seriously discontented, and Arbuthnot awaited the *coup de grâce*.[3] Among their opponents there was hourly expectation of change, and even of a new ministry with Grey at the head.[4] The decision to cancel the king's visit to the city caused further unpopularity and a further loss of support, the funds dropped heavily, and by 11 November there were numerous reports that the prime minister was anxious to resign and was kept back only by the wishes of the king himself.[5]

Nearly all the speculation concentrated on Brougham's forthcoming motion. Durham tells his wife that 'all the world are speculating as to the division on Brougham's motion on Tuesday —on which the fate of ministers is supposed to depend'.[6] Expec-

[1] Bank of England Letter Book no. 6, 1824/31, p. 187. Governor of Bank of England to Birmingham Branch, 15 November 1830.

[2] C. W. Wynn to H. W. Wynn, 10 and 28 October 1830 (Wynn, 4817); *Quarterly Review*, xliv. 315. See also Lowther to Lansdowne, 27 October 1830 (Lowther MSS.).

[3] Lady Granville to Devonshire, 9 and 15 November 1830 (Devonshire); C. S. Parker, *Peel*, ii. 167; Broughton, iv. 57–58.

[4] Durham to his wife, 9 November 1830 (Lambton); Countess of Carlisle to Devonshire, 8 November 1830 (Devonshire); Mrs. Hardcastle, *Lord Campbell*, i. 484–5.

[5] Howick, Journal, 8 November 1830 (Grey); Lady Granville to Devonshire, 9 and 11 November 1830 (Devonshire).

[6] Durham to his wife, 10 November 1830 (Lambton).

tations were confused; Denman and other whigs expected that the ministers would be defeated, Campbell, Abercromby, and Wellington himself that they would have a majority, and Grey was open-minded.[1] Possibly the motion would have been defeated, for next year, with the full backing of a government, and a massive agitation in the country, an admittedly more radical measure passed by only one vote. Yet the very discussion of the question was bound to make the government's position far more difficult by exciting the country and stimulating new pressures.[2]

The discussion about reform was hypothetical. One motion stood before Brougham's, Sir H. Parnell's motion for referring the civil list to a select committee, due for discussion on 15 November. Although far from being as much discussed as Brougham's, this motion too, produced difficulties for the government, though not such as were expected to lead to defeat.[3] The whigs were united in urging their traditional views on the civil list, the pressure for economy was strong, and some government supporters were committed on the question. It also provided an opportunity for ultras and tory country gentlemen to demonstrate their hostility to the government, and their readiness to respond to the demands of the nation without the need to go as far as reform. On the morning of 15 November a group of nearly forty ultras met at Knatchbull's and decided to vote for the motion.[4] It was carried against the government by 233 votes to 204. Wellington resigned promptly to avoid discussion on reform.[5]

As the only possible alternative leader, Grey was asked by the

[1] J. Arnould, *Denman*, i. 321; Mrs. Hardcastle, *Lord Campbell*, i. 486; Abercromby to Devonshire, 15 November 1830 (Devonshire); G. Le Strange, *Lieven*, ii. 115–17; Broughton, iv. 59; Mrs. Hardcastle, *Lord Campbell*, i. 487; Brougham to Devonshire, 8 November 1830 (Devonshire). Brougham himself states that Scarlett, the attorney-general, was to have voted for the motion, pencil note by Brougham on Abercromby to Brougham, n.d. [1830] (Brougham).

[2] Abercromby to Devonshire, 15 November 1830 (Devonshire); Durham to his wife, 12 November 1830 (Durham); Mrs. Hardcastle, *Lord Campbell*, i. 486; Lord Colchester, *Ellenborough*, ii. 432.

[3] Mrs. Hardcastle, *Lord Campbell*, i. 486; Lord Colchester, *Ellenborough*, ii. 435.

[4] *Spectator*, 20 November 1830; Lord Colchester, *Ellenborough*, ii. 434.

[5] Wellington, *Despatches*, vii. 361. Expectations that the duke would hang on, though defeated, all centred on reform: Durham to his wife, 10 November 1830 (Lambton). See also H. Brougham, *Life and Times*, iii. 73.

king to form an administration. In it he brought together the groups who had defeated the Wellington government, his object being 'to unite as many efficient persons as possible in the public service, entirely disclaiming every principle of exclusion'.[1] Yet though it was a coalition, Grey's administration was still essentially whig. The leaders in lords and commons were whigs, the leading figures of the party took office in it, the bulk of its support came from the old whig party. The principles on which it was founded, reform, retrenchment, and peace, were whig principles; and people at large called it a whig government. The long exclusion was over.

[1] Grey to Devonshire, 17 November 1830 (Devonshire). Grey added: 'my chief hope of support must be derived from persons like yourself.'

XI

CONCLUSION

THE history of the early-nineteenth-century whig party falls into three phases. The brief spell of power from 1806 to 1807 was a period of disillusion. A period of decline lasted until the end of the Napoleonic war, which ushered in the period of deadlock described in this study. Stronger in numbers, more united in views, and probably more effectively organized than previous oppositions, the whigs could also claim to be a 'popular' party in view of their strength in the largest constituencies, and could attempt to carry this popularity further by encouraging agitation through the traditional channels. They opposed a government which faced serious unpopularity, could be defeated in the house of commons, and differed both internally and, at times, with the king. Yet the whigs did not achieve office until 1827. Even then it was a brief tenure lacking real power.

The party had come to office in 1806 because the break-up of Pitt's old party had provided them with allies in the Grenvilles, the Sidmouths, and the 'old whigs'. Since then Pitt's party had been slowly rebuilt, until finally the Grenvilles and Canning took office in 1821 and 1822. Reconstruction gave the government new strength and leeway for minor reshuffles, and deprived the whigs of all hope of allies: tory groups might disagree among themselves and within the cabinet, but they all disliked the whigs more than each other. Even Canning was prepared to ally with whigs only when all else had failed. The old days of achieving power by building pyramids of factions appeared to have passed. So had hopes from crown or reversionary interest. The king had accepted the whigs in 1806 because there was no alternative, but monarch and party proved incompatible. George IV assumed all his father's prejudices against whig principles and personnel, while the whigs learned not to take office on uncertain or restricted tenure.

Without hopes from coalition or crown the party had only one prospect of power; to bring the government down by making the commons impossible to control. This could be facilitated by exploiting popular discontent and pressure on the house. Session after session the whigs organized or participated in campaigns of meetings. Session after session their hopes rose at symptoms of discontent among country gentlemen or of government weakness. Session after session it proved impossible to do more than inflict occasional defeats. Until more liberal sentiments began to spread, popular support for the whigs was confined to certain issues, chiefly those relating to economy. Even here the political system was such that the house was subject only to occasional and badly sustained pressure, while the waverers, who did respond in some measure to the stimuli from outside the house, still preferred the government, on balance, to the opposition. Until the system of representation was changed the whigs could not hope to gain much more than a temporary advantage from popular agitations. Nor could the changes taking place in the climate of opinion in the country at large make their due impact on the house.

By 1822 seven years of conflict had demonstrated the unattainability of office. This coincided with the beginning of a period of political change, new ministerial attitudes, and new policy departures. Whig hopes of displacing all men and changing all measures were replaced by hopes of supporting some measures and some men and prospects of a future alliance between whig and liberal tory. This was realized in 1827, but insecurely, since George IV was not prepared to make concessions on the catholic question; nor Canning to accord whigs more than junior positions; nor part of the old opposition to trust king or Canning. Had Canning survived, growing trust and battles shared might have saved the union. Under the weak Goderich it was doomed, and the break-up of the administration became the political nadir of a shattered whig party.

Disunity continued, even increased, through 1829, and into 1830, but at the same time all the obstacles between the whigs and power were disappearing. Wellington smashed the tory party, breaking with the liberal tories and incurring the hostility of the ultras. These groups went into opposition, recreating the system of faction politics and the possibility of alliances for the whigs, and so weakening the government that its forces were probably less numerous than those of the groups outside.

George IV died, and William IV had no hostility to the whigs, collectively or individually. Finally came a revival of distress and discontent, of a type which had always encouraged opposition and produced parliamentary difficulties in the past. Affecting manufacturing areas and agricultural community simultaneously, the impact of distress began to fuse together the independent groups in the house of commons against a government which had neither strength nor solutions. Discontent among waverers inevitably reappeared and could not be conciliated as easily or as quickly as Liverpool had managed to do.

As the whigs drew together to oppose the government in 1830, an opposition and ministerial clash of the old pattern reappeared, with outside discontent once more cheering on opposition. In extreme situations in the past fear of revolution had rallied support to the government: Wellington never seemed strong enough to guide the country through such difficulties. Liverpool had made tactical concessions: Wellington was prepared to economize, but not drastically enough, and he stood firm against parliamentary reform. Liverpool had underlined the dangers of ministerial weakness so as to gather strength: Wellington was not disinclined to go. Liverpool's government had been strong enough to act as a rallying point: Wellington's was weaker. Liverpool had been prepared to accept the odd defeat: Wellington resigned precipitately on the first.

Since Grey and the whigs were the only possible alternative to Wellington the way to office was open. Power removed the remaining problems. Althorp's primacy in the commons was recognized by making him leader of the house, while Brougham, who had declined to accept the title of leader in opposition and had failed to challenge Althorp's growing primacy, went to the lords. As for the over-all leadership, Grey was the only possible leader for the whole party, and Burdett's comment that he was fitted for power rather than the doubts and hesitations of opposition proved to be partially justified.[1] Office changed Grey into a temporarily more zestful and dynamic figure than had been seen in opposition since the 1790's. Finally, public pressure solved the problem of the waverers. Their loyalties were still uncertain and old suspicions of the whigs remained, so that the new ministry could still be defeated. Yet popular pressure for

[1] Broughton, iii. 79.

the reform bill was so strong in 1831 that many of the waverers were compelled either to support it or to lose their seats in the election. This support was all that was necessary to a one-issue government. When the party took office J. N. Fazakerly, whig M.P. for Peterborough, prophesied to his patron:

nor do I believe that the existence or strength of the ministry will so much depend on the common parliamentary combinations for votes, as on the measures which they produce. If those measures are as good as the promises which they have made, they may defy any opposition in parliament, or appeal with confidence to the country. The country is tired of the mere conflict of parties, and wants certain measures, and will support whoever brings them forward. Among these the principal is a reform in parliament.[1]

His prediction proved to be completely accurate.

The breaking of the barriers brought the whigs to power and enabled them to stay in office once they had reached it. It also made the reform bill inevitable. The whigs were committed to reform by their past; the terms on which they took office in 1830 were much the same as those formulated from 1820 to 1822, during a very similar agitation. They believed immediate concession necessary and had said so at the beginning of the session. Finally, their hand was forced by public agitation; as Parkes of Birmingham predicted, 'the whigs *must* and therefore will do something real'.[2] Circumstances dictated a reform bill; logic ordained its nature—the most that would get through the house, and the least that would satisfy the country; public pressure compelled its passage. The resolution of the deadlock was the prelude to a new pattern in politics. If modern historians have tended to minimize the impact of the reform bill and emphasize the elements of continuity in the electoral system, they would not be justified in doing the same for the effects on the house. There the temporary prop of popular pressure which had supported the whig government was replaced by a more permanent one through the reshaping of the pattern of representation. The strengthening of the new urban element, and the elimination of the smaller boroughs, shifted the parliamentary balance permanently. The new system created an environment favourable to the whig-liberals, just as the old system had supported tory governments in power.

[1] J. N. Fazakerly to Milton, 3 December 1830 (Fitzwilliam, G. 68).

[2] Parkes to Francis Place, 5 December 1830 (Place Papers, Add. MSS. 35,148, f. 77).

APPENDIX

The Analysis of M.P.s

FOR the two parliaments not analysed in the text the relevant figures are:

	Double divisions	Vote govt.	Vote oppn.	Votes mixed	Other divisions	Threshold
1812–18	7	320	225	120	114	12
1818–20	2	380	185	11	38	4

In the first of these parliaments forty-two members voting with government on the seven motions gave one or two opposition votes on the others, and are added to thirty-six members giving mixed votes on the seven, who only included in these one opposition vote and did not give any more. They form a government fringe of seventy-eight. Seven members giving mixed votes on the seven motions gave only one government vote and enough opposition votes on the 114 to cross the threshold. They are transferred to the opposition fringe, where they are joined by seventy-six members giving opposition votes on the seven, but falling below the threshold. Ten members giving one opposition vote on the seven motions, but with no more votes recorded at all, are transferred to the waverers, as are twenty-five giving government votes on the seven motions but adding more than two opposition votes on the other motions.

In the second parliament 261 members voting with government, on one, or both, of the two motions on which both sides are listed, gave no other opposition votes at all: eighty gave one or two and became the sole members of the government fringe. Of the members giving mixed votes, five gave enough opposition votes to carry them over the threshold and are transferred to the opposition fringe. There they are joined by eleven members who voted with the opposition on the two motions, but did not give enough opposition votes to cross the threshold on the others. The waverers are made up of the six remaining, who gave mixed votes, three who gave an opposition vote on one of the two motions, but also gave more than two opposition votes on the others. Two slight adjustments are made in this parliament. The usual practice of halving the threshold for those sitting for less than half the life of parliament is not adopted, since this particular parliament sat for too short a time. The other is that members giving one government vote and one opposition vote on the two motions, who gave the government vote on Tierney's motion on the state of the nation, are not transferred to opposition fringe if they gave enough other opposition votes to pass the threshold. Tierney's motion was a major trial of party strength, and to vote against it was in effect to secede from the opposition.

One weakness of this method of analysis is that the three parliaments are not fully comparable in view of the rather different motions for which the votes are recorded. Those for which both sides are listed in the 1812–18 parliament are all on questions of taxation and economy. The popularity of these questions means that the opposition and opposition fringe groups are rather larger than they would be if more 'ideological' questions had been included. For the parliament of 1818–20 only two divisions are listed in full, and the most important of these is a major party clash. In combination with the very low threshold and the diminished tendency to waver in the winter session of 1819, this has tended to push members into the two extreme categories of government and opposition, leaving the intermediate groups unnaturally depleted. The parliament of 1820 to 1826, in which more divisions, and a wider variety of issues, are covered by full lists, is, therefore, the most accurate representation of the situation.

The three parliaments are considered together because the trends are exactly the same in each, a multiplicity of tables is avoided, and there is a satisfactory degree of continuity about the analysis despite the differences between the parliaments. Among the members in the analysis 287 have been classified in two parliaments and a further 297 in three. The changes in their classification are shown in the following table:

	No change							
	Govt.	Govt. Fr.	Waverer	Oppn. Fr.	Oppn.	Total	*Drift into adjacent group*	*Jump into non-adjacent group*
Two parls.	76	14	9	8	61	168	76	43
Three parls.	82	3	7	2	58	152	92	53

The fact that 59 per cent. of those sitting in two parliaments and 51 per cent. of those sitting in three are constant in their classification is satisfactory, particularly when taken with the further fact that most of the remainder had moved only into a neighbouring group. Given the somewhat artificial nature of the boundaries, particularly between government and government fringe and between the latter and waverer, such slides were extremely easy to make. Even among the total of ninety-six who actually changed their classification by moving over one or more groups, nearly thirty of the transfers can be put down to known changes of political viewpoint among groups like the Grenvilles and individuals who were moving towards, or away from, the opposition. A further nine appear to be due to fluctuating attendances produced by absences or illness on the part of opposition members. The largest single category among the remainder is composed of forty-five, whose category changes abruptly because of the less satisfactory classifications in the 1818 to 1820 house. Members who were in opposition fringe or waverer categories, in the previous or the subsequent parliament, have jumped to government fringe or government because of the rigidity of these categories.

BIBLIOGRAPHY

MANUSCRIPT SOURCES

British Museum

Auckland Papers
Broughton Papers
Thomas Grenville Papers
Holland House Papers
Huskisson Papers
Liverpool Papers
Peel Papers
Place Papers
Lord John Russell Papers
Wellesley Papers
Sir Robert Wilson Papers

Public Record Office

Ellenborough Papers
Lord John Russell Papers

In Other Libraries, in Record Offices, and in Private Hands

Althorp Papers, Althorp, Northamptonshire
Bromley–Davenport Papers, John Rylands Library, Manchester
Brougham Papers, University College, London
Sir Francis Burdett Papers, Bodleian Library, Oxford
Carlisle Papers, Castle Howard, Yorkshire
Devonshire Papers, Chatsworth, Derbyshire
Fitzwilliam Papers, Reference Library, Sheffield
Fitzwilliam Papers, County Record Office, Northamptonshire
Graham Papers, Microfilm, Bodleian Library, Oxford
Grenville–Newport Correspondence, Bodleian Library, Oxford
Grey Papers, Prior's Kitchen, Durham
Halifax Papers, Hickleton, Yorkshire
Horner Papers, British Library of Political and Economic Science, London
Hume Papers, Oxford.
Lambton Papers, Lambton Castle, Durham
Lansdowne Papers, Bowood, Wiltshire
Middleton-Monck Papers, County Record Office, Northumberland
Minute Book of the Manchester Representation Committee, Central Reference Library, Manchester
Monteagle Papers, National Library of Ireland, Dublin
Newport Papers, National Library of Ireland, Dublin
Ridley Papers, Blagdon, Northumberland

Roscoe Papers, Picton Library, Liverpool
Lord John Russell Papers, Public Record Office, London
Shuttleworth Scrap Book, Central Reference Library, Manchester
Wallace Papers, County Record Office, Northumberland
Wynn Papers, National Library of Wales, Aberystwyth

In Transcript

Mr. Michael Brock very kindly allowed me to use his transcripts from the following collections:

Bank of England Papers, Bank of England, London
Bedford Papers, Woburn Abbey, Bedfordshire
Creevey Transcripts, in the possession of Sir John Murray
Ellice Papers, National Library of Scotland, Edinburgh
Hatherton Papers, Staffordshire County Record Office
Hardinge Papers, South Park, Kent
Londonderry Papers, Wynyard, County Durham
Lowther Papers, Estate Office, Lowther, Westmorland
Wellington Papers, Apsley House, London.

I have not been able to see any of these collections myself.

NEWSPAPERS AND PERIODICALS

London
The Globe
The Morning Chronicle
The Times
The Traveller

Provincial
The Alfred or West of England Advertiser
Bristol Gazette
Bristol Mercury
Bristol Mirror
Devizes and Wiltshire Gazette
Dublin Evening Post
Felix Farley's Bristol Journal
Gloucester Chronicle
Ipswich Chronicle
Leeds Mercury
Liverpool Mercury
Manchester Chronicle
Manchester Guardian
Manchester Mercury
Newcastle Chronicle
Norfolk Chronicle
Northampton Mercury
Tyne Mercury
Scotsman

Periodicals *The Annual Register*
The Edinburgh Review
The Examiner
The Independent Whig
The Pamphleteer
Political Register
The Quarterly Review
The Spectator
The Westminster Review

BIOGRAPHICAL AND ELECTORAL MATERIAL

An Alphabetical List of Members of the Commons House of Parliament, London, 1822

An Analysis of the British House of Commons as at Present Constituted, London, 1823

An Analytical Review of the Composition of the New House of Commons, Birmingham, 1830

W. W. Bean, *The Parliamentary Representation of the Six Northern Counties of England from 1603 to the General Election of 1886*, Hull, 1890

A Biographical List of the House of Commons Elected in October 1812, London, 1813

The Black Book: or Corruption Unmasked, London, 1820

The Black Book: Supplement to the Black Book, London, 1823

The British Parliament, Containing an Alphabetical List of the Members of the House of Commons, London, 1819

Sir E. Brydges (ed.), *Collins's Peerage of England*, London, 1812, 9 vols.

J. Burke, *A Genealogical and Heraldic History of the Commoners*, London, 1834–8, 4 vols.

J. Burke, *A Genealogical and Heraldic Dictionary of the Peerage and Baronetage*, London, 1828, and subsequent editions

J. Cartwright, *Letters to the Lord Mayor*, London, 1817

The Elector's Remembrancer, or a Guide to the Votes of Each Member of the House of Commons, London, 1822

An Exposition of the British House of Commons as at Present Constituted, London, 1823

The Extraordinary Black Book, London, 1832

The Extraordinary Red Book, London, 1817

R. S. Ferguson, *Cumberland and Westmorland M.P.s from the Restoration to the Reform Bill of 1867*, London, 1871

A Full View of the British House of Commons as Constituted in the Nineteenth Century of the Christian Era, London, 1821

G.E.C.: *The Complete Peerage*, edited by Vicary Gibbs, London, 1910–59, 12 vols.

G. P. Judd, *Members of Parliament, 1734–1832*, New Haven, 1958

A Key to Both Houses of Parliament, London, 1832

The Late Elections: An Impartial Statement of all the Proceedings, Connected with the Progress and Result of the Late Elections, London, 1818

Links of the Lower House, Or an Alphabetical List of the House of Commons, London, 1821

New Parliament: An Appendix to the Black Book, London, 1826

T. H. B. Oldfield, *A Key to the House of Commons*, London, 1820

T. H. B. Oldfield, *The Representative History of Great Britain and Ireland*, London, 1816, 6 vols.

W. D. Pink, A. B. Beaven, *The Parliamentary Representation of Lancaster County and Borough, 1258–1885*, London, 1889

The Royal Kalendar, or Complete and Correct Annual Register, 1812–26

W. A. Shaw, *The Knights of England*, London, 1906, 2 vols.

H. S. Smith, *The Parliaments of England*, London, 1844–50, 3 vols.

T. W. Whitley, *The Parliamentary Representation of Coventry, from the Earliest Times to the Present Date*, Coventry, 1894

W. R. Williams, *The Parliamentary History of the County of Gloucester*, Hereford, 1898

W. R. Williams, *The Parliamentary History of the County of Worcester*, Hereford, 1897

J. Wilson, *A Biographical Index to the House of Commons*, London, 1808

INDEX

PRINTED IN GREAT BRITAIN
AT THE UNIVERSITY PRESS, OXFORD
BY VIVIAN RIDLER
PRINTER TO THE UNIVERSITY